Beyond Stock Options

**Phantom Stock, Restricted Stock,
Stock Appreciation Rights,
and Other Equity Alternatives**

Fifth Edition

Beyond Stock Options

Phantom Stock, Restricted Stock, Stock Appreciation Rights, and Other Equity Alternatives

Fifth Edition

The National Center for Employee Ownership
Oakland, California

Beyond Stock Options, Fifth Edition

Book design by Scott Rodrick

Copyright © 2007 by The National Center for Employee Ownership. All rights reserved. No part of this book may be reproduced or transmitted in any form or by any means, electronic or mechanical, including photocopying, recording, or by any information storage and retrieval system, without prior written permission from the publisher.

ISBN: 1-932924-27-2

First printing July 2003.
Second edition, January 2004
Third edition, February 2005
Fourth edition, January 2006
Fifth edition, January 2007

The National Center for Employee Ownership
1736 Franklin St., 8th Flr.
Oakland, CA 94612
(510) 208-1300
Fax (510) 272-9510
www.nceo.org

Contents

Introduction

Corey Rosen

1. Basic Issues in Plan Design

Corey Rosen

2. Phantom Stock and Stock Appreciation Rights
Helen H. Morrison, Kay Kemp, and Joe Adams

3. Restricted Stock Plans
Barbara Baksa

4.   Performance Award Plans

Helen H. Morrison, Kay Kemp, and Joe Adams

5.   Direct Stock Purchases in Closely Held Companies

David R. Johanson

6. Accounting Issues

Corey Rosen and Helen H. Morrison

7. ESOPs, ESPPs, 401(k) Plans, and Stock Options: When the Old Standbys Still Make Sense

Corey Rosen

8. A Tiered Approach to Equity Design with Multiple Equity Compensation Vehicles

Martin Staubus, Blair Jones, Daniel Janich, and Clare Hatfield

Appendixes

Introduction

Corey Rosen

Employee ownership has become commonplace in the U.S. economy and, increasingly, worldwide. We at the NCEO now estimate that at least 25% of the U.S. workforce owns stock in its employer through an employee stock ownership plan (ESOP), stock option plan, 401(k) plan, or stock purchase plan. Employee ownership can be found in companies of all sizes and in all lines of business. From the two-person start-up to the 1.6 million employees of Wal-Mart, employee ownership has become just part of the business fabric.

This growth is not surprising in light of consistent research showing that companies that share ownership broadly with employees consistently outperform those who do not, especially if they combine ownership with a highly participative management style that shares both corporate financial information and the right to make decisions concerning work-level issues (these issues are addressed in detail in the NCEO book *Ownership Management: Creating a Culture of Lasting Innovation*). It is also consistent with a changing economy in which speed, innovation, and information are essential business resources. For companies to succeed, they need to engage their employees in a daily effort to come up with better products and services, more efficient processes, improved quality control and customer service, and more creative ways to reach new markets. The more people who can be thinking and acting along these lines—thinking and acting like owners—the more successful a company will be. Even the employers who most famously succeed at this still see more opportunity; as Bill Hewlett famously noted, there is no telling what Hewlett-Packard could have done if it had only known what its employees knew. And this from a company leader who was considered the model of getting employees engaged in creative enterprise.

At the same time, the growth of employee ownership builds a momentum of its own. As more employees get ownership, more employees ask for and expect it. Sharing ownership becomes a prerequisite for attracting and retaining quality people.

For many companies, the route to employee ownership will be through a formal employee ownership plan such as an ESOP, 401(k) plan, stock option, or employee stock purchase plan (ESPPs—a regulated stock purchase plan with specific tax benefits). But for others, these plans, because of cost, regulatory requirements, corporate considerations, or other issues will not be the best fit. Or, some companies may have one or more of these plans but want to supplement them for certain employees with another kind of plan. For these companies, phantom stock, stock appreciation rights, direct stock purchase plans, performance awards, or restricted stock may work better. This book is written for these companies.

There are a number of situations that might call for one or more of these plans:

- The company's owners want to share the economic value of equity but not equity itself.

- The company cannot offer conventional kinds of ownership plans because of corporate restrictions, as would be the case, for instance, with a limited liability corporation, partnership, or sole proprietorship.

- The company already has a conventional ownership plan, such as an ESOP, but wants to provide additional equity incentives, perhaps without providing stock itself, to selected employees.

- The company's leadership has considered other plans but found their rules too restrictive or implementation costs too high.

- The company is a division of another company, but it can create a measurement of its equity value and wants employees to have a share in that even though there is no actual stock.

- The company is not a for-profit stock corporation—it is a nonprofit or government entity that nonetheless can create some kind of measurement that mimics equity growth that it would like to use as a basis to create an employee bonus.

This book provides an overview of the design, implementation, accounting, valuation, tax, and legal issues for the plans it covers, and also provides sample plans. It is not, however, a comprehensive manual. None of these plans should be set up without the detailed advice of qualified legal and financial counsel. Sharing equity is a major step that should be considered thoroughly and carefully.

Note to the Fifth Edition

In the fifth edition, most of the chapters have been revised (as of late 2006) to account for new developments and to explain various matters in greater detail. Chapter 8 (on using multiple plans) and the model plans did not need to be revised because they are still current, having been updated as needed at the end of 2005 for the fourth edition. The book has now been typeset to use footnotes instead of endnotes for easier reference.

CHAPTER ONE

Basic Issues in Plan Design

Corey Rosen

Contents

For many companies, the idea of sharing equity growth with employees is appealing. Often these companies will turn to a formal employee ownership plan such as an ESOP (employee stock ownership plan), 401(k) plan, or tax-qualified employee stock purchase plan. But many company owners or corporate boards may be put off by the complexity, costs, or regulations that govern these plans, or by the legal and practical issues for their company in having employees own actual shares. Many of these companies have turned instead to stock options. Options became common currency in the 1990s, covering about 10 million employees. Their (then) favorable accounting treatment, steadily rising stock prices, and the fact that "everyone else" was doing it seemed to make them the equity vehicle of choice. But the favorable accounting treatment for options ended in 2005 (2006 for private companies), and investors and the press started looking at options more skeptically. Options reward volatility more than any other corporate factor (it's better to have an option on a stock that can reach great highs, even it is also can reach deep lows, because you can exercise at the highs and ignore the lows). While options still make sense for many companies, there are other equity alternatives worth considering, either to replace options and/or other ownership plans or to supplement them by providing a different kind of equity reward, either just to certain people or to everyone.

This book is designed to discuss alternative approaches. It focuses on five types of plans: phantom stock, stock appreciation rights (SARs), restricted stock, direct stock purchase plans, and performance awards. Each of these plans is briefly defined below.

1.1 Types of Plans

1.1.1 Phantom Stock

A reward paid to an individual for the value of a defined number of shares. The award is not actually made in shares but in a promise to pay the employee the value of the shares at some point in the future. The award is usually paid in cash, but could be paid in shares. For instance, a company might provide that an employee will have the right to an amount of money equal to a certain number of shares after a specified number of years of employment, but would not actually get the shares.

1.1.2 Stock Appreciation Rights (SARs)

A stock appreciation right (SAR) provides the right to the monetary equivalent of the increase in the value of a specified number of shares over a specified period of time. As with phantom stock, this is normally paid out in cash, but it could be paid in shares.

1.1.3 Restricted Stock

Any shares whose sale or acquisition is subject to restrictions. In employee ownership plans, this typically would mean that an employee would be given shares or the right to buy shares (perhaps at a discount), but could not take possession of them until some time later when certain requirements have been met (or, to put it differently, restrictions have been lifted), such as working for a certain number of years or the company reaching a certain size. While the restrictions are in place, the employee could, if the plan allows it, still be eligible for any dividends paid on the shares and could be allowed to vote them as well. If the employee does not fulfill the terms of restrictions, the shares are forfeited. Some plans allow the restrictions to lapse gradually (for instance, an employee could buy 30% of the stock when the shares are 30% vested); others provide the restrictions lapse all at once.

1.1.4 Restricted Stock Units

A restricted stock unit (RSU) is equivalent to a phantom stock plan paid out in shares. Employees are given a restricted right to receive shares at some future date or subject to some performance condition. They cannot make a Section 83(b) election (a potentially favorable tax decision) on an RSU as they can on restricted stock. The accounting, tax, and securities laws issues for RSUs are identical to those for stock-settled phantom stock.

1.1.5 Direct Stock Purchase Plans

In a direct stock purchase plan, employees can purchase shares with their own funds, either at market price or a discount. In some cases, employers provide below-market or non-recourse loans to help employees purchase the shares. Employees then hold the shares as individuals with the same rights as other holders of the same class of securities.

1.1.6 Performance Awards

While most of the book focuses on these equity or equity-like plans, a separate chapter looks at performance awards, which are essentially profit or gain sharing plans that are designed to pay out (in cash or stock) for performance over a few to several years, rather than annually. These plans provide an alternative to rewarding performance based on the long-term improvement in share price, substituting instead a measure such as improvement in EBITDA, sales, quality, or any other measure deemed critical. Some companies may want to combine equity-based and performance awards.

1.2 Basic Issues in Choosing a Plan

One of the great advantages of the plans we are discussing in this book is their flexibility. But that flexibility is also their greatest challenge. Because they can be designed in so many ways, many decisions need to be made about such issues as who gets how much, vesting rules, liquidity concerns, restrictions on selling shares (when awards are settled in shares), eligibility, rights to interim distributions of earnings, and rights to participate in corporate governance (if any). In this chapter, we discuss some of the considerations in deciding on these plan rules. Before turning to these details, however, we need to discuss why a company would choose one plan or another in the first place.

Because all the details about these plans can become complicated, it is helpful to map out their basic dimensions. In deciding how to provide equity or equity-like awards to employees, companies need to think about three sets of issues:

- Will the award be paid in stock or cash?
- Will the employee get the value of the shares, only the increase in the value of the shares, or an award based on something other than share value?
- Will the employee have to pay anything for the stock?

Table 1-1 provides a quick visual overview of the plans described in this book by showing what kind of plan results from the decisions made on the above issues. In many cases, we have found that corporate boards or owners have very fixed views about issues such as whether employees should be required to pay something for an equity award or whether they want employees to be able actually to own shares. By looking first at these core issues, you can focus specifically on the kind of plan that will work best for you.

1.3 Corporate Organizational Form Issues

Companies using these plans can be organized in any of the standard corporate forms: C corporations, S corporations, limited liability companies (LLCs), partnerships, and even sole proprietorships. In some cases, even nonprofit entities or government entities might consider one of these plans. If employees are actually going to own stock, now or in the future, however, the company must be one that actually has stock. Only C and S corporations have stock. Partnerships have partnership interests, and LLCs have member interests; sole proprietorships have neither stock nor partnership nor member interests because only one person, by definition, owns the assets. For C corporations, any of the forms of ownership discussed in this book are possible.

That is also true for S corporations, but subject to two important caveats. First, S corporations can only have 100 shareholders. Employee holders of restricted stock can be considered owners for this purpose unless (1) the stock is "substantially unvested" ("substantially" is a confusing word here; it just means that the shares can still be forfeited), and (2) the employee has not made a Section 83(b) election for the

Table 1-1. Choosing an Individual Equity or Equity Equivalent Award Plan

Type of plan	Employee pays for all or part of award	Employee does not pay for all or part of award	Award normally paid in cash	Award paid in stock	Award based on share value	Award based on increase in share value	Award based on profit or other non-equity measure
Phantom stock settled in cash		■	■		■		
Phantom stock settled in shares (RSUs)		■		■	■		
Direct stock purchase	■				■		
Stock appreciation right (SAR)[a]		■	■			■	
Stock-settled stock appreciation right		■		■		■	
Restricted stock[b]		■		■	■		
Performance award[c]		■		■			■

a. While SARs are normally paid out in cash, they occasionally are paid out in the form of shares.

b. With restricted stock, the employee may or may not pay for the award on grant.

c. Performance awards may pay out in cash or shares.

shares (a Section 83(b) election allows the employee to pay capital gains tax on increases in stock value from the date after which the election is made in return for paying ordinary income tax on the value of the shares awarded minus any consideration the employee paid for them). Second, S corporations can only have one class of stock, although the same class can have different voting rights for different shares. This means that if some shares have benefits other shares do not, they are not allowed. Stock appreciation rights, phantom stock, and restricted stock granted to employees as compensation for services are not considered to be separate classes of stock, provided they are not transferable (i.e., holders cannot transfer them to others) or are subject to buy-sell or redemption agreements that are structured so as to circumvent the one-class-of-stock rule. Buy-sell agreements or redemption agreements that provide for repurchase at book value, appraised value, or a formula value established by the board of directors that can be shown to have a reasonable basis all are considered not to violate the one-class-of-stock rule.

Paying distributions on restricted stock that is not vested is not required under the regulations governing the one-class-of-stock rule for S corporations, but once the shares are actually fully owned by employees, they would have to receive the same economic benefits other shareholders do. Companies can, however, pay distributions before vesting, as would be common with restricted stock. They would be paid pro-rata to distributions on other shares, but normally they would be paid as a bonus and taxed as compensation rather than as a distribution of earnings. A potential problem can come up if holders of restricted stock (or phantom stock or SARs that are paid out in the form of stock) actually take full ownership of the shares in S corporations that have previously taxed but undistributed earnings (this is called the "accumulated adjustment account"). If amounts from this account are distributed to owners, the employees who exercised their rights now are entitled to a pro-rata share of the distributions, *even though the other owners have already paid taxes on them.* So it is usually advisable to pay out the earnings prior to employees taking ownership of the shares.

For LLCs and partnerships, there cannot be restricted stock or direct stock purchase because there is no stock. However, an employee can have a right to a capital interest in the company through a restricted capital interest award (the right to a capital interest that is subject to certain restrictions lapsing), a capital interest appreciation right, or a phantom capital interest right. If these rights can convert to an actual membership interest, however, it is important to consult with your attorney over how the income of the employee will be taxed. If the employee is not considered a limited partner in the entity, then the employee could be considered self-employed and have to pay the entire payroll tax obligation of his or her salary, rather than just half. LLCs and partnerships can offer phantom stock or SARs without these issues if, as is usually the case, the awards are paid in only in cash. In that case, the employee is not really an owner, but is just getting a bonus based on an equity measurement. Similarly, if employees do end up with actual membership interests, companies need to be very clear about just what their rights will be with respect to being a partner in the firm.

A sole proprietorship would be limited to SARs and phantom stock because if employees actually became owners, the company would not be a sole proprietorship any more. Instead, these companies will want to pay employee in cash based on the growth in or value of the company's assets or other measurement of worth.

Finally, keep in mind that certain professional corporations (medical practices and law firms, most notably, and also accounting firms, subject to some flexibility in some states) are prohibited by state laws from being owned by anyone who is not a member of that corporation.

1.3.1 Divisions of Companies, Nonprofits, and Government Entities

While not common, it is possible for some nonprofit organizations and government entities to use these plans. For instance, the Katz School of Business developed a phantom "stock" plan that rewards employees for the school's measurable goals. If an organization can create some kind of measurement like this, it can then reward employees with phantom units of value based on them or the right to a value linked to their growth (the equivalent of a stock appreciation right).

Similarly, a division of a company that has no stock of its own may nonetheless have a very specific way of measuring its own performance. For instance, a division may have its own income statement or even its own balance sheet (or can construct one), as might be the case in a division that makes or provides a service that it sells, either to the parent, the market, or both. Even if the division could not be conceptualized as an independent for-profit entity, it may still have measurements of contribution to the parent corporation. For instance, it might track its "equity" growth in terms of a multiple of the margins on the products or services it provides to the parent, or create a stock value equivalency measure based on what the parent would have to pay for these services or products on the marketplace. To the extent the division beats what the market can provide, this could be considered "profit"; a multiple of the profit can be applied consistent with what the multiple would be for similar companies, and an equity value is thus created. Establishing these formulas, of course, takes expert advice and the input and acquiescence of the parent.

1.4   Picking a Plan

A separate chapter of this book looks in some detail at why a company might *not* want one of these plans, focusing particularly on a comparison of these plans to ESOPs and 401(k) plans. While these more formal plans have many advantages, companies may choose a phantom stock plan or other alternative plan for a number of good reasons. In all of the plans below, a major advantage is flexibility in deciding who gets how much under with what rules. We have not repeated that as an advantage in the description of specific pros and cons of each plan, however.

1.4.1 Phantom Stock Plans and Stock Appreciation Rights Settled in Cash

For phantom stock plans and stock appreciation rights (SARs) plans, the most common arguments are:

- Some companies do not want employees actually to own shares or, in some cases, have no shares to make available. For instance, as noted above, limited liability companies, partnerships, and sole proprietorships do not have stock, but they could give employees a right to a capital interest in the company. These companies have equity value, and owners may want to share this in some way with employees without actually making them partners in the firm.

- In companies that do have stock, owners may be concerned about employees owning actual shares. In some cases, this may be for fear of losing control, although, in fact, other kinds of stock plans can usually handle the control issue with little or no difficulty.

- Closely held company owners may be concerned that there is no foreseeable market for actual shares given to employees. It may be simpler in these cases just to give employees cash rather than to buy shares back from them or try to find other buyers. Such sales may also raise securities law compliance issues. Even the issuance of shares can trigger securities law compliance issues, although it is usually a fairly simple process to obtain an exemption from these rules.

But there are also arguments against phantom plans and SARs:

- They provide no significant tax benefits to employers or employees, especially relative to such tax-qualified employee ownership plans as ESOPs, 401(k) plans, and incentive stock options.

- They may be difficult to communicate to employees who are skeptical about whether the plans will really deliver value. Whereas stock comes with specific contractual and general corporate law rights, and carries the same value as shares of the same class held by other owners of the company, phantom stock or SARs are based only on a contractual agreement to pay out based on management's determination of what the company is worth.

We have presented the arguments for phantom stock and SARs together because they generally have the same pros and cons. Stock appreciation rights, however, provide value only if the stock price rises. On the one hand, this can be a positive in that employees benefit only if corporate stock performance improves; on the other hand, phantom stock allows employees to get some reward if the company's own performance improves but its stock price or equity value, because of broader market factors, does not.

Also note that phantom stock awards are subject to the requirements of the deferred compensation rules under Section 409A of the Internal Revenue Code (described in more detail below). Restricted stock that does contain a deferral feature as part of the grant, incentive stock options, stock appreciation rights, and non-discounted nonqualified stock options all are exempt from these rules. Closely held companies, however, must follow specific valuation guidelines to assure that SARs and options are priced at fair market value.

1.4.2 Stock-Settled Stock Appreciation Rights and Restricted Stock Units

Stock-settled stock appreciation rights (SSARs) are stock appreciation rights paid in shares, and restricted stock units (RSUs) are equivalent to phantom stock paid in shares.

Many advisors have speculated that SSARs may become very popular in public companies due to the new accounting rules that treat stock options the same as other equity compensation. The economic benefit to employees is equivalent to a nonqualified option that is exercised at vesting, but SSARs are less dilutive than options because the company issues only enough shares to equal the difference between the price of the stock at the award date and the price at vesting. Normally, a company will also deduct the shares needed to satisfy payment of ordinary income tax. In addition, employees get actual shares, usually net of taxes, which may encourage them to remain shareholders. By contrast, options count as issued shares when calculating dilution at the time the options are granted, which by definition is a much higher number.

RSUs also generated some buzz a few years ago, although their adoption rates have been fairly slow. Because RSUs are now subject to deferred compensation tax rules, they may gain even less popularity. RSUs delay any dilution until the shares are paid, but at that point, they are as dilutive as the issuance of any other face-value stock award. Unlike restricted stock, they rarely pay dividends or carry other stock rights until the shares are paid out (these rights would have to be assigned in some way other than attaching them to actual shares, however).

From a tax standpoint, both of these kinds of awards are deductible to the company when paid out, but taxed to the employee as ordinary income. Both types of plans could also encourage employees to hold on to shares if they are paid out in shares net of taxes, an approach that also minimizes dilution.

1.4.3 Direct Stock Purchase Plans

Direct stock purchase plans also have their pros and cons. Among the arguments for these plans are the following:

- If employees own shares as individuals, as opposed to through some kind of trust or similar arrangement, they may feel more like real owners.

- If employees have to buy shares, they are making more of a real commitment to the company.

- The purchase of shares infuses new capital into the company.

- Ownership is held only by people interested enough to make a financial sacrifice.

On the other hand:

- If employees have to buy shares, how many will be able to do so? Will ownership end up being distributed mostly to higher-paid people? While this may be the company's objective, it will mean the company will be unlikely to be able to develop an ownership culture in which most or all employees will think and act like owners. Some owners think just making stock available to people is enough to accomplish this purpose, even if they do not buy it, but there is little reason to believe this is the case.

- If a company asks employees to buy shares, will they feel pressured to purchase them even when they are not in a financial position to take that risk? Will they resent what they may perceive as subtle—or not so subtle—pressure? Will they rush to sell shares at the first opportunity to minimize their financial risk?

- Will employees who own shares directly be able to sell them when they like, thus reducing the incidence of employee ownership in a company? If they cannot sell when they like, will this make them less interested in owning shares?

- If there are stock registration or other legal forms and procedures to comply with, will the costs of compliance justify the amount of investment employees make?

- Direct stock purchases must be made with after-tax employee dollars; other plans can arrange for more favorable terms.

1.4.4 Restricted Stock

Restricted stock plans have a number of advantages:

- They provide some kind of service or performance target for employees to achieve before actually receiving shares or having the right to buy them. For instance, a seniority target can help assure that people don't "take the money and run" before making a contribution to the company. A profit or growth target can be a useful way to focus the attention of employees as a group on an objective.

- They can carry dividend or voting rights, if the company chooses.

- Unlike stock options or stock appreciation rights, restricted stock retains some value for employees even if the price goes down.

- Employees can receive capital gains treatment on all or part of the gain on the shares, provided they make a Section 83(b) election, as described in the chapter on restricted stock.

There are, of course, disadvantages as well:

- The restrictions may make ownership seem like an unlikely benefit. If an employee purchases shares, especially at the market price, but then cannot actually take possession of them until certain events occur, buying the shares may not seem very attractive.

- Restricted stock has no value unless there is a market for the shares at some point. Employees must believe this is a real possibility, not just a corporate intention.

- The company cannot take a tax deduction for the value of the gain employees eventually realize if employees have made a Section 83(b) election to have the gain taxed as a capital gain.

- Relative to other plans, restricted stock is a more complicated approach and can involve significant financial risks for employees if they choose to make a Section 83(b) election to obtain capital gains treatment on any increase in share value they eventually realize.

1.4.5 Performance Awards

Performance awards have several advantages:

- They can be settled in cash or stock.
- They are directly linked to performance targets.
- They are infinitely flexible in design.
- When settled in cash, they can more specifically link what an employee does to a desired result than do stock awards because part of the value of shares is created by things beyond the employee's control.

Among the disadvantages are:

- Awards settled in cash do not provide an ownership stake.
- Determining accurate and acceptable measures of performance can be tricky.
- Focusing employee effort on one or more goals, such as sales, quality, or profit, may lead the employee not to focus on other important objectives.
- Individually based awards may discourage teamwork.

1.5 Deciding on Key Plan Features

The sections below explore a variety of issues that affect all kinds of employee ownership plans. Subsequent chapters look at specific issues that affect stock option plans, stock purchase plans, profit-sharing type plans, and phantom plans.

1.5.1 How Much of Your Company's Equity or Equity Value Will You Share?

The first question you must ask is how much stock will be available for employees or, if you have a phantom stock plan or SAR plan, how much equity value you will share. It may seem at first blush that if you are not actually giving up stock, then you are not really giving people equity value, but rather just a bonus based on equity performance. In fact, however, if you pay people out based on equity value, you are giving up an important part of ownership. The value of a company is, in most companies, a function of the present value of future cash flows or earnings. If you pay people based on equity value or appreciation, your future stock value is being reduced in exactly the same way as if you gave them shares or stock options (the realized value of an option to an employee is the same as SARs on an equivalent number of shares). So whatever kind of plan you have, if it is based on equity in any way, you should think of it in terms of sharing ownership or its equivalent. Deciding how much ownership to share is obviously an essential, if difficult, first step in setting up a plan.

Generally, companies approach this issue in one of two ways. The most common is to determine in advance some percentage of total shares or equity value that the existing owners are comfortable in sharing. Unless employees pay fair value for the stock in a direct share purchase plan, sharing ownership or equity value dilutes the economic value of the ownership already held by dividing the claims on the company's assets into more pieces. If employees have to purchase shares at a fair market value, however, this economic effect is offset by the infusion of cash, so all owners end up having a smaller share of a larger company. Any ownership plan that allows employees to vote their shares or their share equivalents (such as phantom stock), however, dilutes control rights.

Owners' tolerance for stock or equity value dilution will depend in part on what they see as the alternatives. For instance, assume that owners are willing to share 10% of the stock or equity value of their company. What if this turns out to provide an insufficient incentive to attract, retain, and motivate those employees targeted by the plan? What else can be done? Will more current cash be needed to reward people, either with straight pay or bonuses? If more cash is spent, how will that affect future share price? Would it be better to share more of the company's future growth through some form of ownership than to deplete current cash that can be used to help the company grow?

Other factors come into play as well, however. In companies listed on stock exchanges, there are often informal norms about how much dilution is acceptable, as well as formal rules requiring shareholder approval for dilution. For any particular company, the range of acceptable dilution will vary with industry norms, company performance, the makeup of shareholders (some institutional shareholders, for instance, are more opposed to dilution than others), and the distribution of ownership rights to employees (generally, shareholders are more tolerant of broadly distributed ownership rights than concentration of ownership rights among a few key people). Going beyond what shareholders or the broader market of potential stock buyers find acceptable may be a signal to investors that the company wastes too much of its assets on excessive compensation.

Companies now can partially address this issue by paying in phantom stock or SARs (settled in cash or shares). These plans had been subject to very unfavorable accounting rules in that they required a current charge to earnings, whereas options did not (this changed with the new accounting rules effective in 2005). As a result, public companies especially tended to use these plans on a very limited basis (closely held companies tend to be less concerned with dilution). Shareholders will not look kindly on what they perceive as attempts to disguise stock ownership by providing it in an equivalent form. Public companies need to evaluate their total equity compensation package and be prepared to justify that to their investors. Of course, it should be said that in recent years, investors have shown remarkable tolerance for extraordinary levels of executive pay. That may be a disappearing artifact of a booming stock market, however.

In closely held companies, owners may have plans or obligations to provide family members, partners, or investors with a specific percentage of the company, either for control or economic reasons. Or, in many cases, they may have a conviction that they cannot share more than a certain percentage of total ownership rights. In some closely held companies, there are venture capital investors who may place strict limits on how much equity value can be shared, in whatever form. They may also have *minimum* guidelines from these investors for how much ownership they want key employees, or even all employees, to have, either by corporate contribution or by employee purchase. Companies with significant debt may also want to check whether there are any loan covenants that would make it difficult or impossible to pay out employees for their equity awards during the term of the loan.

The most common approach to this problem is to set a fixed ceiling on how much ownership or equity value can be shared, such as 10% of the shares or 5% of the equity value of the company (earned in shares or in cash) in any two-year period. Deciding in advance on a fixed percentage, however, is probably the least rational way to make a decision on this issue. First, companies that are growing often make the error of setting aside a certain percentage of stock ownership or equity value for employees and giving out most or even all of these shares to whoever is there early on. As the company grows, it then has only a small and shrinking pool of stock ownership or equity value to make available to new employees. The result is that a two-class system emerges of owners and those owning little or nothing, even among people doing the same jobs.

Another problem with the fixed percentage approach is that even if employment remains fairly stable, the job market can change. While departing employees may surrender their shares to the company to give out to new employees, the new employees may now expect more stock ownership or equity value than the company can make available. Similarly, company philosophy can change, calling for a greater emphasis on equity awards.

There are three principal methods of dealing with this. The first provides an initial percentage of stock ownership or equity value for employees that is below what the company expects to need in the long run. An upper parameter is also set, but set high enough to leave enough for expected contingencies. For instance, the company's board of directors may agree that in no case should employee ownership exceed 25% of the company's total shares or, over a 10-year period, more than 25% of the value of the company being given out to employees in the form of phantom stock or SAR payments. The employee ownership plan might start by providing half of this for employee plans, providing additional reserves as the company grows. If market conditions or a change in company philosophy demands more, the company can reconsider its positions and ask existing owners to authorize more stock ownership or equity value as needed. This ad hoc approach is simple and flexible, but shareholders often come to resent repeated requests for further dilution, seeing it perhaps as a sign of management incompetence or employee greed.

One solution to this is that within the fixed limit for additional share or equity award issues, a company might create some automatic devices for issuing stock ownership or equity value that will not require periodic shareholder approval. For instance, in our example, shareholders might agree that not more than 15% of the stock ownership or equity value can be given out. As long as the company stays under that number, however, it might be authorized to issue enough additional stock ownership or equity value each year so that any equity awards that are cashed in are used to provide opportunities for other employees. Or the formula might be adapted so that the total amount of stock ownership or equity value available will increase with employment up to a limit, with additional awards issued as needed to supplement those that are cashed in.

A second approach would be to base the amount of stock ownership or equity value given out on employee compensation or job responsibilities. Owners can be told at the outset that they should expect the amount of stock ownership or equity value available to increase as the total number and composition of the work force changes. If owners can agree that the formulas used to provide stock ownership or equity value to employees make sense for the current work force, they might agree that the same guidelines would make sense for a future work force. If the employment composition changes more dramatically than anticipated when a calculation was made about how much dilution this formula would cause—because of growth or hiring more higher paid or specialized people—this would normally be a sign of company success and, hopefully, share value growth, so owners may be persuaded to share some of the unexpectedly good performance.

A third approach is to base the total pool of stock ownership or equity value available on corporate performance. Owners would agree in advance, perhaps on a periodic basis, that if performance exceeded certain targets, employees would get a percentage of the resulting increment in the form of additional equity rewards, based on whatever formula is being used to allocate them. Because the owners dilute their position only if employees help create more value for that position, they should be more willing to share than if some automatic formula gives out awards regardless of performance. It also gives employees a more specific reason to focus on performance targets.

1.5.2 Liquidity

An equity sharing plan has no value if the shares that are awarded cannot be sold or the promised cash payments for phantom stock or SARs cannot be made. Generally, this is not a problem in companies listed on stock exchanges, but this is true only if there is an active market for the shares and the employee receives a class of shares that can be sold. If employees get non-voting shares, for instance, these shares might not be among those traded and may have little if any value. Securities rules may also restrict the ability of key employees to sell their shares, at least for certain periods of time.

Liquidity is a more serious issue for closely held companies. By definition, there is no ready market for shares of these companies. In the case of restricted stock, directly purchased shares, performance awards paid out in shares, or the unusual case of phantom stock or SARs paid out in shares, liquidity can be provided in these cases in a number of ways:

- *Share repurchase by company:* The company can agree to repurchase the shares from employees at stated intervals (every so many years, every time share value exceeds a certain amount, when the employee leaves the company, when the company has more than a certain amount of cash on hand, or some other rule). Companies can modify this in a variety of ways. If shares are held a certain number of years, for instance, employees may be paid full value, but if an employee leaves before then, the company might only pay the employee back what the employee paid for the shares, perhaps with interest. Or the company might agree to a reduced price buyback feature but allow the employee to sell the shares elsewhere for full price. Note, of course, that money used to buy back shares is a non-productive expense providing the company with no new investments it can use to make more money. On the other hand, either of the two methods below risk that employees will not get paid or, almost as bad, believe that they may not be paid.

    If the company does buy the shares, it should consider an employee stock ownership plan (ESOP). As explained in the final chapter of this book, an ESOP can provide a way to buy out owners with tax-deductible corporate dollars. If the owners bought their shares at full price in a direct share purchase program, and have held them for at least three years before the sale, they can also defer taxes on the gain by reinvesting the proceeds in the securities of domestic corporations not receiving more than 25% of their income from passive investment. This benefit applies only if the company is a C corporation, however.

- *Internal market:* The company can try to set up an internal market for employees to buy and sell from one another. This can supplement other approaches or be the entire approach (which will probably mean some employees will not be able to sell their shares for longer than they want). Securities rules may impose onerous requirements on such market making, however, so these laws need to be investigated. Short of a formal market, of course, employees may informally be allowed to buy and sell from one another.

- *Liquidity only on the occurrence of certain events:* The company can allow liquidity only on certain events occurring—for example, the shares may be sold only if someone else buys the company, the company goes public, or a major investor is brought in. In the interim, the company might agree to buy shares from employees at a fixed lower price if they did not want to wait. Not allowing liquidity unless one of these events occurs, however, may be risky if employees do not believe that the event is likely in the reasonable future. This is especially true with respect to IPOs. Although thousands of companies believe they are good IPO candidates, over the last 30 years, only about 7,000 companies have gone public, a number of them spin-offs of large companies.

If the awards are made in cash rather than shares, the company has to arrange for funds to be available. One approach is to set up a corporate sinking fund. Companies simply can set aside cash to be used to pay off their obligations under employee awards. These accumulated earnings, however, could be subject to an excess accumulated earnings tax. The law provides that earnings accumulated in excess of reasonable business needs are subject to the highest marginal tax rates. Virtually any corporation can accumulate up to $250,000 ($150,000 for service-type corporations) without this tax applying, but amounts above this could be taxable. Many advisors argue that accumulating earnings for the purpose of paying out employee awards such as phantom stock or SARs, however, is a legitimate business purpose. It is advisable to discuss this matter with counsel before creating a reserve fund.

If a company does establish a fund to pay for employee awards, the fund would most likely be a "rabbi trust" or "secular trust." A rabbi trust holds funds that must be paid to employees at the time the plan states they can get paid for their equity awards. This may be when they exercise an award or could be after some required post-exercise holding period. While the funds are being held, the employer cannot use them to fund ongoing business needs. However, if there are creditor claims against the company, the fund can be used to satisfy them if other funds are not available. The advantage of a rabbi trust is that the fact that the availability of the funds is contingent means employees will not be taxed on the employee's pro-rata portion of the earnings or contributions to the trust.

By contrast, a secular trust actually sets aside money for the employee and is not subject to claims of corporate creditors. As a result, the employee is taxed on contributions to the trust and earnings of the trust as they occur. The employer, however, can take a tax deduction for contributions to the trust when they are made, while in a rabbi trust the company only gets a deduction when the funds are paid out. Secular trusts also provide more certainty to employees that they will actually get paid for their equity interests than do the more contingent rabbi trusts.

In practice, most deferred compensation plans, whether based on equity or other measures, use rabbi trusts. Taxing employees currently on a benefit they will receive later (or may not receive at all if they do not vest in the award or forfeit the award subject to some condition in the plan) may be a significant demotivator.

There is, of course, a more basic problem with accumulating earnings this way, namely that they are not being used to help the business grow. An alternative would be to plan to borrow money as the need arises. The argument here is that rates of return on invested capital in corporate operations should, almost by definition, normally exceed rates of return on debt. The risk is that the company will be unable or unwilling to borrow the funds needed when they are needed. Telling employees their awards will be funded this way will also not generate a lot of confidence.

As with actual stock ownership, it is possible to write the plan so that the award of phantom stock or the exercise of SARs is available only if there is a liquidity event, such as going public or a sale to a third party. Similarly, companies could restrict the sale of shares acquired under any of the plans described in this book until a liquidity event occurs. Because employees do not have the same legal claim with these awards that they would have if they actually owned shares, however, companies need to write into their governing contracts with employees that liquidity will occur on these events. Employers then need to commit to negotiate with buyers to make sure they agree to pay for these awards. Remember, because employees do not own stock, the buyer is not legally obligated to honor the award; it is, after all, a contractual agreement between the selling employer and the employee, not the buying employer and employee. If the company goes public, then investment bankers must be agreeable to having the company provide liquidity on or soon after the IPO, and this information will have to be disclosed in a prospectus. These elements of uncertainty can make employees more skeptical about the potential value of the awards.

Finally, if employees do actually end up with shares, companies should consider whether they want to have a "right of first refusal." This allows companies to require an employee to sell shares back to the company, rather than to another buyer, provided the company matches the competing offer within a specific reasonable period of time. If such a right is created, companies should have employees sign an agreement granting this right when the equity award is made.

1.5.3 Deferred Compensation Rules Under Section 409A

In the American Jobs Creation Act of 2004, a complex change was made to the treatment of deferred compensation by the addition of Section 409A to the Internal Revenue Code. Employees can now defer the receipt of a vested (and thus taxable) deferred compensation award, such as one of the equity awards described here, by making an election. So, for instance, an employee might elect to defer receipt of a phantom stock payout for some years after it vests, paying tax only at the time the award is actually paid out. This approach has been used by (and generally only offered to) executives. Under Section 409A, employees will be able to elect to defer only if several conditions are met:

1. The employee dies, becomes disabled, there is a change in control, there is an unforeseen emergency (as rigorously defined in the law), or there is a fixed date or schedule specified by the plan.

2. Elections for deferral must be made not later than the close of the preceding taxable year in which the award would vest or, if made in the first year of the award, within 30 days after the employee first becomes eligible for an award. If the employee is a key employee (as defined by statute) of a public company, receipt of the benefit must be not earlier than six months after separation.

3. If the award is performance-based, the election must come not later than six months before the end of the performance period.

4. There can be no acceleration of benefits once a deferral election has been made.

5. Any subsequent elections for an award must be at least twelve months after the prior election and must defer receipt for at least five years in the future.

Section 409A does not apply to qualified benefit plans, such as ESOPs or 401(k) plans, as well as sick leave, death benefits, and similar arrangements. Existing rules for incentive stock options or employee stock purchase plans (ESPPs) qualifying under Section 423 of the Internal Revenue Code are not changed by this law. If the employee is granted an option on stock at not less than the fair market value, normal deferral features of such plans are not covered. The effective date of the rules initially was set at January 1, 2005, but that has been changed in regulations to January 1, 2008. Existing plans, however, are subject to transition rules that are beyond the scope of this discussion.

In proposed regulations, the IRS has clarified that stock appreciation rights, including stock-settled stock appreciation rights, can be used in both closely held and public companies, provided the rights are granted and awarded based on a fair market value. Restricted stock that does not contain a deferral feature as part of the grant is also exempt from the requirements. Phantom stock, restricted stock units, and performance units, however, are covered by the rules.

For closely held companies, one critical consideration is that the rules require a reasonable method of determining fair market value for any kind of option or stock appreciation right. Companies with an appraisal for an employee stock ownership plan (ESOP) can use that price; other companies can follow the rules for ESOP appraisals. These require an independent, outside appraisal performed at least annually by a qualified appraiser using standard methods of business appraisal (that is, determining what a willing buyer would pay a willing seller, generally determined by an analysis of comparable transactions, capitalization of earnings or cash flow, net asset value, and other considerations). Start-up companies in their first 10 years can use a somewhat simpler method. Formula appraisals can be used only under certain circumstances, including that the same price be used consistently for corporate transactions and that the formula be based on reasonable assumptions.

1.5.4 Who Will Be Eligible?

Deciding who is eligible depends on the company's goals and the kind of plan it operates. For instance, if the company is simply allowing employees to buy shares, it may want to base eligibility rules on how many shareholders it is willing to have, how it can structure an offer to avoid costly securities law requirements, or which employees it believes can legitimately take the risk. The tax and financial planning complexities of restricted stock and direct stock purchase plans generally make them more appealing as key-person plans. Phantom stock and SARs, by contrast, can more easily be used as broad-based plans. Performance awards, which can function much like a bonus, can be made to anyone, as well as to teams or groups.

Corporate goals for the plan raise even more important questions. For instance, the company may just want to provide an incentive for exceptional performance. By definition, then, only some employees will get stock awards in any one year. If the company is trying to establish a culture in which most or all employees think and act like owners, however, such restrictive practices may create a few winners and lots of losers. Even if everyone is eligible for an award, but in practice only a few people actually get one, there will inevitably be resentment and concern about favoritism. Another common corporate goal with an equity award plan is to attract and retain specific talented employees. In most cases, these plans will then only be made available to a few people, although a company may offer a different plan more broadly.

1.5.5 Arguments for Broad-Based Ownership Rights

Many readers of this book will have purchased it to help figure out how to attract, retain, and motivate key people. While this is a legitimate goal, it is also worthwhile to consider expanding ownership more broadly. In the last 20 years, broad-based employee ownership has become a mainstay of American business and, increasingly, of multinational companies as well. About 25 to 30 million U.S. employees now participate in one kind of broad-based plan or another (or about 25% of the non-governmental work force), primarily ESOPs, stock options, ESPPs, and 401(k) plans with employer stock as an investment alternative. Employers of all sizes, industries, and regions are participating in this trend.

While tax incentives account for some of this growth, most of it is a result of a growing belief that broad-based employee ownership helps companies perform better. More and more, companies are relying on their employees to share ideas and information about how to move the company forward. Employees at all levels have more responsibility, often working in teams to make an increasing number of decisions. Ownership, it turns out, is a very effective reward for employees who are making the effort to improve the corporate bottom line. Research from a variety of academic studies shows that companies that set up broad-based employee ownership plans grow 2% to 3% per year faster in employment, sales, and productivity than would have been expected otherwise. When broad ownership is combined with a high involvement work style, companies perform even better still.

For instance, DPR Construction is a Redwood City, CA, company that made all non-union and some union employees (about half its work force) eligible for phantom stock awards. Actual awards, however, are based on merit. Founders Peter Nosler, Doug Woods, and Ron Davidowski felt strongly that an informal, egalitarian environment would encourage creativity and enthusiasm that would translate into more efficient planning and procedures as well as a happier and more productive work force. As a result, DPR has no titles, no private offices, no hierarchy, and plenty of camaraderie. The company also has experienced phenomenal growth: from the proverbial "three men and a dog" to a privately held company of over 2,500 employees with 18 offices and revenues of over $1.2 billion.

As many as 90% of the eligible staff members have received grants during a year, from which they might reasonably expect, after fully vesting, an annual bonus equivalent to about 20% of their ordinary compensation. A five-year vesting schedule allows the employees to secure 20% of their total grant for each full year of employment. The holders of phantom stock do not receive any payment on a particular grant, however, until the entire five years elapse or they leave the company (in which case they are paid on a pro-rata basis for the percentage of time completed). Moreover, most eligible employees receive additional grants, thereby achieving a "rolling" equity interest. While DPR is now a very large company, it started its phantom plan when it just had a handful of employees. One of the most appealing things about phantom plans and similar approaches, in fact, is that they can fit companies of any size.

Many companies will choose instead some kind of gainsharing (a system of awards for employees, as individuals or groups, in which employees get a specified percentage of gains resulting from meeting preset performance targets) or profit-sharing mechanism to reward non-management employees; many others will provide no incentive pay. The research on these issues strongly suggests, however, that broad ownership is the most effective way to create a more innovative and productive corporate environment.

1.5.6 Key Issues in Thinking About Eligibility

Once a decision is made about how broadly the coverage of the plan should be, employers need to consider several other issues, as described below.

1. *Tenure:* At the simplest level, companies can require that people can get awards only after they have worked a minimum amount

of time, often one year. This assures at least some commitment on the part of the employee to the company.

2. *Full-Time/Part-Time:* In the past, it was unusual to provide equity incentives to part-time employees. Innovators like Starbucks, however, have provided awards to everyone (in Starbucks' case, stock options), arguing that many of their part-time people would (or if properly rewarded could) be long-term employees. Changes in both the work force and the nature of some jobs have made part-time workers more an integral and, in some cases, stable part of a company's total employment. Given the high cost of training and recruitment, providing an incentive for part-time people to stay makes sense for them. In making this decision, companies need to consider how important enough it is to retain part-time people, or whether these employees are more seasonal and short-term and thus very unlikely to stay with the company more than a short time under any circumstances.

3. *Merit:* One of the most common ways to define eligibility is some assessment of merit. This can be done in a variety of ways. Company or unit managers may be given the authority to decide who will get a stock award that year. There may be specific criteria established that measure employee performance (such as employee review ratings, personal sales or production goals, not missing days of work, or some other measure). Merit might also be defined at a team or group level so that if that unit meets certain performance targets, everyone will get an award.

4. *Position:* Many companies provide awards only to people above a certain position. This may just be managers or it could go much further down, such as technicians, assistant store managers, production supervisors, etc. Companies need to consider, however, that such an approach may make it very difficult to establish a culture of ownership that affects the entire company.

5. *On-Hire or Promotion:* For some companies, awards are granted to people only when they are hired or promoted. This can create something of a lottery effect, however, because the awards could have very different value depending on when the employees joined or were promoted. A company could end up with employees doing the same job with very different amounts of equity.

6. *Avoiding ERISA Requirements:* The "Employee Retirement Income Security Act" (ERISA) governs retirement plans such as ESOPs, pension plans, 401(k) plans, and profit sharing plans. Plans that fall under its control must follow specific guidelines for eligibility, allocations, distributions, and other matters of plan operation. They must also file periodic reports and, for plans with over 100 participants, have annual plan audits. Phantom stock, SAR, and restricted stock plans can all fall under ERISA if they are designed to benefit more than just key employees (this issue is discussed more in the chapter in this book on phantom stock and SARs) *and* they are designed to pay out benefits on retirement or, some advisors say, after long periods of employment even before termination. Restricting coverage requirements is thus one way to avoid being subject to ERISA, but plans can avoid these rules by following the approach of DPR and paying out awards on a periodic basis.

1.5.7 How Much Will Each Person Get?

The same criteria that might be used for eligibility might also be used for determining how much ownership people will get (tenure, promotion, position, and merit). Awards can also be made equally or based on hours worked or, as is common in qualified employee ownership plans such as ESOPs, according to relative pay. Each of these approaches, of course, has very different consequences for the kind of ownership culture the company is creating. The issue of allocation also applies primarily to stock award programs, not programs where employees buy shares.

A formula that indicates that people will get equity awards in proportion to relative pay (someone with 1% of pay would get 1% of the total stock award) sends a message the awards are simply part of the overall compensation system. If people regard current salary, benefit, and bonus systems as fair, they will probably view the equity award allocation formula as fair as well. Companies can also combine the relative pay approach with another formula, such as tenure or equal allocation, or can cap the amount of pay that is eligible.

A formula that indicates awards will be allocated on the basis of hours worked, on the other hand, says that ownership is more a basic right in the company and that everyone's contribution is valued equally.

This can be helpful in creating a culture of common ownership, but may also cause some resentment, and perhaps recruitment and retention problems as well, among higher-paid people.

A third formula provides awards based on promotion or a merit assessment. The message here is meritocracy. If employees believe that the system for judging merit or giving out promotions is fair, this may work well; if not, they may see ownership as just another way to enrich the undeserving. These approaches also send a message that all employees are not thought deserving of ownership, something that could make it harder to create an ownership culture. Some companies address this issue by creating merit award systems in which everyone is expected to earn ownership at some time in their tenure—or not stay with the company.

A fourth approach is seniority. This obviously encourages people to stay with the company, but may mean that only the very long-tenured people will see much benefit. It may also be discouraging to hard-working younger employees who may see the years required to get much stock as daunting or unrealistic.

Finally, the amount allocated may be based on the position held. Of all the formulas, this is the least likely to help create an ownership culture because it reinforces the notions of hierarchy that an effective ownership culture seeks to undermine. On the other hand, this approach may be appealing as a strategy to help attract and retain keep people.

Of course, these formulas can be combined in a variety of ways. A point system may give so many points for pay, so many for merit, etc. A multiple system approach may award some shares based on merit, some on tenure, and some on position.

1.5.8 Holding Periods and Forfeiture Rules

Where plans make awards in shares, a common concern of executives is that employees will not hold on to their shares long after they are awarded them or buy them. These executives believe that unless employees hold the shares, they won't ever think of themselves as owners. This may not be as obviously true as it seems, however. If employees are being awarded shares or even some equity equivalent on a periodic basis, they have an ongoing interest in the future share value of the company. The ability to cash in their shares periodically may be a very attractive plan feature. It also allows employees to avoid excessive risk from a concentration of their assets in company stock.

If companies do want employees to hold on to their shares, however, they can either require a minimum holding period (which may cause some resentment if share prices are volatile or fall) or provide incentives to hold shares, such as awarding bonus shares or options if the shares are held beyond a certain point. That way, employees are themselves making the investment decision. Of course, in many closely held companies, the issue of whether people hold their shares after their award may be moot because the company has no plans for providing any immediate cash value for them.

An important consideration in phantom, RSU, and SAR plans for setting requirements on holding periods after the award or exercise is whether employees will have to pay tax at the exercise of the award. The doctrine of constructive receipt states that an employee is taxable on a benefit once the employee has the right to control the timing of its payment. So if the plan structure says that employees have the right to the value of their SAR, RSU, or phantom stock once vested but can defer it to a later point, they would be taxable at the time this right becomes effective. The employee could defer the taxation by agreeing before earning the award (prior to its vesting) to defer its actual receipt until a later point, but this is much less practical under the new deferred compensation rules, which require the employee to specify in advance the date to which it will be delayed. Alternatively, if the employee has to pay something to get the award after it is exercised, that could also defer taxation. The issue of the taxation of the equity awards described in this chapter is discussed in detail in subsequent chapters of this book. The point here is that in designing these plans, companies must consider carefully how plan design can effect employee taxation.

On the flip side of the rules for holding shares is the requirement that employees disgorge the gains made on some or all of any equity award, share or cash-based, if they are fired for cause or go to work for a competitor. In the stock option arena, a number of companies have tried to institute what are known as "claw-back" agreements that require forfeitures of gains made if these conditions are met. These kinds of agreements can be hard to enforce. Many states (most notably

California) have very strict limitations on non-compete agreements that make most of them unenforceable. Forfeiting benefits on termination for cause, while it may be spelled out clearly in an employment agreement and/or equity award contract, can lead to lawsuits if the amounts involved are significant. Employees have sued employers over these provisions, for instance, claiming that they were fired only to prevent them from realizing significant gains. On the other hand, employers are understandably concerned about enriching employees who, in their view, have damaged the company. Finally, aside from legal concerns, "claw-back" agreements may raise employee doubts about the awards when they are granted.

1.5.9 Vesting

Most employee ownership plans have some kind of vesting provisions. Vesting is the term used to describe the amount of time an employee must work for the company after getting an equity award (or, in some cases, buying shares) before actually having a right to them. Vesting can either be all-at-once (after five years, for instance, someone has the right to 100% of the award) or gradual (an employee might get a right to 20% of the awards for every year worked, for instance). When plans are first set up, some companies give partial or full credit for prior years worked, while others start everyone from the date the plan is started.

Vesting obviously encourages employees to stay with the company. The trick is to find a schedule that retains good people without making them think that the chance of vesting is so remote that the stock awards are irrelevant. Careful attention to company turnover patterns is also essential. If the company has very high, and unavoidable, turnover in the first three years, it might want to not start vesting till the third year. If turnover is very low anyway, faster vesting can be an attractive benefit that has few negative consequences for the company. Giving credit for prior service will be well received by employees, but can increase plan costs and raise the risk that some people may get their benefit and leave. Not giving credit for prior service, however, may cause serious resentment among senior employees.

In any event, the analysis for all these issues should be combined with an assessment of who the company really wants to end up owning shares, as vesting schedules can preclude whole classes of people this way.

1.5.10 Voting and Control

Perhaps the most contentious issue about employee ownership is whether employees will have the right to vote their shares or other ownership rights and/or have other representation rights in company management. To some people, the notion that employees can really be owners without voting or control rights seems absurd; it's one of the basic rights of ownership. Others note that there are different kinds of ownership, and that ownership rights are largely a function of what people have contributed to get them. Owners who have made an investment of capital, time, and/or risk, they say, deserve control rights in a way that employees who get actual ownership or ownership equivalency rights as a benefit of employment do not.

Our research at the NCEO indicates that this is a less important issue than it seems. Employees generally do not care intensely about whether they can vote for members of the board or other typical corporate voting issues and usually have only mild interest in being represented on the company's governing bodies. When employees do have control rights, they tend to exercise them very conservatively, and their board representatives tend to act very responsibly. They almost never use their power to throw out management. Where employees buy shares or make concessions to get them, their attitude would certainly be different. In a direct stock purchase plan, for instance, employees would most likely argue that they should have the same rights as any other shareholder.

1.5.11 Dividends

Dividends can be paid on shares that have been delivered to employees. In fact, dividends are often paid on unvested restricted stock.

Under the deferred compensation rules of Internal Revenue Code Section 409A, the right to receive accrued dividends upon the exercise of a stock option, stock appreciation right (SAR), or restricted stock unit is tantamount to a discount from the grant date fair market value.

However, arrangements for dividend-like payments that are separate from the award ("dividend equivalent rights") are acceptable under the proposed regulations under Section 409A. For those arrangements, the date at which the dividend equivalents will be paid must be determined in advance to avoid the payment itself being taxed as deferred compensation.

When a dividend equivalent right is paid, the amount is taxed as ordinary income. The company must withhold taxes and is eligible for a corresponding tax deduction.

Because restricted stock usually pays out when it vests, it is not treated as deferred compensation under Section 409A, and as a result recipients can be, and usually are, paid dividends on unvested shares.

- *Stock options:* Typically there are no dividends or dividend equivalents on unexercised awards. Once options are exercised, the holder receives dividends like any other shareholder as long as he or she holds the stock.

- *Restricted stock:* They typically carry dividend rights even before vesting. Dividends paid on unvested awards for which no Section 83(b) election has been filed are taxed as ordinary income. The company must withhold taxes on these, and it can take a corresponding tax deduction. Dividends paid on awards for which a Section 83(b) election has been made are taxed as dividend income. In that case, no withholding is required, and the company is not eligible for a tax deduction on the dividend payment.

- *SARs:* Dividend equivalent rights can be offered only as separate arrangements not tied to the exercise of the SAR, even if the employee has control over the SAR's exercise date.

- *Phantom stock/RSUs:* There are no dividends; there may be dividend equivalent rights.

1.6 Making the Plan Effective

Designing the plan well is only the first part of the battle. An effective employee ownership plan requires an ownership culture. The first step in creating this culture is good communications. On the most basic level, employees need to understand how the plan works. In most companies, this means providing material that outlines legal rights and responsibilities. Employees sign off on documents acknowledging they have received and read these materials. These "rules of the game," however, are no more effective as communication tools than, say, the rules for a board game are effective means to get people to know how to play. How many of you read the rule book first? So in addition to these legal documents, companies need to provide plain-English explanations, hold employee meetings, and, if needed, meet with employees one-to-one to explain how the plan operates. On an ongoing basis, updates on company activities, changes in the plan, corporate performance, equity value growth, and other key ownership issues need to be provided. Larger companies often create an employee committee charged with the task of finding effective ways to keep this communication going.

While a strong communications program is a good start, research is very clear that economic performance will not significantly improve just because people have a financial incentive, even if they are really tuned in to how it works. Part of this is because of the so-called "1/n" problem. Scratch up just about any economist and ask about employee ownership, and he or she will tell you about this dilemma. It's the argument that if an incentive is provided to a group of people to achieve a collective aim (such as improving the stock price), the value of that incentive to any individual employee will diminish directly in proportion to the number of employees. It assumes employees will look at all the other people they work with and say "look, I'm just one of 10, or 50, or 1,000, or 100,000." The bigger the n, the less they are motivated by the reward.

It seems like a very compelling argument. Why should I put in a lot of extra physical or mental effort when my efforts alone really won't affect the stock price in any meaningful way? Moreover, I can always rely on the efforts of other people to get the stock price up, so I can be a "free rider." People who make the 1/n argument say that it is better to design incentive systems that apply to smaller groups of people and that provide rewards for specific things that they do.

The argument seems persuasive if one assumes people act (1) only for their own narrow economic self-interest and (2) they believe that their self-interest is not furthered by cooperative behavior. But ownership is a more complicated motivation than an "if I do this, I'll get that" calculation. In an effective employee ownership or equity sharing program, people's behavior changes not so much because they perceive that there is an incentive to do x or y, but because the company has changed its organizational approach so that certain kinds of cooperative behaviors are now structured into the work place. In return for people living up to higher expectations, they get ownership as a reward.

When people identify with an organization, they see its success as their own. In this sense, as the organization grows (and "n" usually becomes larger), each individual feels more successful. To get to that point, organizations need to show that they value each employee. Employee ideas are sought out in active and ongoing ways. Employees have opportunities to implement projects they and their colleagues create, provided they can make a good case for them. There are opportunities for individual growth and learning. And the company makes an effort to respect the needs of the individuals as people with lives outside their jobs. This kind of loyalty to employees usually engenders a return loyalty to and identification with the organization.

But motivation itself is not enough. Just getting people to work harder or more carefully at the same things is less valuable than getting people to think about how things can be done better. That requires what organizational development experts now call "high-involvement management." The studies on employee ownership and corporate performance could not be clearer on this point. It is the combination of employee ownership and a highly participative management style that distinguishes successful employee ownership companies from less successful ones. For instance, the NCEO found that companies that combine ownership and employee participation in work-level decisions grow 8% to 11% per year faster than they would have been expected to grow without this combination. Subsequent academic studies in New York and Washington confirmed both the direction and magnitude of these findings. A U.S. General Accounting Office study of ESOPs found that productivity growth rates jumped 52% when ownership and participation were combined. Neither ownership nor participation, on their own, make much difference.

Employee involvement can take many forms. Employee task forces, ad hoc and permanent, can be established to solve problems. In larger companies, permanent teams might be set up in discrete work areas, such as warehousing, customer service, marketing, and production. In smaller companies, periodic staff meetings might serve this purpose. Employees can be given greater authority over their own jobs as well.

Aside from getting employees more involved in decisions, companies need to give them the kind of business information they need to make decisions intelligently. At Springfield ReManufacturing in Springfield, MO, for instance, employee owners are taught to read detailed financial and production data. Meeting in workgroups, they go over the numbers then figure out ways to improve them. The company has grown from 119 employees in 1983 to over 1,000 today, while its stock price has gone from 10 cents to over $85. It also is important to share not just financial information with employees, but also "critical" numbers that look at measures of their own work processes. These measurements help employees assess the effectiveness of their efforts and create a kind of "game" environment that is motivating on its own.

1.7 Conclusion

Sharing the rewards of equity has repeatedly been shown to have the potential to improve corporate performance in a variety of ways, especially when shared broadly and in combination with the creation of an "ownership culture." Even when only shared with specific employees, however, it can still help companies attract and retain critical talent. As this chapter has made clear, however, sharing equity cannot be just a "back of the envelope" exercise. It requires careful deliberation about the form equity sharing should take, plan structure, legal and tax issues, and corporate culture. The input of qualified advisors is essential. Just as there is much to gain, there is also much to lose. Disgruntled employees who believe they have not received what they were promised not only will be demotivated themselves but also can poison the atmosphere for other employees. In the worst case, they can sue over the plan. Most lawsuits in this field are generated from just a few kinds of disputes:

- Improper valuations of the stock.
- Failure (or perceived failure) to live up to the terms of the plan.
- Promises made (or perceived) that were not delivered.

- Employees who are terminated prior to their equity interest vesting who claim their terminations were to prevent them from getting an award.

Companies can never fully insulate themselves against these potential problems. Careful plan design, clear and thorough communication with employees, and a willingness to operate the plan in a way that is genuinely fair to all parties can avoid most problems, however. There are few, if any, attributes of a business more important than ownership. Sharing it deserves the most thoughtful consideration.

CHAPTER TWO

Phantom Stock and Stock Appreciation Rights

Helen H. Morrison
Kay Kemp
Joe Adams

Contents

Virtually all public and many private companies reward their key employees with equity-based awards. A growing number of companies now make these awards to employees below the key employee level as well, and many make stock available to most or all employees. The simple explanation for including equity grants as part of an employee's compensation package is to provide the employee with the incentive to improve the company's financial performance and increase shareholder value. This objective is straightforward, but the selection of the appropriate equity-based incentive program to achieve the objective is much more complicated. Equity grants come in many forms, such as stock options, stock grants, stock appreciation rights (SARs), and phantom stock. In addition to choosing the right equity compensation vehicle, choosing the right program design is equally important. For example, will the employee vest in the grants with the passage of time or based on performance achievements? Will payments be made during the term of employment or deferred to termination or retirement? Which employees should receive the equity-based grants and in what amount? Another critical objective for any company that implements an equity-based program is to increase shareholder value, not to dilute it.

Fundamentally, equity-based programs may be separated into two types of awards:

1. Awards that provide the employee with appreciation, if any, in the value of the underlying stock, Stock options with an exercise price based on the fair market value of the underlying stock are the classic example of an award that provides a benefit equal to the appreciation in the underlying stock. If the value of the underlying stock fails to appreciate before the expiration of the option, the employee receives no benefit but is not harmed because no investment was required. SAR grants are similar to stock options, with the exception that the employee generally has no obligation to pay an exercise

price, and the award is generally paid in cash, rather than shares of stock (although, as discussed later in this chapter, stock-settled SARs may become more common in the future given changes in accounting rules).

2. Awards that provide the employee with the underlying value of the stock, *plus* the appreciation, if any, following the award date. Restricted stock grants are a basic example of an award that provides the employee with the benefit of the underlying value from the date of grant, plus the appreciation, if any, thereafter. Phantom stock awards are similar to restricted stock awards with the exception that the award is generally paid in cash rather than shares of stock.

Within these two broad types of awards, there is a follow-up question as to whether the award should be paid in cash or in shares. The answer depends on a number of factors, such as whether the company is private or public and whether the objective is employee retention or providing a performance incentive. Public companies are more likely to make actual stock awards, either in the form of a stock option or in the form of a (restricted) stock grant, because their stock is already widely held and the value can be more easily determined. Private company owners may prefer not to provide their employees with actual stock awards, but they may still be interested in providing the employees with an incentive to increase shareholder value with equity-based grants. In this case, a SAR or phantom stock award would be more appropriate. Although it may be an overgeneralization, programs that provide the employee with the underlying value of the stock (e.g., restricted stock or phantom stock) have a stronger retention element, whereas appreciation right programs (e.g., stock options or SARs) are designed to motivate employees to improve financial performance and grow shareholder value.

The focus of this chapter is "phantom equity" awards: SARs and phantom stock awards. The chapter will define SARs and phantom stock awards, and distinguish them from each other and from other forms of equity-based grants, such as stock options and stock grants. It will discuss the reasons for implementing a SAR or phantom stock program and the plan design issues that should be addressed. The income tax, securities law, and ERISA consequences of making SAR or phantom stock awards are critically important to the understanding and success of the program and will be discussed in detail. Accounting issues are addressed in this book's chapter on accounting.

Practitioners use the terms "phantom stock," "phantom award," "phantom share plan," "phantom share unit," "phantom stock option," and "SAR" interchangeably to describe an incentive compensation program similar to either a stock option or restricted stock. In this chapter, we will use the term "SAR" to refer to a phantom award that provides a benefit equal only to the appreciation (if any) in the underlying stock. The term "phantom stock" award or grant will denote an award similar to restricted stock that provides the value of the underlying stock plus any appreciation.

2.1 Distinguishing SARs and Phantom Stock

A SAR is a right to be paid an amount equal to the difference between the value of the employer's underlying stock value on the date of exercise and the value on the date of grant. SARs reward the participant only for the appreciation in the underlying stock value. By contrast, participants in a phantom stock program are entitled to receive payment for the underlying stock value, as well as the appreciation, if any, in such stock. Under a phantom stock program, the participants receive an award of hypothetical shares of company stock and are entitled to payment at a specified date for the full value of the underlying shares. Generally, SARs and phantom stock awards are designed to provide for a cash payment of the benefit rather than payment in the form of shares of company stock. However, as discussed later in this chapter, certain employers may now have reason to design a SAR with payment in the form of company shares (a "stock-settled SAR").

2.1.1 Stock Appreciation Rights (SARs)

A SAR is a variation of a stock option. Like a stock option, a SAR provides the grantee with the appreciation, if any, in the value of the underlying stock from the date of grant to the date of exercise.

A SAR program has traditionally included the following features:

- Participants do not make a capital investment in the company but instead have a contractual right to receive a future payment from the company, pending satisfaction of the terms and conditions of the program.

- Participants generally have the right to "exercise" and realize the value of their SARs at their election (once vesting has occurred) or upon the occurrence of a payout event, which can include any or all of a specified date in the future, termination of employment, a change in control, or a public offering.

- Participants are rewarded based only on the excess, if any, of the value of the company as of a future payout event over the value of the company as of the date of grant (the "exercise price").

- Participants generally receive a cash payment for their award and do not become shareholders of the company. However, SAR programs may be designed to provide for payouts in shares of company stock.

The American Jobs Creation Act of 2004 included new deferred compensation tax rules that affect the design of SAR programs. The new rules are contained in Section 409A of the Internal Revenue Code of 1986, as amended (the "Code").[1] Code Section 409A (referred to here simply as Section 409A) provides two general approaches to SARs: (1) the SAR program can be designed to be *exempt from* the requirements of Section 409A, or (2) the SAR program can be designed to *comply with* Section 409A. A SAR program that neither is exempt from nor complies with Section 409A will result in severe tax penalties for participants.

A SAR program can be designed to be exempt from Section 409A and thus can continue to make grants and otherwise operate as in the past, provided the program meets the following requirements:

---

1. "Section 409A," as referred to here, includes the applicable guidance issued by the IRS for that section—specifically, Notice 2005-1 and proposed regulations issued in September 2005. The Section 409A rules are complicated and comprehensive. A complete discussion of Section 409A is beyond the scope of this chapter. However, a brief discussion of the important Section 409A rules that are applicable to SARs and phantom stock is included.

- The SAR must provide for payment not greater than the difference between the fair market value of the underlying common stock on the date of exercise and the fair market value of the underlying common stock on the date of grant. The proposed regulations under Section 409A define "fair market value" for this purpose. (See section 2.3.3 below for a discussion of the definition of "fair market value" under the proposed regulations.)

- The "exercise price" cannot be less than the fair market value of the company's common stock on the date of grant.

- The number of shares covered by the grant must be fixed at or before the date of grant.

- The SAR cannot provide for a deferral of income beyond the date the SAR is exercised.

This chapter refers to a SAR program that meets the above requirements as a "409A-exempt SAR."

If the above requirements are not met, then SARs that are granted or that vest after 2004 must comply with the requirements of Section 409A.[2] Generally, this means that participants will not be permitted to exercise their SARs freely. Instead, the SAR grant will have to specify the applicable payment events, which could include one or more of the following: a specified payment date, separation from service, death, disability, or a change in control (as defined in Section 409A). SAR awards that comply with the requirements of Section 409A are not required to be valued in accordance with the strict "fair market value" definition of 409A-exempt SARs. Instead, the employer may designate the valuation methodology based on an objective formula (e.g., a multiple of cash flow, EBITDA, operating earnings, net earnings, or book value; or another

---

2.   SARs that were granted and vested before 2005 are grandfathered, i.e., they remain subject to the old tax rules, provided they are not materially modified in any way. Grandfathered SARs can continue to be exercised at the participant's election much the same as the 409A-exempt SARs discussed in this chapter. However, in the event a grandfathered SAR is materially modified in any way, the SAR would automatically become subject to the requirements of Section 409A (and would likely be immediately in violation of Section 409A). Accordingly, employers desiring to preserve the grandfathered status of pre-2005 SARs should take care to not inadvertently materially modify those SARs.

financial measurement such as a trailing average of the last three years' net earnings) or a good-faith determination by the board of directors. This chapter refers to a SAR program that meets the applicable requirements of Section 409A as a "409A-compliant SAR."

An employer will want to comply with all requirements of Section 409A if its SAR program will not qualify for the exemption because the penalties for failure to comply are extremely onerous. In the event of a failure to comply:

- The employee[3] is taxed on the value of the SAR award in the year of the failure (or the year of vesting, if later) and is subject to a 20% income tax penalty. Further, the IRS has suggested that the tax may occur each year the non-compliant SAR is outstanding.

- Interest is also payable, in an amount equal to the underpayment rate plus one percentage point, imposed on the underpayments that would have occurred had the compensation been includible in income for the taxable year when first deferred, or if later, when no longer subject to a substantial risk of forfeiture.

- All "like" arrangements are generally treated as a single arrangement for purposes of these rules. The IRS has established four categories of arrangements: account-based arrangements, non-account-based arrangements, separation pay, and other types of arrangements (generally including SARs and other forms of equity-based arrangements). If a failure occurs with respect to an arrangement in one of these categories, then all other arrangements in that same category are deemed to have failed as well, so the aforementioned penalties would apply to all arrangements in that category.

- The penalties for failure to satisfy Section 409A are imposed entirely on the affected employees, except for penalties that would be assessed on the employer for failure to satisfy applicable reporting and withholding requirements.

---

3. Section 409A applies to nonqualified deferred compensation arrangements involving common-law employees as well as other service providers, such as independent contractors, consultants, and non-employee directors. Throughout this chapter, the term "employee" or "participant" should be understood to include all types of service providers when the requirements of Section 409A are being addressed.

If there is a Section 409A failure, the employer must report the deferral amount includible in income on the individual's Form W-2 or Form 1099-MISC (for a non-employee) for the year in which the failure occurred. Generally, the employer must withhold income tax on the deferral amount in the year of income inclusion, but not later than the date on which the amount is actually or constructively received by the employee. Penalties and interest would likely be payable by the individual when he or she files Form 1040 for the applicable year, but, as of this writing, the Internal Revenue Service (IRS) has not issued specific guidance on this aspect of the new rules.

Table 2-1 provides a brief summary of the different tax and reporting characteristics for 409A-compliant SARs and 409A-exempt SARs.

2.1.2 Phantom Stock

Phantom stock awards are analogous to restricted stock grants but provide no actual shares to employees. Such awards provide the recipient with the benefit of the value of the underlying company stock, not just the appreciation in stock value.

Like a SAR program, a phantom stock program does not usually require or permit the participants to make a capital investment in the company. Instead, a participant has a contractual right to receive future payments from the company, subject to satisfaction of the program's terms and conditions. However, in some circumstances, companies do have modified phantom share programs in connection with their executive deferred compensation plans. In such cases, the executive's deferred compensation is "invested" in phantom shares.

Some of the features of a phantom stock award that are different from the features of a SAR award include the following:

- Participants receive a bonus award of units in the form of hypo- thetical shares of stock, usually with no "exercise price" or required employee investment except in the case of a deferred compensation plan investing in phantom shares.

- Participants have phantom stock units credited to their accounts.

- Generally, the participant's phantom stock account will also be credited with any future cash or stock dividend equivalents and

Table 2-1. Characteristics of 409A-Compliant SAR vs. a 409A-Exempt SAR

	409A-Compliant SAR	409A-Exempt SAR
Strike price must be no less than fair market value on the date of grant (no formula value)	No	Yes
Participant can receive payments on a vested SAR at any time, at his or her discretionary election	No	Yes
Payments may be made over a period of years	Yes	No (payment must be made in a lump sum)
Must comply with 409A distribution timing and deferral election requirements	Yes	No
Failure to comply with 409A distribution and deferral election requirements results in immediate taxation upon vesting and 20% excise tax to the participant	Yes	No
Employer is required to report and withhold income tax, FICA, and Medicare when payment is made[a]	Yes (provided that SAR is compliant; if not, SAR is subject to income tax reporting and withholding and 20% excise tax when vested [FICA and Medicare taxes unchanged])	Yes

[a] Under Code Section 409A, any deferral of compensation must be reported by the employer in the year of deferral, regardless of whether the amount is then taxable to the employee. As of this writing, the IRS has provided only limited guidance on this requirement, but it is expected to issue regulations on this subject soon.

any stock splits attributable to the shares, although in some cases participants are not entitled to dividend equivalents until they vest in the phantom shares.

- Participants are generally entitled to payment at a specified date in the future (e.g., the earliest of a date certain, termination of employment, change of control, or a public offering).

Section 409A generally applies to phantom stock awards granted or that vest after 2004. Section 409A requires all applicable non-qualified deferred compensation, including phantom stock awards, to comply with strict distribution and deferral election requirements. For example, payment of the participant's benefit may be paid only upon a permissible distributable event, which includes a specified payment date, separation from service, death, disability, and a change of control (as defined in Section 409A). Initial deferral elections as well as redeferral elections are subject to specific timing requirements set forth in Section 409A.

2.2 When Would an Employer Establish a SAR or Phantom Stock Program?

Before establishing any equity-based compensation program, an employer must assess several threshold issues:

- Which employees will receive the grant? Is the program intended only for executives and key employees or is it intended to be a broad-based program?
- What are the principal objectives of the program, e.g., to encourage retention, increase performance, etc.?
- What is the financial statement effect of the program? Does it matter whether the employer is privately held rather than publicly traded?

2.2.1 Key Employee Program vs. Broad-Based Program

SAR and phantom stock awards are typically made only to executives and key employees as part of their long-term compensation packages.

Because SAR and phantom stock programs may (but need not) be designed to provide for a cash payment at the participant's termination of employment or later, employers would be justifiably concerned that the program could be considered an ERISA retirement plan and, if the program were offered to a broad-based group of employees, it would be subject to all of the ERISA funding, eligibility, vesting, and fiduciary requirements.[4] (The ERISA issues related to SARs and phantom share plans are addressed later in this chapter.)

While SARs and phantom plans are generally only made available to key employees, if they are properly designed, they can be made available broadly. See chapter 1 for an example of a broad-based phantom stock plan at DPR Construction.

Historically, public companies that were interested in providing a broad-based equity compensation program would make stock option grants, create a discounted stock purchase program (under Code Section 423), or contribute company stock to an ESOP (employee stock ownership plan) or 401(k) plan. Stock options or discounted employee stock purchase plans have been perceived as a more acceptable form of non-retirement plan broad-based equity compensation because the financial accounting rules in effect before 2006 were more favorable for those plans than for SARs or phantom stock.[5] In addition, stock option grants may generally be exercised during the grantee's term of employment; as a result, they are not subject to the same ERISA concerns as SAR or phantom plans that allow payout only at termination of employment.

---

4. "ERISA" refers to the Employee Retirement Income Security Act of 1974, as amended. Section 3(2)(A)(ii) of ERISA defines an "employee pension benefit plan" as any plan that "results in a deferral of income by employees for periods extending to termination of covered employment or beyond."

5. Under the most commonly applied financial accounting standard in effect before 2006, APB Opinion No. 25, stock option grants, unlike SARs and real or phantom stock awards, did not result in compensation expense on the company's income statement. However, effective in 2006, a new accounting standard, FAS 123(R), became effective, requiring all companies to report stock option grants as a compensation expense. (See chapter 6 of this book for a more complete discussion of equity-based accounting issues.)

2.2.2 Performance vs. Retention

SAR grants and phantom stock awards are generally made to encourage employee retention, provide an incentive to grow shareholder value, or a combination of both.

If the employer's principal objective is to motivate the participants in the program to grow the value of the business, a SAR grant is typically more appropriate. The holder of a SAR award receives no benefit unless the underlying stock value appreciates. As a result, the holder has an incentive to improve financial performance with the expectation of growing the stock value. SAR grants are frequently made subject to a vesting schedule to encourage retention, as well as to provide an incentive to grow value. However, the vesting element of a SAR grant is successful as a retention tool only to the extent that the stock continues to appreciate. If the underlying stock declines in value from the date of grant so that the SARs have no value, the employee might be more susceptible to entertain an offer to go elsewhere because he or she forfeits no value upon departure. For example, assume an employer makes annual SAR grants with a graded five-year vesting schedule for each grant. Assume further that the underlying stock value appreciates each year during the first four years from $10 to $15, $20, $25, and then $30. If, at the end of five years, the underlying stock is valued at $40 per share, the employee would have a significant unvested build-up of the early awards. In this case, the annual SAR grants, with their five-year graded vesting schedules, become a valuable retention device. If, however, the underlying stock is more volatile and the value at the end of five years, based on the prior example, drops to $20, the retention value is more limited.

Phantom stock awards are more valuable if the objective is to promote employee retention. Phantom stock awards are universally subject to a vesting schedule for several reasons, not the least of which is to encourage retention. The vesting schedule may be designed with specific objectives in mind. If the employer's sole objective is retention, the forfeiture provisions may be based solely on the passage of time (e.g., a five-year cliff vesting schedule, meaning the award does not vest at all until the end of the fifth year, at which time it becomes 100% vested). In this case, for example, if 500 units of phantom stock are granted when the underlying stock is worth $100 per share, the initial value of the award is $50,000. Even if the value of the stock drops in half to $25 per share, the employee would forfeit significant value if he or she left the company during the five-year period before the units become fully vested. Forfeiture provisions may also be designed to assure that the employee remains in the service of the company during a critical period. For example, the vesting provisions may be tied to the repayment of the company's outstanding senior loan. In addition, if the objective is a combination of retention and performance, the vesting provisions could be tied to the achievement of certain financial targets (e.g., EBITDA targets). For example, some plans use relatively long vesting schedules (e.g., six to seven years) for grants, but provide that vesting will accelerate if certain performance measures are satisfied.

2.2.3 Public vs. Private Companies

The economic value of a SAR essentially is identical to a stock option. Although SARs do not have the obligation that a stock option holder has to pay the exercise price, many stock option plans have cashless exercise or other features that essentially relieve the optionholder from paying cash out of his or her pocket to exercise the shares.

Despite the economic similarities, stock options have traditionally been more popular with public companies because the accounting treatment of stock options in effect through 2005 was much more favorable than the accounting treatment for SARs. Specifically, under APB Opinion No. 25 ("APB 25"), stock options that were granted at fair market value and had a service-based vesting schedule did not trigger any compensation expense on the employer's financial statements. In contrast, SARs with similar features were subject to variable accounting expense, resulting in a charge to earnings equal to the value of the SAR "spread" for the period of time that the SARs were outstanding, which could negatively affect earnings per share. This spread was "marked to market" over the life of the SAR so that prior appreciation reduced current year charges. It was also adjusted for vesting, regardless of whether the SAR had a service-based or a performance-based vesting schedule.

Starting in 2006, all companies (public and private) were required to expense the value of their stock options under the new accounting standard, Statement of Financial Accounting Standards No. 123 (revised 2004) ("FAS 123(R)"). The advent of the requirement to expense stock options may cause a resurrection of the popularity of SAR grants in public companies because SARs have some attractive advantages. Under the current stock exchange rules, public companies can avoid the shareholder approval requirements by forgoing the issuance of stock if they have a stand-alone, cash-settled SAR program. In contrast, if the SARs are stock-settled SARs, which avoid the need for the holder to produce the exercise price, the plan may use fewer shares than traditional stock options. (See section 2.4 below.) For these reasons and others, SAR grants may become more prevalent in public companies.

SAR and phantom stock awards are generally a more appropriate incentive compensation program for private companies. Closely held businesses are generally less concerned about the earnings charge, but may have understandable concerns about retaining the outstanding shares in the family or a limited group of shareholders in order to avoid possible securities registration requirements. SAR or phantom stock awards permit a private company to reward employees based on the underlying appreciation in the company stock but without awarding actual shares of stock.

The use of SARs and phantom stock in privately held S corporations that are owned in whole or in part by an ESOP has increased dramatically.[6] The grant of a SAR or a phantom stock unit is not a grant of an actual share of stock for purposes of the S corporation rules. As a result, such an incentive compensation award does not jeopardize the favorable tax and cash flow structure of an ESOP-owned S corporation, but does motivate management to grow the ESOP's and other S corporation shareholders' value.[7] However, the grant of a SAR or phantom stock

---

6.   An employee stock ownership plan (ESOP) is a tax-qualified retirement plan under Code Sections 401(a) and 4975(e)(7).

7.   An ESOP trust is an eligible S corporation shareholder and, by virtue of a being a Code Section 501(a) tax-exempt trust and a special provision under Code Section 512(e), the portion of the corporate earnings attributable to the ESOP's ownership is not subject to income tax or unrelated business income tax. Because an S corporation is permitted to have only a single class of stock, any S corporation distributions that are made to the taxable S corporation shareholders in order for them to pay the tax on their proportionate share of the corporate earnings must be paid to the ESOP trust even though the ESOP

unit, or any form of deferred compensation for that matter, must be taken into account in performing the required anti-abuse tests under Code Section 409(p).[8] Employers that maintain S corporation ESOPs will need to consider the anti-abuse testing requirements when deciding on the level and form of any deferred compensation provided to employees.

2.3 SAR and Phantom Stock Award Design

Following are a number of plan design issues that must be considered before adopting a SAR or phantom stock award program.

2.3.1 Eligible Participants

The employer (typically through the compensation committee of the board of directors) must determine who is eligible to participate in the program. Because SAR and phantom stock awards may be treated as nonqualified deferred compensation programs, the employer retains much discretion to determine eligibility.

2.3.2 Number of SARs or Phantom Shares

The number of SARs or phantom shares need not be the same for each participant and can be based on any criteria the employer may determine to be appropriate. In setting the number of SARs or phantom shares to be awarded in connection with initial grants, the employer should also consider whether the program will be an ongoing plan, with additional awards being made in the future. The employer may also want to establish a maximum number of SARs or phantom shares that can

---

trust is not subject to tax. In order to minimize the required S corporation distributions (and consequent cash out-flow), many ESOP-owned S corporations design their management compensation programs to avoid providing a grant of actual stock ownership.

8. These tests are intended to ensure that an ESOP is made available to a broad-based group of employees. The tests are extremely complicated and beyond the scope of this book, but employers will want to be sure their plans comply, as the penalties for failure to do so are quite severe.

be granted to all participants in order to limit the percentage interest in future appreciation that will be made available to all participants.

2.3.3 SAR Strike Price

Presuming that the SAR is intended to deliver a benefit from future appreciation only, the SAR strike price would be set at an amount representing the "value" of the employer's common stock at the time of grant. For a 409A-compliant SAR, this value can be set in any manner the employer determines. For a 409A-exempt SAR, this value must be based on the fair market value (FMV) of the employer's stock at the grant date. As noted above, FMV is specifically defined under Section 409A.

For publicly traded companies, FMV can be determined using any reasonable method for deriving fair market value from actual transactions as long as that method is consistently applied. FMV can be based on the last sale price before the grant, the first sale price after the grant, the closing price on the trading day before the grant or on the grant date, or an average price over a period of up to 30 days before or after the grant.

For companies that are not publicly traded, determining FMV is more challenging. In general, Section 409A requires use of a reasonable method based on reasonable assumptions. In addition, the selected valuation method must be used consistently.

A method will be considered reasonable based on the facts and circumstances as of the selected valuation date, but a reasonable valuation method will likely take into account the value of tangible and intangible assets, the present value of future cash flows, the market value of the company's competitors, and other relevant factors (such as control premiums or discounts for lack of marketability). The proposed regulations under Section 409A establish three safe harbor methods for determining FMV:

1. An independent appraisal that meets the requirements for valuing stock help by an ESOP, if that valuation is issued not more than 12 months before the SAR's date of grant.

2. A formula price that is used to determine the price of common stock subject to transfer restrictions, provided that the formula price is

used for all transfers of stock and for all purposes requiring valuation of the stock, including regulatory filings, loan covenants, and issuances to and repurchases of stock from individuals other than employees.

3. For start-up companies with illiquid stock, a reasonable, good-faith valuation that is evidenced by a written report issued by someone with significant training in performing valuations.

The company will be deemed to use a valuation method consistently if the same method is used for all equity-based compensation arrangements, including for determining the SAR strike price and the FMV of the SAR on exercise.

2.3.4 Exercise and Payout Events

A SAR and a phantom stock program differ in the way in which grants are "exercised" and paid out. In addition, the "exercise" of a SAR will differ depending on whether it is a 409A-exempt SAR or a 409A-compliant SAR.

With a 409A-exempt SAR grant, the participant will have the right to exercise vested SARs at any time. Typically, however, the participant will be required to exercise by the earliest of the following events: (1) a fixed or specified date, (2) 30 days after termination of employment, (3) a change of control, or (4) an initial public offering (IPO).

With a 409A-compliant SAR grant, the participant does not have the right to exercise the SAR freely. Instead, the "exercise" or payout date must be specified no later than the time of grant. The SAR program may provide for payment on one or more of the following events: (1) a fixed or specified date, (2) separation from service,[9] (3) death, (4) disability,[10]

---

9. As defined in Prop. Treas. Reg. § 1.409A-1(h), but subject to a six-month wait for specified employees of public companies, as defined in Prop. Treas. Reg. § 1.409A-1(i).

10. As defined in Code Section 409A(a)(2)(C) and Prop. Treas. Reg. § 1.409A-3(g)(4).

(5) unforeseeable emergency,[11] or (6) a change in control.[12] The program may provide for payment on either the earlier or the later of the specified events. A participant can elect to delay a previously scheduled payment provided certain requirements are met:

- The election is made at least 12 months before the scheduled payment,

- The election does not become effective until 12 months after it is made, and

- The delay is for an additional period of five years. Note, however, that during the five-year period, distributions can be made, if the plan so provides, for any of the other specified distribution events. For example, if the participant is to receive payment on the earlier of age 55 and separation from service, and he or she elects to delay payment (in accordance with the above rules) from age 55 until age 60, payment will be made on the earlier of separation from service and age 60.

Phantom stock awards typically do not give the participant the discretion to elect the timing of payment. Instead, a phantom stock program will provide that the payments commence on the earliest of: (1) a specified date, (2) a change of control, (3) an IPO, or (4) the termination of employment. To the extent that the plan provides for a deferral of payment to a taxable year after the taxable year in which the phantom stock award vests, the phantom stock award program must comply with Section 409A.

As discussed below, a payout event will only apply to a participant's "vested" SARs or phantom stock awards; unvested awards are forfeited upon termination of employment for no consideration.

---

11. As defined in Code Section 409A(a)(2)(B)(ii) and Prop. Treas. Reg. § 1.409A-3(g)(3).

12. A change in control may be a change in the ownership of the corporation, a change in effective control of the corporation, or a change in the ownership of a substantial portion of the assets of the corporation, as defined in Notice 2005-1 (Q&A 11-14) and Prop. Treas. Reg. § 1.409A-3(g)(5).

2.3.5 Payout Amounts

For SARs, the amount payable to a participant following exercise or occurrence of a payout event is the product of (1) the number of *vested* SARs exercised or subject to payout, multiplied by (2) the excess, if any, of the value of an SAR as of the date of the payout event over the SAR strike price. As noted earlier, the SAR strike price can be determined in a number of ways. The method used for determining the SAR's value as of a payout event is generally the same as the method used for setting the strike price, but it could be based on different criteria. To be a 409A-exempt SAR, however, the SAR must determine the value as of the exercise date under a valuation method that meets the requirement of Section 409A, as discussed above.

For phantom stock awards, the amount payable is equal to the value of the employer's underlying common stock.

Some plans will provide for a different measure of the value of the SARs or phantom stock awards if the payout event is triggered by a change of control (in which case the change of control consideration per share can be substituted for the value based on the method that would otherwise be used) or a liquidity event resulting from an IPO (in which case the market capitalization of the company could be used instead of the general valuation method).[13]

2.3.6 Vesting

As noted above, a participant may receive payment only on vested SARs and vested phantom stock awards. Any SARs or phantom stock awards that remain unvested following the employee's termination of employment or other payout event are typically forfeited for no consideration. Vesting schedules can vary by individual in the discretion of the employer.

SARs and phantom stock awards typically provide for vesting based on the passage of time, meaning the participant will vest on specific dates if he or she remains employed by the employer. However, vesting

---

13. Note that a 409A-compliant SAR must be paid out on a permissible payment date (e.g., a fixed date, termination of employment, death, etc). An IPO liquidity event is not a permissible payment date.

can also be based on the achievement of company and/or individual performance goals, either alone or in conjunction with a vesting schedule based on the passage of time.

If vesting is based on the passage of time, the vesting schedule should set forth the period over which vesting will occur. This is typically a three- to five-year period, but it can be made longer or shorter if appropriate. The vesting schedule also states whether vesting will occur in equal or unequal installments, and the frequency of vesting (e.g., annually, quarterly, or monthly).

2.3.7 Acceleration of Vesting

The employer must determine whether all or part of an unvested SAR or phantom stock unit will automatically vest upon the occurrence of certain events, such as upon a change in control or an IPO.[14]

Acceleration of vesting can also occur upon a termination of a participant's employment for certain reasons, such as a termination by the company without "cause," or upon a termination of the participant's employment due to his or her death, permanent disability, or qualified retirement. For arrangements that are subject to Section 409A, if an acceleration of vesting also accelerates payout to the participant, a violation of Section 409A could occur, so the employer should consult with its legal advisor in this regard.

2.3.8 Payout Period

Payments of vested SARs and phantom stock units are often made in installments following the payout event (with or without interest), but lump-sum payments also can be made. For arrangements that are subject to Section 409A, the initial election regarding the form of payment must be specified no later than the time the award is made. If more than one form of payment is available, an employee may change his or her election of the form of payment, subject to the "re-deferral" rules discussed above (see section 2.3.4 of this chapter). By definition,

---

14. If the vesting of a SAR or phantom stock grant is accelerated upon a change of control of the employer, it may be deemed a "parachute" payment and could possibly expose the employee to an excise tax under Code Section 280G and result in a loss of deduction for the employer.

however, a 409A-exempt SAR can make payment only in a lump sum upon exercise of the SAR.

The payout period may vary depending on the circumstances surrounding the payout event. For example, it is common to provide for a lump-sum payout in the event of a change in control or termination of employment due to death or disability.

Different installment payouts can also be provided for in different payout circumstances. For example, payouts can be made over a three-year period following a termination of employment by the company without cause, but over a longer period, such as over five years, in the event of a payout following a participant's voluntary termination of employment.

2.3.9 Forfeiture of SAR or Phantom Stock Award upon Termination for Cause; Violation of Restrictive Covenants

The plan may provide that a participant will forfeit his or her SARs or phantom shares (vested as well as unvested) if the participant's employment is terminated for "cause." Cause can be narrowly or broadly defined.

In addition, the SARs or phantom stock plan can provide for a forfeiture of any remaining installment payouts following the participant's termination of employment in the event the participant violates any applicable restrictive covenants relating to the participant's employment with a competitor, solicitation of employees or customers, etc., following the participant's termination of employment. Note, however, that some states, particularly California, provide very narrow grounds for these "non-compete" clauses, although ERISA might preempt such laws. Note too that courts have ruled that, with respect to such covenants, employment agreements do not automatically also cover agreements for equity awards, which should have their own contractual terms agreed to by both parties.

2.3.10 Dividend Equivalents

Participants can be provided with an additional payout based on any distributions that might have been received by the participant had the

SARs or phantom shares been actual shares of company stock. However, a deemed distribution is not generally provided to the extent of any actual distributions to the shareholders of an S corporation in amounts intended to allow the members to satisfy their tax obligation on allocable income; in other words, if actual shareholders get a distribution, the SAR or phantom stock holder usually does not get a distribution nor is he or she deemed to receive one for tax purposes.

If the SARs and phantom share awards are subject to vesting and they carry dividend equivalency rights, then the plan or award agreement must specify whether the dividend equivalency rights also will be subject to vesting. If the dividend equivalency rights are subject to vesting, the amount of dividend-equivalent payments are usually held in escrow and paid out when the associated SAR or phantom share award vests.

Section 409A will apply to dividend equivalents that are credited after 2004. To comply with the requirements, the arrangement will have to specify the timing of payment of dividend equivalents, subject to the same general rules as apply to payments of the associated SAR or phantom share award. For a 409A-exempt SAR, however, the payment of dividend equivalents will not be tied to the exercise of the SAR but rather will be treated as a separate arrangement for which form and timing of payment must be specified at the date of grant.

2.3.11 Unfunded Plan

No assets need to be segregated or otherwise set aside for payments under a SAR or phantom stock plan, and the participants will be general unsecured creditors with respect to their interests. This is necessary to avoid constructive receipt of the SAR or phantom stock award. A "rabbi trust" could be funded to provide participants with a greater assurance of payment without triggering constructive receipt. These trusts set aside funds for employees but make them subject to the condition that if they are needed to satisfy creditors, they will be used for that purpose before paying employees.

The rabbi trust should be established with the assistance of qualified legal counsel to ensure the trust does not result in constructive receipt. In addition, care should be taken when selecting the appropriate funding technique; under Section 409A, certain funding techniques can result in immediately taxation to participants (particularly if the company maintains an "at risk" defined benefit plan). Assuming compliance with Section 409A, funds set aside in a rabbi trust are not deductible by the company until paid out. Earnings on amounts funded through a rabbi trust are taxable to the company.

2.4 Future SAR Plan Design: Stock-Settled SARs

Under FAS 123(R), the accounting standard that all companies (public and private) have now implemented, stock options no longer have a preferred status as the one equity vehicle that avoids a compensation charge. Under FAS 123(R), the "fair value" of stock option awards must be reported on the financial statements as a compensation expense. The issue then becomes: if an equity compensation expense must be incurred, what is the most efficient or best way to incur that expense?

Stock-settled SARs may prove to be an efficient alternative. A stock-settled SAR is an appreciation right that is satisfied solely with stock—no cash is paid by the company (or, for that matter, the employee). If service-vested, this type of award is treated under FAS 123(R) in the same way as stock option awards, with minor changes. If the award is performance-vested, the company calculates an estimate of the present value of the grant at the award date. If the performance condition is market-based (based on something related to stock prices), the charge cannot be reversed if the condition is not met, but it can be reversed if the award's vesting is based on other criteria, such as company, unit, or individual economic performance. For purposes of determining the "fair value" of SARs, the Black-Scholes or lattice valuation calculation is completed in the same manner as for stock options. Thus, 1,000 stock-settled SARs in Company X awarded to employee A on the same date as 1,000 Company X stock options awarded to employee B have exactly the same values for purposes of the earnings charge.

Why would a company consider a stock-settled SAR rather than a stock option? First, it is arguably less dilutive, which is an important consideration at many companies. Consider the three cases in table 2-2.

Table 2-2

	Stock option	Stock option	Stock SAR
Fair market value at exercise	$25	$25	$25
Exercise price	$10	$10	$10
Spread	$15	$15	$15
Number of options/SARs awarded	100	100	100
Aggregate spread	$1,500	$1,500	$1,500
Exercise price paid in cash	Yes	No	N/A
Exercise price paid in shares	No	Yes	N/A
Net shares delivered (taxes not considered)	100	60	60

In the first case, the shareholders have clearly been diluted by 100 shares. In the second case, if the exercise price was paid through a cashless exercise, then again there are 100 new shares in the marketplace. If, however, shares were tendered to the company in this second case, there would be 40 shares added back to the pool for future awards, i.e., future dilution. In the case of the stock SAR, the dilution is 60 shares, but no possibility of future dilution. Stock SARs also eliminate the need for the optionee to produce the exercise price. Thus, no open market sales are needed to finance the exercise, which most companies would prefer. Similarly, cashless exercise programs would not be needed.

There is no economic difference to the employee between a stock option and stock SAR. Both the leverage until exercise and the economic benefit or spread are the same.

Finally, with a stock option, the company often receives cash for the exercise price. To some extent, therefore, positive cash flow would be adversely affected if stock SARs are used in lieu of stock options. On the other hand, if the exercise price proceeds were used to buy shares to minimize the dilution, then the result becomes the same as the stock SAR.

2.5 Taxation of SARs and Phantom Stock

Assuming a SAR complies with the requirements of Section 409A or is otherwise exempted from those requirements, the SAR does not trigger any taxable income to the employee at the time of grant. Instead, an employee has taxable income when the SAR becomes payable to the employee.

The income from a 409A-compliant SAR is taxed when the payment is made. If, by the terms of the SAR, the employee receives payment for its value over a period of years, the employee will be subject to tax in the year that payment is made.

A 409A-exempt SAR is taxed when the employee exercises the SAR and receives payment. The taxation of the income received by the SAR is governed by the constructive receipt rules under Code Section 451. Treas. Reg. § 1.451-1 provides that "[g]ains, profits and income are to be included in gross income for the taxable year in which they are actually or *constructively* received by the taxpayer" (emphasis added). Treas. Reg. § 1.451-2 goes on to say that "income is not *constructively* received if the taxpayer's control of its receipt is subject to *substantial limitations or restrictions*" (emphasis added). Even though an employee may have the right to exercise and receive payment for a SAR at any time, the IRS held in Revenue Ruling 80-300 that it does not result in constructive receipt of income.[15] The IRS concluded that there is a "substantial limitation" on the exercise and payout of a SAR. The economic position of the holder of a SAR is significantly changed after it is exercised and the holder receives payment. Before the exercise and payment, the holder enjoys the prospect of benefiting from all future appreciation in the underlying stock. If, instead, the holder were to exercise the SAR, take his profit and immediately reinvest it in the same stock, he or she would be entitled to future appreciation on a smaller number of shares. Suppose, for example, that an employee holds SARs with respect to 1,000 shares whose market value was $10 on the date of grant. The stock's value rises to $20 per share. If the employee were to cash out the SARs, he or she will receive $10,000, with which the employee can purchase only 500 shares. Therefore, each one-dollar rise in the stock value will gain the employee only $500, compared to $1,000 that he or she had

---

15. This analysis continues to apply to 409A-exempt SARs and grandfathered SARs. However, 409A-compliant SARs do not permit free exercise by the participant, so the more traditional application of the constructive receipt rule applies to those SARs. The result is the same, i.e., payments are taxable to the participant as received.

before the cashout. The IRS concluded that the leverage provided in the SAR creates a substantial limitation to its exercise and, as a result, the employee has no taxable income until the SAR is exercised and payment is made.[16]

Phantom stock awards must comply with and are taxed under Section 409A. To ensure compliance, the phantom stock award must define the date upon which the award will be paid (e.g., the earlier of five years from the date of grant and termination of employment, death, disability, or change in control). Phantom stock awards also may be designed to pay out as soon as they become vested. In this case, the payment will be treated as a permissible "short-term deferral" that is exempted from the Section 409A requirements as long as the payment is made within 2½ months of the later of the end of the employer's taxable year or the end of the participant's taxable year.[17] A phantom stock award may be designed to permit the employee to elect when to receive payment, but the employer must be careful to ensure that providing such an election does not result in constructive receipt of the value of the shares and that the election otherwise complies with the deferral requirements of Section 409A.

From the employer's standpoint, the timing of its tax deduction is the same for SARs and phantom stock awards. The employer is entitled to a tax deduction at the time and in an amount equal to the income realized by the employee.[18]

For Social Security and federal unemployment tax purposes, employees are deemed to have compensation income under a SAR when payment is made. Under a phantom stock program, employees are deemed to have compensation income on the later of the date that the

---

16. See PLR 8829070 for the IRS's explanation of this point.

17. The requirements of Code Section 409A are complicated and beyond the scope of this chapter. However, chapter 4 of this book provides a more complete discussion of the Code Section 409A "short-term deferral" rules.

18. Code Section 162(a). If a SAR is settled in cash, the exercise of the SAR fixes the employer's liability so that an accrual basis taxpayer can deduct the liability under the all events test. However, if the payment of cash is not fixed at the time, no deduction is allowed under Code Section 404(a)(5) until the cash is paid. If the SAR benefit is satisfied with the payment of shares of stock, the employer will be entitled to a deduction at the time the service provider has income under Code Section 83(h).

services relating to the compensation are performed or the date that there is no longer a substantial risk of forfeiture.[19]

SARs and phantom stock awards have been attractive forms of equity-based compensation programs for S corporations because they are not treated as outstanding stock and are not deemed to be a second class of stock.[20] SARs and phantom stock are tested under the deferred compensation rules, which provide that a grant will not be deemed to be "stock" if it (1) does not convey the right to vote; (2) is an unfunded and unsecured promise to pay compensation in the future; (3) is issued to an employee or an independent contractor in connection with the performance of services; and (4) is issued under a plan with respect to which the employee or independent contractor is not taxed currently on income.[21] If the S corporation maintains an ESOP, however, equity-based compensation programs and other deferred compensation are taken into account in determining whether the ESOP satisfies the Code's anti-abuse rules,[22] thus making equity-based compensation less attractive than it has been in the past. Section 409A provides some relief by permitting distribution of deferred compensation in certain instances to avoid a failure of the anti-abuse rules.[23]

2.6 ERISA Coverage

A SAR or phantom stock plan is designed to provide participants with deferred compensation the value of which is tied to the value of the employer's stock. Whether a deferred compensation benefit of this sort is an "employee pension benefit plan" within the meaning of ERISA is a fact-specific determination.

An "employee pension benefit plan" is defined as a plan or program maintained by an employer that by its express terms or as a result of the surrounding circumstances results in a deferral of income by the employees for "periods extending to the termination of covered employ-

---

19. Code Sections 3121(v)(2) and 3306(r)(2).

20. Code Section 1361(b)(1)(D).

21. Treas. Reg. § 1.1361-1(b)(4); see also PLR 9803023.

22. Code Section 409(p).

23. Prop. Treas. Reg. § 1.409A-3(h)(2)(ix).

ment or beyond."[24] An ERISA pension benefit plan must comply with ERISA's strict vesting, funding, and disclosure requirements, as well as ERISA's heightened fiduciary duties of loyalty, care, and prudence.

ERISA provides a widely used exemption for a "top-hat plan." Under this exemption, a deferred compensation plan is exempt from the basic ERISA requirements if the plan is unfunded and maintained primarily for the purpose of providing benefits to a select group of management or highly compensated employees.[25] Most SAR and phantom stock plans are designed to comply with this "top-hat plan" exemption.

If, however, the employer desires the SAR or phantom stock plan to benefit a broad cross-section of employees, the "top hat" exemption would not apply. In this case, the key inquiry is whether the plan has the effect of systematically deferring income until termination of employment or beyond.[26] To avoid ERISA coverage, the employer should design the broad-based SAR or phantom stock plan to compensate participants while they are actively employed rather than deferring the income to termination of employment or retirement. For example, a plan that is intended to compensate employees while they are still employed and provides that each year's award pays out five years later should not be considered an ERISA retirement plan.[27] On the contrary, a plan that results in the majority of the recipients retaining their benefits through their late fifties and up to their retirement is likely to be an ERISA plan.[28]

---

24. ERISA Section 3(2)(A)(ii).

25. ERISA Sections 201, 301, and 401. If the plan is designed as a "top hat plan," the sponsor must be sure that the underlying benefit is not considered to be "funded." See *Dependahl v. Falstaff Brewing Corporation,* 653 F.2d 1208 (8th Cir. 1981) (court held excess benefit plan was "funded" with whole-life insurance policies. The court stated: "Funding implies the existence of a res separate from ordinary assets of the corporation . . . [In this case,] the employee may look to a res separate from the corporation in the event the contingency occurs which triggers the liability of the plan.").

26. ERISA Section 3(2)(A)(ii); see also 29 C.F.R. § 2510.3-2(c).

27. See *Murphy v. Inexco Oil Company,* 611 F.2d 570 (5th Cir. 1980); *In re Tucher Freight Lines, Inc.,* 789 F. Supp. 884 (S.D. Mich. 1991).

28. See *Darden v. Nationwide Mutual Insurance Company,* 922 F.2d 203 (4th Cir 1990); *Petr v. Nationwide Mutual Insurance Company,* 712 F. Supp. 504 (D. Md. 1989).

2.7 Securities Law Issues

SAR and phantom stock programs have generally been designed so that the holder has only the right to a cash payment. SARs and phantom stock awards that pay out solely in cash do not involve the issuance of any security, so no securities registration or disclosure is required. As a result, compliance with the securities law rules is not an issue.

However, in light of the current regulatory scrutiny and the pressure to report stock option expense, the use of stock-settled SARs may become more popular. In this case, attention to the securities law rules will be important.

2.7.1 Registration and Disclosure

If the holder of a SAR or phantom stock unit is entitled to elect to receive payment in either stock or cash and controls the time at which the shares or cash will be distributed, the holder is treated as making an investment decision when he or she makes the election.[29] By exercising a SAR and making an election with respect to the form of payment in the case of a SAR or phantom stock unit, the holder is effectively buying the shares received or, if he or she receives cash, selling derivative rights to the stock. Consequently, SARs and phantom stock awards that are potentially payable in stock and for which the holder controls the timing and manner of payment must be registered under the Securities Act of 1933 (the "1933 Act"), unless an exemption from registration exists.

Without an exemption, any registration statement covering this type of SAR or phantom stock award must be effective not later than the first date at which the SAR is exercisable or the phantom stock is payable. Companies with publicly traded securities may use a Form S-8 registration statement to register the SAR or phantom stock programs. This form offers the simplest method of compliance with the 1933 Act. Under the Form S-8, the actual registration statement merely entails the cover sheet, certain required undertakings, the exhibit sheet, and the signature pages. Although a prospectus is required, the contents of the prospectus is limited in scope generally to disclosure of the mate-

---

29. An elective choice of this sort (cash or stock payment) would be an unusual (but not impossible) plan design feature for a SAR or phantom stock program.

rial terms of the SAR or phantom share award plan or program. The prospectus, however, is not required to be filed with the registration statement.

Private companies that grant SARs or phantom stock awards that permit the holder to elect a stock or cash payment may rely on one or more of several exemptions from registration: (1) a private placement;[30] (2) an offering in compliance with Regulation D (commonly referred to as a "Reg D Offering");[31] or (3) Rule 701.[32] Of these exemptions, Rule 701 provides the greatest flexibility with the least amount of burden.

2.7.2 Insider Trading

SARs and phantom stock awards that offer the holder the right to elect to be paid in cash or shares of stock are derivative securities that may be reportable under Section 16(b) of the Securities Exchange Act of 1934. The grant of a SAR or phantom stock award will be an exempt transaction for purposes of Section 16(b) if granted with the approval of the independent members of the board of director's compensation committee. In addition, the SAR grant is exempt if it is held, or if any shares issued upon its exercise are not sold, for six months from the date of grant.[33]

---

30. Section 4(2) of the 1933 Act exempts from registration any offer to sell not involving a public offering of the securities.

31. Regulation D is an exemption that provides a safe harbor with respect to a private placement under Section 4(2). Pursuant to Regulation D, securities may be offered for sale to up to 35 nonaccredited investors, plus an unlimited number of accredited investors. 17 C.F.R. §§ 230.501 et seq.

32. Rule 701 allows companies to make offers to sell their securities to employees under compensatory plans with limited restrictions and limited filing requirements. The maximum value of securities that may be sold in a 12-month period in reliance on Rule 701 is an amount equal to the greatest of (1) $1 million, (2) 15% of the employer's total assets, and (3) 15% of the outstanding securities of the class being offered. Offerings in excess of $5 million require the issuer to provide certain disclosure to each purchaser. Note that none of these exemptions provides an exemption from the general provisions of federal common law and state securities laws against fraud or deception in the sale of securities. Thus, disclosure of liabilities and adequate financial information is required to preserve a defense against a claim of fraud if the securities decline in value.

33. 17 C.F.R. § 240.16b-3(d) and (e).

2.7.3 State Blue Sky Laws

State securities or "blue sky" laws may also affect the design and/or grant to employees of SARs or phantom share awards. Most states have exemptions similar to Rule 701, a Regulation D offering, or a private placement. However, several states, in particular California,[34] have special requirements that the SAR or phantom share awards must satisfy in order to conform with such exemptions. Some states have requirements that the SAR or phantom share awards must be filed with an appropriate regulatory body. Thus, it is important to make sure that the grant of SAR or phantom share awards not only complies with federal securities laws but also meets the requirements for applicable state securities law exemptions.

---

34. California Corporations Code Section 25102(o) provides an exemption similar to Rule 701. However, the regulations issued under Section 25102(o) contain several requirements that must be contained in the plan in order for the exemption to be met. See California Corporations Code Regulation Section 260.140.42.

CHAPTER THREE

Restricted Stock Plans

Barbara Baksa

Contents

A restricted stock arrangement provides the recipient with the right to acquire a specified number of shares of stock. The recipient may be required to pay for the stock or may receive it at no cost. If the stock must be purchased, the purchase price is typically the fair market value of the company's stock on the date of grant ("grant" here is used in its formal sense in a restricted stock plan and can refer to either the award of shares for no consideration or the award of the right to buy shares).

Privately held companies that offer restricted stock to their employees typically require the employees to pay full fair market value for the stock. While the company is private, the value of the stock is often relatively low, so that this price is not a significant obstacle to the employee's purchase, and requiring payment can alleviate administrative difficulties that might otherwise arise from the tax treatment of these arrangements. In addition, the employee's investment provides the company with additional cash that could be valuable to the operation of the company.

In a publicly held company, however, there is little incentive to employees to purchase restricted stock at full fair market value, since, presumably, they could buy the same stock on the open market at essentially the same price without regard to the restrictions. Because of this, publicly held companies that offer restricted stock to their employees typically offer it at no cost or at a discount from the current fair market value.

Unlike employee stock options, which might provide up to 10 years for employees to purchase stock, the recipient of restricted stock must make a decision with respect to acquiring the shares of stock within 10 to 30 days after the arrangement is granted. Where payment for the shares is required, generally the recipient may purchase the shares of stock with cash, a promissory note, or other consideration approved by the company.

Alternatively, the company may simply award restricted stock at no cost to employees. If the stock is awarded at no cost, it may be issued at grant subject to restrictions or may be awarded in the form of units that convert to shares of stock (usually on a one-for-one basis) upon distribution to the recipient.

In both publicly and privately held companies, the arrangement is granted subject to restrictions or risk of forfeiture. That is, the recipient's right to the shares of stock covered by the restricted stock arrangement (i.e., the "restricted shares") is contingent on continued service or contribution to the company for a specified period of time (the "vesting period"). Alternatively, the recipient's right to the restricted shares may be contingent upon the achievement of one or more specified performance goals.

If shares are issued at grant, the restricted shares are not transferable and are usually held by the company in an escrow or custodial arrangement during the vesting period. The recipient may have some of the rights of a shareholder with respect to the restricted shares during the vesting period, including the right to vote and to receive dividends. If the recipient fails to satisfy the vesting conditions (for example, by terminating employment before the completion of the vesting period or failing to achieve the performance targets), the company has the right to repurchase any unvested (unearned) restricted shares at a price equal to the shares' initial cost to the recipient. If, at the time of forfeiture, the shares are worth less than the recipient's initial investment, the repurchase price is typically the current fair market value of the stock. This repurchase right lapses cumulatively over the vesting period.

If the award is granted in the form of units, no shares are issued until the units are converted into stock (upon distribution to the recipient). The recipient does not have voting or dividend rights with respect to the underlying stock until this time (although some companies pay dividend equivalents on unvested units). If the recipient fails to satisfy the vesting requirements, the units are simply forfeited with no payment to the recipient.

Table 3-1 compares the various forms of restricted stock.

Table 3-1. Comparison of Various Forms of Restricted Stock

Restricted Stock Purchase	Restricted Stock Award	Restricted Stock Units
Price is typically equal to market value at grant.	Price is typically $0 or a nominal amount.	Price is typically $0 or a nominal amount.
Shares are issued at grant and held in escrow until vested.	Shares are issued at grant and held in escrow until vested.	Shares are not issued until distribution.
Underlying shares are considered issued and outstanding before vesting.	Underlying shares are considered issued and outstanding before vesting.	Underlying shares are not considered issued and outstanding until distribution.
Recipient has voting rights even before vesting.	Recipient has voting rights even before vesting.	Recipient does not have voting rights until distribution.
Recipient typically receives dividends on unvested shares.	Recipient typically receives dividends on unvested shares.	Recipient does not receive dividends on unvested units but may earn dividend equivalents.
Section 83(b) election can be filed at grant.	Section 83(b) election can be filed at grant.	Section 83(b) election is not applicable.
Taxation cannot be deferred beyond vesting.	Taxation cannot be deferred beyond vesting.	Taxation can be deferred beyond vesting if distribution of underlying shares is deferred (either mandatorily or through a valid deferral election).

Characteristics of Restricted Stock Plans

- Employees are generally required to accept awards or purchase shares (if payment is required), within 10 to 30 days of grant.

- If offered by a privately held company, the purchase price is usually at or near the fair market value of the company's stock on grant date. If offered by a publicly held company, the shares are usually awarded at no cost or at a discount.

- Shares or units are usually subject to vesting restrictions. If shares are issued at grant, they are usually held in escrow until vested.

- Upon termination of employment, unvested shares are forfeited or subject to repurchase at the employee's original cost.

- Both purchases and awards (of both stock and units) are generally subject to tax upon vesting, at which time the difference between the purchase price (if any) and the fair market value of the stock is treated as compensation income to the employee.

- If shares are issued at grant, an election under Section 83(b) of the Internal Revenue Code (the "Code") can be filed at the time of purchase or award. If a Section 83(b) election is filed, the difference, if any, between the purchase price and the fair market value of the company's stock on the purchase or award date is compensation income to the employee. No taxable income is recognized on the vest date.

- If the award is made in the form of units, it may be possible to defer payment of income tax by deferring distribution of the underlying shares. The deferral and distribution is subject to Section 409A of the Code, and employment taxes (FICA and FUTA) will still be due upon vesting.

- Withholding tax obligations arise at the time compensation income is recognized.

- The company receives a tax deduction equal to the compensation income recognized by employees.

3.1 Advantages of Restricted Stock

From the company's perspective, restricted stock arrangements have many of the strengths of employee stock options. They enhance the company's ability to recruit and retain talented employees. They may be granted to specific individuals in different amounts and subject to different terms and conditions, enabling the company to tailor the arrangements to meet specific corporate objectives. If the arrangements require an immediate purchase of stock, they result in cash inflow to the company (assuming that the employees do not tender payment in the form of a promissory note or previously acquired shares of stock). The company may receive a corporate tax deduction (for compensation expense) when the restricted shares vest. And, as with other equity arrangements, restricted stock arrangements allow the company to align the interests of the employees with those of its shareholders.

For employees, restricted stock provides a relatively low-risk way to acquire and maintain an equity interest in the company. It may provide a strong motivational tool, as employees recognize that their individual performance can directly affect the company's prospects and, therefore, the value of the company's stock.

3.1.1 Advantages Distinct to Restricted Stock Issued at No Cost

Restricted stock that is awarded at no cost offers a distinct advantage over employee stock options and stock appreciation rights in that, regardless of fluctuations in the company's stock price, it always retains some value. Employee stock options and stock appreciation rights have little value (and do little to retain and motivate employees) when the current value of the company's stock is less than the option price. This disadvantage does not apply to restricted stock that is awarded at no cost; because employees have not paid for the stock, whether the company's stock price increases or decreases, the restricted stock always has value to them.

Some practitioners believe that restricted stock awarded at no cost provides a better incentive for long-term growth since these arrangements are not as leveraged as stock options (and therefore do not benefit as much from short-term spikes in stock value).

Finally, some practitioners believe that employees place a higher value on stock that they receive at no cost than they do stock options or stock appreciation rights, which inherently involve more risk. Where this is the case, restricted awards can be significantly smaller than stock options, reducing the company's overall expense for the plan (even though the per-share expense may be greater than for stock options) and plan dilution.

3.2 Disadvantages of Restricted Stock

There also can be drawbacks to using restricted stock arrangements as a compensation tool. The grant of restricted shares gives rise to a compensation expense if the purchase price is less than the fair market value of the company's stock on the date of purchase. If the shares are awarded at no cost, then the entire value of the grant is treated as a compensation expense. Moreover, if the recipient files a Section 83(b) election in connection with the purchase of the restricted shares at fair market value, the company may forego a compensation expense deduction for income tax purposes. And, as with any equity arrangement, the issuance of restricted stock will dilute the interests of the company's shareholders.

If employees are required to pay for the restricted stock, employees are making an immediate investment decision, and assuming the risk of a decline in the value of the stock before the stock is transferable. Employees may be unwilling to make this investment (especially when their ability to sell the stock is restricted subject to vesting requirements) and may incur substantial risk by doing so. Moreover, if the granting company is privately held, the restricted shares will be illiquid, further limiting the employee's ability to realize any appreciation in the value of the shares.

Unlike employee stock options, restricted stock arrangements offer employees little control over when the stock is subject to taxation. If a Section 83(b) election is not filed, each vesting date under the arrangement is a taxable event to the employee. Upon vesting, employees recognize compensation income equal to the difference, if any, between the purchase price of the restricted shares and the current fair market value of the company's stock, with a commensurate withholding tax obligation.

Only with an award in the form of units is there any opportunity for the employee to defer taxation past vesting, and even there the deferral is severely limited by new Section 409A of the Code. The stock may vest at a time when the employee is already in a higher than normal tax bracket or when the employee does not have cash available to pay the withholding taxes. In some cases, employees may be forced to sell some of the restricted shares to satisfy this tax liability. When vesting occurs during blackout periods or other periods where employees are not able to sell the stock, satisfying the tax liability can be particularly problematic for employees. For companies that offer restricted stock at no cost, collecting the requisite tax withholding and assisting employees with their tax obligations is often one of the most significant administrative challenges that must be overcome; this is especially true when the plan is offered to a large group of employees.

3.3   Restricted Stock Plan Design

When a company decides to implement a restricted stock program, management usually instructs the human resources department and/or benefits personnel to design an appropriate plan. Typically, the plan's structure, as well as specific terms and conditions, are determined in consultation with the company's legal counsel, accountants, and outside compensation or benefits specialists. Factors taken into consideration in designing the plan include the cost to the company and proposed participants, the potential liquidity for participants, and the income tax and financial accounting consequences arising from the operation of the plan.

Some companies adopt a separate plan, under which only restricted stock can be offered; other companies adopt "omnibus" plans, under which a variety of equity vehicles, including restricted stock, can be offered. The omnibus plan clearly provides the company with maximum flexibility, allowing the company to determine what types of arrangements to actually offer to employees as the arrangements are granted. Unfortunately, shareholders are sometimes uncomfortable with this approach, and where shareholder approval is necessary or desired, the company may find it advisable to implement a separate plan for the restricted stock program.

In most cases, the company's legal counsel prepares the actual plan documents. Once management has approved the restricted stock plan, it is presented to the company's board of directors for consideration and adoption. Under the corporate laws of most states, the board has the authority for all issuances of the company's stock, so board approval is generally required before implementing a restricted stock plan.

Following adoption by the board of directors, the plan is usually submitted to the company's shareholders for approval. Shareholder approval may be a requirement under state corporate law or the company's charter documents. If the company is publicly traded, shareholder approval is almost always required by the exchange where the company's shares are listed. Even where shareholder approval is not required, there may be advantages to obtaining shareholder approval of the restricted stock plan for tax and/or securities law reasons.

Most restricted stock plans expressly provide that the board of directors can amend the plan from time to time, or even suspend or terminate the plan before the expiration of the plan term. Any such action is typically accomplished through a formal board resolution and results in an appropriate revision of the restricted stock plan document.

The restricted stock plan may expressly provide that certain types of plan amendments must be approved by the company's shareholders before becoming effective. These include amendments to increase the number of shares of stock authorized for issuance under the plan, to change or expand the categories of eligible participants in the plan, to extend the term of the plan, to reduce the purchase price at which shares of stock may be sold under the plan, or to increase the benefits available to participants in the plan. Even if not expressly required in the plan, it may be necessary to submit certain amendments for shareholder approval to ensure compliance with relevant laws or listing requirements.

3.3.1 Plan Participation/Eligibility

Restricted stock arrangements are not subject to statutory eligibility restrictions. Therefore, restricted stock can be offered to non-employees—such as outside directors, consultants, advisors, and other independent contractors—as well as to employees (both full-time and part-time), subject only to any eligibility restrictions contained in the restricted stock plan itself. Moreover, restricted stock can be offered pursuant to a restricted stock plan or as individual arrangements outside any formal plan.

Under a restricted stock plan, both the selection of recipients and the timing of grants are typically at the discretion of the board of directors. Companies use a wide variety of different approaches and/or policies for determining which employees should receive restricted stock. In some instances, only senior management is eligible to receive restricted stock. Other companies grant restricted stock to some or all managers. Still other companies grant restricted stock to all employees, regardless of job description.

3.3.2 Number of Shares Granted

Under a restricted stock plan, the number of shares of stock offered to each employee is typically determined by the board of directors. Companies use a wide variety of different approaches and/or policies to determine the size of a restricted stock arrangement. For example, the number of shares of stock may be determined on an employee-by-employee basis, by job classification or based on the company's overall performance over a specified period of time. The number of shares of stock may also be determined as a percentage of the employee's annual salary.

3.3.3 Purchase Price

Restricted stock can be offered at no cost or employees can be required to pay for the stock. If required to pay for the stock, the price can be the full fair market value of the stock or can be discounted. Typically, privately held companies offer restricted stock at a purchase price equal to the fair market value of the company's stock on the date of grant. Publicly held companies usually offer restricted stock at no cost or at a discounted price.

3.3.4 Expiration

If the stock must be paid for, employees typically have a limited period of time in which to complete the purchase. Typically, a decision to acquire the restricted shares must be made within 10 to 30 days after the restricted stock purchase arrangement is granted.

Although not legally required when the restricted stock is offered at no cost, for administrative purposes, the company may require employees to accept the offer of stock within 10 to 30 days after the offer is made. While the company could forego requiring acceptance from employees in this situation, it may be advisable to require employees to acknowledge the terms and conditions under which the stock is offered.

3.3.5 Vesting

The process of earning the restricted shares is commonly referred to as "vesting." Generally, a vesting schedule provides that, at the completion of designated intervals, or the satisfaction of established performance criteria, a pre-determined percentage or ratio of the restricted shares are earned and thereafter may be transferred by the employee. These interim dates are called "vesting dates." Vesting is typically measured from the date the restricted stock is granted, but it can be measured from any date the company deems appropriate (such as an employee's hire date).

Companies adopt a vesting schedule that best suits the incentive or other objectives of their restricted stock plan. Most restricted stock plans provide for annual vesting schedules; that is, the restricted shares vest in equal annual installments over a period of several years (typically, three, four, or five years). In some instances, monthly or quarterly vesting schedules are used, but because the administrative process of assessing and collecting the taxes that become due as the shares vest can be burdensome, companies may want to avoid vesting schedules where the shares vest in frequent intervals. Where restricted stock is offered at no cost to employees, frequent and/or short-term vesting is often viewed negatively from a corporate governance perspective. It is not uncommon for restricted stock issued at no cost to be subject to a three- to five-year vesting period, with no portion of the award vesting until the end of this period.

Restricted awards also can vest upon the achievement of specified company performance goals (such as earnings per share, revenue, or profitability targets) or based on work unit, individual, departmental, or divisional performance goals.

3.3.6 Termination of Employment

If an employee terminates employment before the restricted shares have vested, the unvested shares or units are typically forfeited or subject to repurchase by the company. Generally, the terms and conditions of forfeiture and the company's unvested share repurchase right are set forth in the restricted stock agreement. Where repurchase is necessary, the company usually must notify the employee in writing within a specified period of time (60 to 90 days following termination is common) of its decision to repurchase some or all of the unvested shares. To avoid a situation where the notice of repurchase is inadvertently overlooked, some plans provide that the company's repurchase option in automatically exercised unless the recipient is notified otherwise with a specified period (usually 60 to 90 days following termination).

If the employee originally paid for the stock, the company generally repurchases the stock at the lower of the employee's original cost or the current fair market value, since guaranteeing repurchase at the employee's original cost can negatively affect the accounting treatment of the plan (and, where the stock has declined substantially in value, could be a disincentive for continued employment). This payment is made in cash or by cancellation of any outstanding indebtedness of the employee to the company. Where the employee received the stock at no cost, any unvested shares are simply forfeited upon termination, with no payment from the company.

3.3.7 Additional Restrictions

Privately held companies occasionally impose restrictions on the ability of employees to transfer or dispose of vested restricted shares. These restrictions are intended to discourage employees from leaving the company, and to enable the company to maintain some control over the identities of its shareholders. Such restrictions may also enable the company to regulate and control the development of a trading market in its securities before its initial public offering.

One common type of transfer restriction is a "right of first refusal." A right of first refusal entitles a company to repurchase restricted shares of stock from the employee on the same terms offered, and at their current fair market value, if the employee proposes to sell or transfer the shares to a third party. Typically, the terms and conditions of a right of first refusal are set forth in the restricted stock agreement. A right of first refusal usually terminates when the company's securities become publicly held.

Another device used by privately held companies to restrict the transfer of shares of stock is a vested share repurchase right. As in the case of an unvested share repurchase right, this provision entitles the company to repurchase any vested shares of stock from an employee upon termination of employment. This allows the company to restrict share ownership to current employees and, provided the repurchased shares are returned to the plan, increases the number of shares the company has available to compensate current employees. On the other hand, employees may feel that once they have earned the stock, they should be entitled to keep it upon departure, and, particularly where the restricted stock serves as a substitute for other forms of compensation, may view this restriction unfavorably. If the company does choose to repurchase the vested shares, generally, the repurchase price is an amount equal to the fair market value of the company's stock on the date of termination of employment. Typically, the terms and conditions of a vested share repurchase right are set forth in the restricted stock agreement. A vested share repurchase right usually terminates when the company's securities become publicly held.

Other repurchase provisions may be triggered upon the death of the employee or in the event of a dissolution of marriage.

3.3.8 Methods of Share Payment

Where payment for the restricted shares is required, a restricted stock plan may provide more than one method for paying the purchase price for the restricted shares. These payment methods include cash (usually in the form of a check), use of a promissory note, or any other consideration approved by the company. Company policy should clarify which methods are available to employees and the relevant guidelines for each.

3.3.8.1 *Restricted Stock Purchase Arrangements*

The most common form of payment for stock issued through a restricted stock purchase arrangement is cash. At the time of purchase, the employee is required to remit the total purchase price for the restricted shares (and any withholding taxes due to the company, if applicable). Generally, payment is made in the form of a check payable to the company. The company should decide whether a cashiers' check is required for payment or if a personal check is acceptable and the permissible time period for remitting payment.

Some companies permit employees to deliver a promissory note to pay the total required purchase price for the restricted shares being purchased. If the use of promissory notes is permitted, such arrangements must provide for the payment of at least the minimum amount of interest required under the Code and current accounting standards. In addition, the promissory note should be a full recourse obligation secured by the restricted shares being purchased or other property acceptable to the company.

If the interest rate charged is less than the applicable federal rate, the Internal Revenue Service (IRS) will treat a portion of the amount repaid as imputed interest, which may have significant income tax consequences to the employee and the company. The applicable federal rates are published by the IRS on a monthly basis. Note that under the Sarbanes-Oxley Act of 2002 public companies are prohibited from offering loans to officers and directors.

3.3.8.2 Restricted Stock Awards and Units

Where stock issued through a restricted stock award or unit arrangement is subject to a par value, award recipients may be required to pay this amount since the par value is a minimum payment the company must receive for the stock. Par value is typically a nominal amount, often times only $.01 per share or less. Under the corporate laws of most states, par value can be paid in cash, property, or services. To alleviate the administrative difficulties associated with collecting such nominal amounts from the award recipients, most companies designate the form of payment to be past service.

To avoid this consideration altogether, some companies fund their restricted stock award or unit plan with treasury stock, since par value is not generally required for stock that has already been issued once and reacquired by the company (generally, the company is required to collect par value only on the first issuance of the stock).

3.3.9 Methods of Tax Payment

Restricted stock arrangements are generally subject to taxation upon vesting (except where the employee has filed a Section 83(b) election for a restricted stock purchase or award or where distribution of restricted stock units is deferred). Since the employee's tax obligation upon vesting can be burdensome, the restricted stock plan may provide for more than one method of meeting this obligation. The most common tax payment methods include cash (usually in the form of a check), use of a promissory note, tender of a portion of the vested stock to the company, or sale of the restricted stock on the open market. Company policy should clarify which methods are available to employees and the relevant guidelines for each.

If the use of promissory notes is permitted, such arrangements must provide for the payment of at least the minimum amount of interest required under the Code and current accounting standards. In addition, the promissory note should be a full recourse obligation secured by the restricted shares being purchased or other property acceptable to the company. Note that under the Sarbanes-Oxley Act of 2002 public companies are prohibited from offer loans to officers and directors.

If employees are permitted to tender a portion of the restricted shares that are currently vesting in payment of the tax obligation, the tax payments should be limited to the statutorily required payments. Allowing employees to tender shares for payments in excess of the statutorily required amounts could cause the company to recognize additional compensation expense for the arrangement and could change the accounting treatment applicable to the restricted stock plan. Where this requirement is complied with, however, from an administrative standpoint, this may be the most expedient method of satisfying the tax obligation. It relieves the employee of the sometimes considerable burden associated with making a cash payment, it does not require coordination with outside vendors (such as a brokerage firm), and generally is permissible even during a company blackout period. The only significant disadvantage to this tax payment method is that the company must pay over the taxes to the IRS in cash and is reimbursed for this cash expenditure with the shares of stock tendered by the employee, rather than with cash.

3.3.10 Dividends

As mentioned above, restricted stock, which is issued at grant, is generally eligible for any dividend payments made to shareholders after its issuance (even those payments made before the stock has vested). Restricted stock units, on the other hand, are not eligible to receive dividend payments until they have been converted to stock (and paid out to the employee). However, many companies provide payments on unvested restricted stock units that are equivalent to the dividends paid to shareholders; these payments are typically referred to as "dividend equivalents." Units are designed to track the value of the company's company stock, and dividends paid to shareholders are part of that value. Therefore, although units cannot receive actual dividends, it is reasonable (although not legally required) to provide an equivalent payment to unit holders.

For both restricted stock and units, dividends or dividend equivalents can be paid on either a current or a deferred basis. If paid on a current basis, employees receive the dividend payment at the same time it is paid to shareholders. If paid on a deferred basis, employees receive the dividend payment when the underlying award is paid out; in this case, the dividend payments are typically subject to the same vesting/forfeiture restrictions as the underlying award. This structure ensures that employees do not receive dividend payments until they have earned the award on which the dividends are paid.

Dividends can be paid either in cash or in stock. Where dividends are paid on a current basis, they are most commonly paid in cash. Where the dividends are paid on a deferred basis, they are most commonly paid in stock.

3.4 Tax Treatment

As is true of most arrangements that provide for the receipt of stock in connection with the performance of services, Section 83 of the Code governs the tax treatment of restricted stock arrangements. Because restricted stock is subject to Section 83 and because it is paid out immediately upon vesting, it generally is not treated as deferred compensation under Section 409A of the Code (enacted under the American Jobs Creation Act of 2004).

Note, however, that restricted stock units, which represent an unsecured promise to deliver stock at a future date, are treated as deferred compensation under Section 409A. Where the units are subject to distribution (and therefore, taxation) upon vesting, there should not be any adverse consequences under Section 409A. If the units are subject to deferred distribution, i.e., the units will be paid out some time after they have vested (either mandatorily or via a deferral election), it is critical for the arrangement to comply with the requirements in Section 409A governing both deferral elections and distributions. A full discussion of Section 409A is beyond the scope of this chapter, and much guidance is still anticipated regarding its application; therefore, companies that wish to offer restricted stock units, especially units subject to deferred distribution, are strongly encouraged to consult qualified tax advisors before proceeding.

3.4.1 Tax Treatment of Employee

Since the restricted shares are, by their terms, not transferable on the date of purchase or award and subject to a substantial risk of forfeiture (that is, the restricted shares are not vested), there is no taxable event at this time, and the compensatory element of the transaction remains open until the restricted shares vest. As the forfeiture restrictions lapse (that is, as the restricted shares vest), the difference—if any—between the purchase price and the fair market value on the date of vesting is compensation income to the employee. If the shares were awarded at no cost to the employee, this means that the full fair market value of the stock as it vests is compensation income to the employee. This compensation income is subject to taxation at ordinary income rates. As with other forms of compensation, such as salary and bonus, the employee must include the compensation income arising from the restricted stock in his or her ordinary income calculation for the year of vesting. The employee may elect to close the compensatory element of the transaction and accelerate the time at which compensation income is realized to the date of purchase or award by filing a Section 83(b) election with the IRS.

Where the restricted shares have been purchased at the full fair market value of the company's stock on the date of grant, generally the employee will make this election and recognize zero compensation income. If the restricted stock was awarded at no cost to the employee or purchased at a discount, filing a Section 83(b) election causes the employee to recognize compensation income equal to the full fair market value of the stock on the date of award or the amount of the purchase discount. This compensation income is subject to taxation at ordinary income tax rates and must be included in the employee's ordinary income calculation for the year. In the absence of an election, the compensatory element of the arrangement is not determined until the date of vesting, as described above. If a Section 83(b) election is filed and the employee subsequently leaves the company before the restricted shares have been fully earned, the employee is not entitled to a refund of the taxes paid at the time of award or purchase, nor is the employee entitled to take a loss deduction for the amount, if any, previously included in income. Likewise, if the stock declines in value after the award or purchase so that the fair market value of the stock upon vesting is less than the fair market value of the stock when the award or purchase occurred, the employee is not entitled to claim a loss deduction unless the shares are sold at the lower value. Thus, where the stock is purchased at a discount or awarded at no cost, filing a Section 83(b) election could cause employees to pay a higher amount of tax than if the election were not filed; few employees choose to file a Section 83(b) election in this situation. But where the employee is paying full fair market value to acquire the restricted stock, many employees do choose to file the Section 83(b) election, since, in this situation, it eliminates any compensation income associated with the arrangement.

The following examples may help clarify the tax treatment.

Example 1: Restricted Stock Purchased at Fair Market Value: An employee is offered the right to purchase 1,000 shares of restricted stock at a price of $10 per share, the fair market value on the date of grant. The stock vests in full one year after the date of grant, when the fair market value is $16 per share. In this example, if the employee does not file the Section 83(b) election, the employee recognizes compensation income of $6,000 in the year the stock vests. If the employee files the Section 83(b) election, the employee does not recognize any compensation income on the stock, since the purchase price is equal to the fair market value at the time the shares are purchased. In this example, the employee would most likely file the Section 83(b) election since it does not present any disadvantages to him or her.

Example 2: Restricted Stock Awarded at No Cost: An employee is awarded 1,000 shares of restricted stock at no cost when the fair market value of the stock is $10 per share. The stock vests in full one year after the date of grant, when the fair market value is $16 per share. If the employee does not file the Section 83(b) election, the employee recognizes compensation income of $16,000 in the year the award vests. If the employee files the Section 83(b) election, the employee recognizes $10,000 of compensation income in the year the stock is awarded, but does not recognize any additional income upon vest. Even in this example, it might be advantageous for the employee to file the Section 83(b) election, since doing so would reduce the amount of compensation income the employee would recognize for the award. But it is impossible for the employee to know that this is the case at the time the shares are awarded to him or her, which is when the Section 83(b) election must be filed. The employee could terminate employment before the vest date, forfeiting the shares, or the stock could subsequently decline in value. Thus, in this example, it is unlikely that the employee would file the Section 83(b) election.

Generally, restricted stock units are subject to the same tax treatment as restricted stock awarded at no cost, with a few important exceptions arising from the fact that stock is not issued at grant under a unit award. For an award to be subject to Section 83, a transfer of property must occur. Because there is no stock issued at grant under a unit arrangement, a transfer of property is not considered to have occurred at grant. Thus, unit awards are taxed under Sections 451 and 409A of the Code rather than Section 83. The first consequence of this treatment is that a Section 83(b) election is not available for unit awards. Some companies consider this to be an advantage, since, as discussed above, it is often inadvisable for employees to file a Section 83(b) election on restricted stock awarded at no cost, yet explaining the election can be cumbersome and confusing to employees.

The second consequence is that the recipient of a unit award does not recognize income until he or she has constructively received the compensation paid under it. Under the Internal Revenue Code, compensation is considered to be constructively received when it becomes available to the employee and the employee has control over receipt of it. Compensation is not considered to be constructively received if the employee's control of its receipt is subject to substantial limitations or restrictions. Likewise, compensation is not considered to be constructively received solely because it will be paid out upon termination.

If the unit is converted to stock and paid out at vesting, constructive receipt occurs at vesting, and the employee is taxed in exactly the same manner as if he or she had received restricted stock issued at grant that was not subject to a Section 83(b) election. If, however, the units are subject to a valid deferral election under which they will not be converted to stock and paid out until some time after vesting, constructive receipt does not occur, and the employee is not subject to income tax until the actual distribution (note, however, that employment taxes, i.e., FICA and FUTA, are still due upon vesting), provided that the deferral and distribution comply with Section 409A.

> *Example 3: Restricted Stock Unit with Deferral Election:* An employee is awarded 1,000 shares of restricted stock units at no cost when the fair market value of the stock is $10 per share. The units vest in full two years after the date of grant, when the fair market value is $16 per share. As permitted under the plan, the employee files a deferral election within 30 days of the grant date, deferring conversion and receipt of the underlying shares until five years after the date of grant, when the market value is $23 per share. When the units vest, the employee will recognize $16,000 of income for FICA/FUTA purposes (and the company is required to withhold the payments on this income and make its matching payments) but will not recognize any income for federal income tax purposes. When the units are paid out pursuant to the deferral election, the employee will recognize $23,000 of compensation income for federal income tax purposes (but will not recognize any further income for FICA/FUTA purposes), on which the company is also responsible for withholding the requisite payments. For capital gains purposes, the stock received under the unit award will have a basis of $23 per share, the fair market value on the date it was paid out to the employee, and the capital gains holding period is measured from the payout date.

The ability to defer distribution is also often perceived as an advantage of unit awards and many companies offer employees the opportunity to elect a deferred distribution. Where this is offered, however, care should be taken to ensure that the deferral feature does not cause the plan to become subject to ERISA. This can particularly be a concern when distribution is deferred to the termination of employment, and it and may necessitate limiting the deferral feature to high-level employees.

In addition, as previously mentioned, any deferral elections must now comply with Section 409A. Under the proposed regulations issued in September 2005, where restricted stock units do not vest for at least one year after grant, the initial deferral election can be made within 30 days after the grant date (provided that the election is made at least one year in advance of when the units are fully earned). Where restricted units vest in less than one year after grant, it may be necessary for the initial deferral election to be made before the end of the calendar year preceding the year in which the units are granted. Alternatively, where the deferral will be for at least five years, the deferral election can be made up until one year before the units vest or were originally scheduled to be paid out. Note, however, that as of the writing of this chapter, these regulations have not yet been finalized and are subject to change. In addition to regulating initial deferral elections, Section 409A also imposes limitations on when and how deferral elections can be changed and on re-deferrals. Finally, whether the deferred distribution is mandatory or elective, the distribution itself must comply with the requirements of Section 409A.

3.4.2 Tax Treatment of Dividend Payments

Dividends and dividend equivalents paid on restricted stock and units are subject to tax at the time they are paid to the employee. Where the dividend is paid in cash, the employee recognizes income equal to the cash received; where a dividend is paid in stock, the employee recognizes income equal to value of the stock on the date it is subject to taxation.

Dividend payments on restricted stock are treated as compensation income, subject to all of the withholding described in section 3.4.3, and are reported on Form W-2 unless a Section 83(b) election was filed on the award. Where a Section 83(b) election was filed on the award, the payment is treated as dividend income, reported on Form 1099-DIV, and is not subject to withholding (note that there is some uncertainty as to whether this treatment applies when the dividends are not paid until the underlying award vests).

Dividend equivalents paid on restricted stock units are always treated as compensation income. In most cases, dividend equivalents are paid on a deferred basis. If so, the payments are not subject to federal income tax until paid out, but they will be subject to FICA/FUTA upon vesting. If the dividend equivalents are vested when they are accrued (i.e., for dividend equivalents paid on vested units that are subject to a deferral election), they are subject to FICA/FUTA at the time the payment is accrued but will not be subject to federal income tax until paid out. Withholding and reporting requirements are the same as for the underlying award.

3.4.3 Employee Tax Withholding

If the recipient is an employee, any compensation income recognized in connection with a restricted stock purchase, award, or unit arrangement is subject to federal and state withholding obligations for income and employment tax purposes. Relevant withholding taxes include:

- Federal income tax
- Social Security
- Medicare
- State income tax (if applicable)
- State disability or unemployment (if applicable)
- Local taxes (if applicable)

For federal income tax purposes, any compensation income recognized for restricted stock is treated as a supplemental wage payment. Where an employee has received less than $1 million in supplemental payments during the calendar year, this payment is eligible for withholding one of two ways. First, the compensation income may be aggregated with the employee's regular salary payment for the period, with withholding computed on the total amount. Alternatively, the compensation income is eligible for withholding at the flat rate for supplemental wage payments. Where an employee has received more than $1 million in supplemental payments (including the current payment) during the calendar year, withholding on the payments, or portion thereof, in excess of $1 million must be at the maximum individual tax rate.

In addition, employment taxes under the Federal Insurance Contributions Act (FICA) and the Federal Unemployment Tax Act (FUTA) may be due. FICA is made up of two separate taxes: old age, survivor, and disability insurance (Social Security) and hospital insurance (Medicare). The Social Security component of FICA is collected up to an annual maximum. The Medicare component is collected against the employee's total earnings. The employer must match these taxes. The FICA rates and their applicable ceilings, if any, are subject to change annually. The company's payroll department should be contacted for notification as to when these rate changes occur.

Under Section 6672 of the Code, a 100% penalty may be imposed for failing to withhold and pay over taxes. There is no withholding required from a non-employee.

In the case of restricted stock purchases and awards, all withholding obligations arise at the time of vesting (or grant, if a Section 83(b) election is filed). Restricted stock units are subject to federal income tax withholding upon distribution (which may occur at vesting or later, if the unit arrangement is subject to either a mandatory or elective deferral) and are subject to FICA withholding (Medicare and Social Security) and FUTA at the time of vesting (regardless of whether distribution occurs at that time).

The withholding taxes collected by the company are only an estimate of the employee's ultimate tax liability. It may be necessary for the employee to make additional quarterly tax deposits depending upon his or her personal tax situation (or to remit additional amounts owed when tax returns are filed).

In addition to the company's withholding obligation, the company must furnish an employee (or former employee) receiving restricted stock with a Form W-2 for the year of vesting (or grant or distribution) reporting the compensation income recognized as "wages." If the recipient is a non-employee, the compensation income is not subject to withholding but must be reported on a Form 1099-MISC for the year of vesting (or grant or distribution).

Most states follow the federal treatment for income tax purposes and may require withholding of state disability or unemployment taxes. Generally, state taxes are determined on the basis of the employee's state of residence. The company may also be required to withhold certain local taxes in addition to federal and state taxes.

3.4.4 Tax Treatment of Employer Company

The company receives a corporate tax deduction (for compensation expense) under Code Section 162 equal to the amount included as compensation income in the gross income of the employee. The company generally is able to take the deduction in the taxable year that includes the close of the taxable year in which the employee recognizes income.

Under IRS regulations, an employer is allowed a deduction only for the amount of compensation "included" in the employee's gross income. This "included" amount is the amount reported by the employee on an original or amended tax return, or the amount included in the employee's gross income as the result of an IRS audit.

The regulations stipulate that timely compliance with the Form W-2 or Form 1099 filing requirements, reporting the amount includible in the employee's income, is deemed "inclusion" of the amount in gross income. The employer company is not required to establish that the employee actually included the reported amounts in his or her income tax return. Where the amount of compensation income recognized meets the requirements for exemption from reporting for payments aggregating less than $600 in any taxable year, or is eligible for any other reporting exemption, no reporting is required in order for the employer company to claim the deduction.

In the case of restricted stock offered to the chief executive officer or one of the four most highly compensated executive officers of a publicly held corporation, the compensation income recognized by the employee is subject to the deduction limit of Section 162(m) of the Code. This limit is not applicable, however, if the restricted stock arrangement qualifies for the exception for "performance-based" compensation.

3.4.5 Disposition of Stock

Upon a sale or other disposition of the restricted shares, the employee generally recognizes a capital gain or loss equal to the difference between the employee's adjusted tax basis in the restricted shares and the sale price. An employee's tax basis in the restricted shares is equal to the total purchase price paid (if any) for the shares plus the amount of compensation income recognized by the employee. Generally, this means that the restricted shares have a tax basis equal to the fair market value of the company's stock on the date of vesting/distribution (or the date of grant, if a Section 83(b) election is filed).

For purposes of computing the holding period for long-term capital gains treatment, the holding period generally commences on the date of vesting. Where a Section 83(b) election is filed, however, the holding period commences on the date of grant or purchase, and where a unit award is subject to deferred distribution, the holding period commences on the date of distribution.

3.4.6 International Tax Considerations

Outside of the U.S., the tax treatment of restricted stock can vary greatly from country to country. Some countries assess income based on any value at the time of grant or purchase (regardless of vesting), but other countries may defer taxation until the arrangement vests or until the underlying shares are sold. In countries where restricted stock awards are taxed at grant (which is generally undesirable), this outcome may sometimes be avoided by granting restricted stock units instead. In some countries, it may be necessary for participants to complete filings with the local tax authorities to defer or accelerate the time at which the stock is taxed. The tax rates applicable to restricted stock may be substantially higher than the tax rates that apply in the U.S.

There may also be significant obligations imposed on the company for the restricted stock. The company may be required to fulfill reporting obligations for the income recognized by participants and may also be required to withhold taxes on this income. Where withholding is required, there may not be a flat withholding rate applicable to stock compensation (as exists in the U.S.), in which case companies will need to work closely with local payroll offices (or apply to the local tax authorities for a flat rate) to determine the appropriate tax withholding rates. Many countries also have substantial social insurance taxes that can apply to stock compensation, often with matching payments required from the company. In some cases, the company's matching payments may not be subject to any maximum and could ultimately become a significant burden for the company.

Many countries provide some form of qualified stock option that is subject to lower tax rates, yet only a few countries provide the same benefit to restricted stock arrangements. Thus, offering restricted stock could be significantly more costly to both participants and the granting corporation (which may have to make matching social insurance contributions that would not apply under a qualified option plan).

The company should review the tax treatment applicable to the plan in each country where it will be offered carefully with its legal advisors before offering restricted stock to any employees outside the U.S. Failure to comply with local laws could ultimately be very costly to the company; it can be difficult to correct errors or minimize the cost to the company after the stock has been granted.

3.5 Securities Law Considerations

Federal and state securities laws affect restricted stock plans of both privately held and publicly held companies. Securities law considerations may arise in connection with a restricted stock plan in at least two situations: (1) at the time of grant or purchase of restricted stock and (2) upon disposition of the shares of stock acquired under the restricted stock plan.

When presented with a securities law question, companies must consider both the federal securities laws, which include the Securities Act of 1933 and the Securities Exchange Act of 1934, and state securities laws, which include the laws of the state of the company's principal place of business and each state in which the company proposes to grant restricted stock arrangements to its employees and sell shares of stock. In addition, if the stock will be offered to employees residing outside the U.S., companies must also consider the securities laws of the countries in which the employees receiving the stock reside.

3.5.1 Registration

Before implementing a restricted stock plan, the company must address the question of whether the offer and sale of securities under the plan is subject to registration under applicable securities laws. It is the offer to sell a security that triggers coverage under securities laws, not the actual purchase. Generally, registration requires that the proposed issuance involve both a "security" and the "offer" or "sale" of the security.

The Securities Act of 1933 governs the offer and sale of securities for federal securities law purposes. Generally, the Securities Act of 1933 provides that it is unlawful to offer or sell a security unless a registration statement containing detailed information about the company and the terms of the proposed offering is in effect or an exemption from registration is available.

Registration of restricted shares of stock is required to the extent that a "sale" is involved. The process of registering securities for offer and sale under the Securities Act of 1933 can be expensive. Accordingly, most privately held companies design their restricted stock plans to fit within one of the available exemptions from registration under the Securities Act of 1933. Before 1988, most companies relied on one of the general exemptions under the Securities Act of 1933 (Section 4(2), Regulation D or Section 3(a)(11)) to cover their employee stock plans. Today, Rule 701, which provides an exemption from the registration requirements of the Securities Act of 1933 for offers and sales of securities pursuant to compensatory employee benefit plans exclusively for privately held companies, is typically used.

Rule 701 covers offers and sales of restricted shares. Shares of stock acquired pursuant to Rule 701 are deemed to be "restricted securities" for purposes of the federal securities laws. Generally, the employee cannot resell these shares of stock unless they are subsequently registered under the Securities Act of 1933 or are sold pursuant to an exemption from registration, such as Rule 144. Ninety days after the company becomes subject to the reporting requirements of the Securities Exchange Act of 1934, however, shares of stock acquired pursuant to Rule 701 may be resold by non-affiliates without regard to Rule 144 (other than the manner of sale condition) and by affiliates in reliance on Rule 144 (but without regard to the holding period condition).

Generally, publicly held companies register the shares of stock to be offered pursuant to their restricted stock plans on Form S-8, a simplified registration statement available exclusively for the employee benefit plans of companies subject to the reporting requirements of the Securities Exchange Act of 1934. Form S-8 reflects an abbreviated disclosure format and incorporates by reference information contained in the company's other publicly available documents. Shares of stock acquired under a restricted stock plan registered on Form S-8 are not considered "restricted securities" for securities law purposes and generally can be more easily resold by employees. Even for restricted stock awards that will be issued at no cost, where registration may not be legally required since the offer does not involve a "sale" of stock, most publicly held companies register the restricted stock plan on Form S-8 to alleviate the resale restrictions that might other otherwise apply to the stock awarded under the plan.

Most states follow the pattern of the federal securities laws and treat restricted stock plans as involving the offer and sale of securities that must either be registered under state law or exempt from registration. Thus, it may be necessary for a company to register its restricted stock plan in each state where restricted stock arrangements are to be offered to employees or to locate suitable exemptions for the arrangements. Many states have specific exemptions from registration that cover the offer and sale of securities pursuant to an employee benefit plan, such as a restricted stock plan. These exemptions may impose specific (and often minor) filing requirements on the company.

The securities laws of other countries can vary significantly from U.S. securities laws. It may be necessary to register the plan (which can sometimes be costly) with the local authorities before offering the restricted stock to employees. In some cases, exemptions from registration may be available for stock offered to certain types of employees or under certain circumstances. If an exemption is available, it may be necessary to seek approval from the local authorities to qualify for it. In addition to the registration requirements, the company may be required to provide a prospectus or make other disclosures to the employees receiving the stock. The securities laws of some countries prohibit ownership of foreign securities, making it difficult or impossible for employees of those countries to receive restricted stock.

Before awarding restricted stock arrangements, a company must take steps to ensure that the restricted stock plan and the proposed offering comply with current federal, state, and/or local securities laws. Particularly when a company is experiencing significant growth and expansion, it is important to make sure that the securities laws of each state and country in which the company intends to extend its restricted stock plan have been reviewed and compliance procedures are in place. Advance planning is critical in this area, since certain exemptions may require filings and/or approval from local authorities in advance of when the restricted stock is granted and adequate time must be allowed to register an offering, if required.

Aside from meeting any applicable registration requirements, companies must provide anti-fraud disclosure statements to anyone receiving an offer to buy securities. These documents provide the purchaser with the information needed to assess the company's financial conditions and risks. The level of detail required varies from state to state as these laws are at the state, not federal, level. These statements may not be required if the offer is made only to top executives or others meeting the definition of "sophisticated" investors.

3.5.2 Resale

Rule 144 may limit the ability of an employee to resell shares of stock acquired under a restricted stock arrangement.

In the case of restricted shares that are acquired under an exemption from the registration requirements of the Securities Act of 1933, such as Section 4(2), Rule 506 of Regulation D, or Rule 701, such shares are considered to be "restricted securities." Generally, restricted securities must be sold in reliance on Rule 144.

In the case of restricted shares registered on Form S-8, the shares may be resold by non-affiliates without regard to Rule 144 and by affiliates in reliance on Rule 144 (but without regard to the holding period condition).

3.5.3 Officers, Directors, and Principal Shareholders

Under Section 16 of the Securities Exchange Act of 1934, restricted stock is subject to both the reporting requirements of Section 16(a) and the "short-swing profits" recovery rule of Section 16(b). Consequently, transactions involving restricted stock offered to directors and officers who are subject to Section 16 ("corporate insiders") must be considered in light of compliance with these provisions. Section 16 applies only to directors, officers, and principal shareholders of companies with registered securities (i.e., publicly held companies).

3.5.4 Reporting Requirements

Both a restricted stock purchase by a corporate insider and an award of restricted stock to a corporate insider are reportable events for purposes of Section 16(a). Currently, the purchase or award of restricted stock is reportable on Form 4 within two business days after the purchase or award occurs. Before August 29, 2002, the proper reporting form and the timing of reporting depended on whether the restricted stock arrangement was exempt from the operation of Section 16(b).

Under the Section 16 rules, neither the vesting of a right to receive a security nor the lapse of restrictions relating to a security are subject to Section 16. Consequently, the vesting of restricted shares is neither a reportable event for purposes of Section 16(a) nor subject to the "short-swing profits" recovery rule of Section 16(b).

If restricted shares are forfeited or repurchased by the company while the insider is still subject to Section 16 (e.g., when the insider fails to achieve performance targets required for vesting), the transaction is reportable for purposes of Section 16(a). The forfeiture or repurchase is reportable on Form 4 within two business days after it occurs. If the forfeiture or repurchase occurs after the insider is no longer subject to Section 16 (e.g., after the insider has terminated employment), it is not necessary to report it, provided that the forfeiture or repurchase is exempt from the operation of Section 16(b).

3.5.4.1 *Application of Reporting Requirements to Restricted Stock Units*

The grant of restricted stock units to a corporate insider is also subject to Section 16(a) and must be reported on a Form 4 within two business days of the date of grant. Where the units are convertible to common stock on a one-for-one basis, the grant can simply be reported as a direct acquisition of common stock. If reported in this manner, there is no further reporting obligation when the units vest and are converted to stock, but if the units are forfeited while the recipient is still subject to Section 16, it is necessary to report the forfeiture on a Form 4 within two business days.

Alternatively, the grant can be reported as the acquisition of a derivative security. If reported in this manner, the conversion of the units to common stock upon vesting or release must also be reported. Both the grant and the subsequent conversion are reportable on a Form 4 within two business days. Under this approach, however, it is not necessary to report forfeitures even if they occur while the recipient is still subject to Section 16. This alternative approach is required for units that do not convert to common stock at a one-for-one ratio.

3.5.5 "Short-Swing Profits" Recovery

Under Section 16(b), a purchase or grant of restricted stock or units is considered a "purchase" of the shares of stock unless the arrangement is exempt from the operation of Section 16(b) pursuant to Rule 16b-3. Thus, a non-exempt restricted stock purchase or grant can be matched with any sale of company stock occurring within six months either before or after the date of purchase/grant to trigger the operation of the "short-swing profits" recovery rule.

Rule 16b-3 exempts certain transactions by corporate insiders conducted under employee benefit plans, such as a restricted stock plan, from the "short-swing profits" recovery rule of Section 16(b) where the conditions of the exemption are satisfied. Under the Rule 16b-3 exemption, a restricted stock purchase or award can be exempted from the operation of Section 16(b), provided that the transaction satisfies *one* of the following conditions (only one condition must be satisfied, not all of the conditions):

- The purchase or award must be approved in advance by either the company's board of directors or by a committee of two or more non-employee directors.

- The purchase or award must either be approved in advance or ratified after the fact by the company's shareholders.

- The restricted shares cannot be disposed of within six months from the date of purchase or award. If this alternative is relied on, a sale of the restricted shares within six months of the date of purchase or award will cause the retroactive loss of this exemption for the grant. A corporate insider may sell shares of stock other than the restricted shares, however, without affecting the exempt status of the restricted stock purchase or award.

The repurchase or forfeiture of restricted shares (such as where a corporate insider terminates employment) is considered a disposition to the company and, unless exempt, can be matched with any non-exempt purchase of company stock occurring within six months either before or after the repurchase/forfeiture date to trigger the operation of the "short-swing profits" recovery rule. A repurchase or forfeiture of restricted shares is exempt if it is approved in advance by the company's board of directors, a committee of two or more non-employee directors, or the company's shareholders. Where the original grant of the restricted stock was approved by one of these three entities, the initial approval covers the subsequent repurchase or forfeiture without any further action.

3.5.6 Disclosure and Reporting

The Securities Exchange Act of 1934 requires that a publicly held company disclose detailed information about the compensation of its executive officers, including compensation under any restricted stock plans in its proxy and information statements, periodic reports, and other filings. In addition, the proxy solicitation rules of the Securities Exchange Act of 1934 require tabular disclosure of the shares outstanding and available for grant under the company's restricted stock plans (additional disclosures are required when a plan is being submitted for shareholder approval).

3.6 Financial Statement Impact

The accounting treatment of restricted stock plans may have a direct effect on the company's financial results. Beginning in 2006, companies are required to account for most forms of stock compensation, including restricted stock and units, under Statement of Financial Accounting Standards No. 123 (revised 2004), *Share-Based Payment* ("FAS 123(R)"). Under FAS No. 123(R), restricted stock plans are viewed as compensatory arrangements that give rise to a compensation expense that must be reflected in the company's financial statements. This expense is generally equal to the fair value of the award on the "measurement date" for the arrangement.

The measurement date is the date the terms of the arrangement are mutually understood by both the company and the employee. For restricted stock granted to employees of the company, this almost certainly is the date of grant, even where the restricted stock is subject to forfeiture based on the completion of performance targets.

For restricted stock or units where vesting is contingent on continued service or performance goals that are not related to the company's stock price (such as earnings or revenue targets), the fair value of the arrangement is generally equal to its intrinsic value—that is, the difference between the purchase price, if any, and the fair market value of the underlying stock on the measurement date. Where dividends are paid on the underlying stock but will not be paid on the unvested restricted stock or units, the fair value can be reduced by the present value of the dividend stream that is expected to be paid to shareholders over the vesting period of the arrangement. For restricted stock where vesting is contingent on market conditions (e.g., stock price targets or shareholder return), the fair value is adjusted based on the probability that the targets will be met. This adjustment must be computed with an option pricing model.

For restricted arrangements granted to non-employees, with the exception of outside directors (who are treated as employees for accounting purposes), under EITF 00-19, the measurement date is typically the date the arrangement vests.

If the restricted stock is offered to employees at a price equal to the fair market value on the date of grant, the company does not recognize any expense for the arrangement. Where a company grants restricted stock purchase arrangements to employees with a purchase price less than the fair market value of the company's stock on the date of grant, or awards the stock at no cost to employees, compensation expense results under FAS 123(R). This expense must be amortized, or "accrued," over the service period for the arrangement. The service period is generally the vesting period for the arrangement, but other factors, such as automatic acceleration of vesting upon retirement, may have an impact on the determination of the service period. Where the arrangement is subject to vesting contingent on performance goals or price targets, the service period is derived based on the time period in which the goals or targets are expected to be achieved.

Where restricted stock is subject to vesting that is contingent on service or non-market performance conditions, expense is accrued only for the portion of the arrangements that are expected to vest. If the expected or actual vesting outcome varies, the expense accrual is adjusted to reflect the new expected or actual outcome so that expense is recorded only for those awards that actually vest. Where restricted stock is subject to vesting that is contingent on market conditions, the expense is not adjusted for expected or actual forfeitures. Because the initial fair value of the arrangement is adjusted to reflect the market conditions, expense is recorded for the arrangement regardless of whether those conditions are met.

3.6.1 Disclosure

To accurately represent a company's financial condition and capital structure in its financial statements, certain disclosures are required under generally accepted accounting principles and the rules of the Securities and Exchange Commission. FAS 123(R) sets forth the specific financial statement disclosures that are required with respect to a company's employee stock option plan.

Under FAS 123(R), the following information must be disclosed about a company's restricted stock plans:

- A description of the restricted stock arrangements, including vesting conditions, price, and the number of shares authorized for issuance under the plan.

- The weighted average grant date fair value of arrangements granted under the plan.

- A description of the method used to calculate the fair value. Where restricted stock vests based on market conditions, this also should include a discussion of how the effect of these conditions on fair value was determined.

- The total compensation cost recognized for the company's equity compensation plans, including restricted stock.

- The remaining unrecognized compensation cost for the company's equity compensation plans, including restricted stock, and the period of time over which it is expected to be recognized.

- A description of any modifications to previously granted restricted stock arrangements, including the terms of the modifications, number of employees affected, and additional incremental cost resulting from the modification.
- The amount of cash received from payments for restricted stock and/or tax benefits realized by the company.
- The company's policy for issuing restricted stock, including the source of shares (i.e., authorized but unissued shares or treasury shares) and the number of shares the company expects to repurchase in the following annual period.

The company should provide the following additional information for restricted stock purchase and award plans:

- The number and weighted average grant date fair value of shares unvested at the beginning of the period.
- The number and weighted average grant date fair value of shares hares unvested at the end of the period.
- The number and weighted average grant date fair value of shares granted, vested, and forfeited during the period.

The company should provide the following additional disclosures for restricted stock units:

- The number and weighted average conversion ratio of units outstanding at the beginning of the period.
- The number and weighted average conversion ratio of units outstanding at the end of the period.
- The number and weighted average conversion ratio of units convertible at the end of the period.
- The number and weighted average conversion ratio of units granted, forfeited, or converted during the period.
- The number, weighted average conversion ratio, aggregate intrinsic value, and weighted average remaining term of units outstanding (for fully vested units and those expected to vest during the current period).

- The number, weighted average conversion ratio, aggregate intrinsic value, and weighted average remaining term of units currently convertible (for fully vested units and those expected to vest during the current period).
- The total intrinsic value of units converted during the period.

3.6.2 Accounting for Tax Effects

The expense that companies recognize for restricted stock differs from the tax deduction they are entitled to for the arrangements both in terms of timing and the amount of the tax deduction. The expense recognized for the arrangement is equal to the fair value of the arrangement (typically the intrinsic value of the underlying stock) at grant and is recorded over the arrangement's service period, typically the vesting schedule. The company's tax deduction, however is generally realized only once the arrangement vests (and, in the case of restricted stock units subject to deferral, not until the shares are distributed) and is equal to the intrinsic value of the stock at this time. These differences must be accounted for in the company's financial statements.

Assuming that a Section 83(b) election has not been filed for the award, the company records an estimated tax benefit (sometimes referred to as a deferred tax asset) as it recognizes expense for the award. This estimated benefit is always equal to the amount of expense recognized multiplied by the company's statutory tax rate (regardless of the current intrinsic value of the stock), and it reduces the company's reported tax expense. Upon realization of a tax deduction (at either vest or release of the shares), the actual tax savings resulting from the deduction is compared to the estimated benefit recorded earlier. Where the tax savings exceeds this benefit, the excess is recorded to additional paid-in capital. Where the tax savings is less than the previously estimated benefit, the shortfall is deducted from paid-in capital, provided that enough paid-in capital is available from the excess tax benefits recorded for prior stock plan transactions. Where insufficient paid-in capital is available from prior stock plan transactions, the shortfall is treated as additional tax expense.

For example, assume a company grants a restricted stock award for 10,000 shares when the market value of the underlying stock is $10 per share. The award vests in full two years after the date of grant, and the employee does not file a Section 83(b) election. The total expense for the award is $100,000 (10,000 shares multiplied by $10 per share). This expense is recorded over the two years that the award is vesting. During this same period, the company records an estimated tax benefit of $40,000 (assuming a combined statutory tax rate of 40%) and reduces its reported tax expense by this amount as well.

Now assume that the market value is $17 per share when the award vests. At this market value, the company recognizes a tax deduction of $170,000, which, at the same 40% tax rate, produces an actual tax savings of $68,000. This tax savings exceeds the previously estimated tax benefit by $18,000, which is treated as additional paid in capital (it does not further reduce the company's tax expense.

On the other hand, if the market value when the award vests is only $8 per share, the company's tax deduction will be only $80,000, and the resultant tax savings is only $32,000. This is $8,000 less than estimate benefit recorded for the award. In other words, the company reduced its reported tax expense by $40,000 for the award but only realized an actual tax savings of $32,000; thus, the tax reflected in its financial statements is less than the amount of tax actually paid. This $8,000 shortfall is merely deducted from paid-in capital, assuming enough exists from prior stock plan transactions. The amount of the shortfall that exceeds the paid-in capital that is available from prior stock plan transactions is treated as additional tax expense.

Where a Section 83(b) election is filed for a restricted stock purchase or award, there will generally be no difference between the expense recognized for the arrangement and the tax deduction realized for it. In addition, the company's actual tax savings will be known at grant; thus, there is no need to reduce tax expense based on an estimated amount. As expense is recorded for the arrangement, the company will simply reduce tax expense based on the amount of actual tax savings realized at grant. Assuming the company's tax deduction equals the expense recognized for the award, no adjustments to paid-in capital will be necessary.

3.6.3 Accounting for Dividend Payments

Under FAS 123(R), dividends paid on restricted stock and units are charged to retained earnings. This applies regardless of whether the dividends are paid on a current basis (i.e., at the same time the dividend is paid to other shareholders) or on a deferred basis (i.e., not until the underlying award is paid out). It also applies whether the dividends are paid in cash or stock and whether they are paid on restricted stock or restricted stock units.

When the award is granted, the market value of the underlying stock already includes the value of the future dividend payments (i.e., when investors are buying and selling the stock, the prices they agree on should take into account the future dividend stream the buyer will be entitled to and the seller is giving up). Since the expense the company recognizes is based on this market value, when the dividends are actually paid there is no need for the company to recognize any further expense.

As mentioned earlier, for restricted stock arrangements that are not entitled to dividends before vesting but where the company does pay dividends on the underlying stock, the fair value of the award is reduced by the present value of the dividends that will be paid over the vesting period of the award. For example, assume that restricted stock units that will vest over four years are granted when the market value is $40 and that the company expects the dividend yield on the underlying stock during this period to be 2%. If the company pays dividend equivalents on the unvested restricted stock units, the fair value of the unit award is $40 per share (the market value on the date the award is granted). If the company does *not* pay dividend equivalents on the unvested units, the fair value of the award is reduced by the present value of the future dividend stream, or approximately $3 per share.

Note, however, that where dividends are paid on awards that are ultimately forfeited, the company will recognize compensation expense for the dividends. In this situation, because of the forfeiture, the company will not recognize any expense for the award itself. However, the employee has received compensation in the form of the dividend payment; that compensation should be recognized as an expense. Another way to think of it is that the original award encompassed both the underlying shares and the future dividend stream that would be paid on them; both of these components contributed to the award's fair value. Now that the underlying shares have been forfeited but the employee retains the dividend payments, the company still must recognize expense for the portion of the award that was not forfeited, i.e., the dividend payments. Thus, the portion of the award's fair value that is attributable to the dividends is recognized as compensation expense.

This scenario is much more likely to occur with dividends that are paid on a current basis. For example, assume that a company grants a restricted stock award that cliff vests in four years on January 1, 2006, and pays a dividend to the grantee in 2007, and then the grantee terminates in 2008, forfeiting the award. In 2007, when the dividend is paid, it is charged to retained earnings. But in 2008, when the award is forfeited, unless the company makes the employee pay back the dividend (highly unlikely), the company will have to recognize compensation expense equal to the amount of the dividend. Just as in other areas relating to forfeitures under FAS No. 123(R), the company would have to estimate forfeitures up front and record expense for dividend payments based on the estimate, truing up for actual outcome. Or rather, the "haircut" that the company applies to its overall expense for estimated forfeitures is reduced by the amount of the dividends that are expected to be paid out on awards that ultimately forfeited.

This is less likely to be a concern with dividend that are paid on a deferred basis because they are typically subject to forfeiture if the vesting conditions of the underlying award are not met.

3.6.4 A Bit of Accounting History

Before FAS No. 123(R), employers were permitted to choose whether to account for their stock compensation plans, including their restricted stock and unit awards, under the original FAS 123 or APB Opinion No. 25.

Issued in October 1972, APB Opinion No. 25, *Accounting for Stock Issued to Employees* ("APB 25") first established the principles that employers would apply to account for stock compensation programs. Under APB 25, a restricted stock and unit award resulted in expense equal to the award's intrinsic value on its measurement date. For awards that vested solely on continued service to the company, the measurement date was the grant date; for awards that were subject to performance conditions (whether or not the conditions related to the company's stock price), the measurement date was the date the awards eventually vested. Just as under FAS 123(R), expense was recorded over the award's service period, and expense was not recorded for awards that were ultimately forfeited.

In 1995, the FASB issued the first version of FAS No. 123. The treatment of restricted stock and restricted stock units under the original FAS 123 was substantively the same as their treatment under FAS 123(R). FAS 123 was intended to supersede APB 25 in its entirety; however, for political reasons, FASB was unable to require this. Instead, FAS 123 originally permitted employers to elect to adopt its provisions or to continue to rely on APB 25 and disclose, on a pro forma basis, the impact FAS 123 would have on the employer's financial statements if adopted. Most employers elected to remain under APB 25, with only pro forma disclosure of the FAS 123 impact. It was not until the issuance of FAS 123(R) in 2004 that FASB was able to require employers to adopt the new standard. Now all employers are required to account for their stock compensation programs, including their restricted stock and unit awards, under FAS 123(R).

Employers were permitted to adopt FAS 123(R) using a modified prospective approach or with a retrospective restatement. Those employers that adopted using the modified prospective approach did not restate fiscal periods ending before they adopted FAS 123(R) for the new standard. Thus, these employers may be continuing to rely on APB 25 to account for their restricted stock and unit awards in these historical periods.

3.7   International Considerations

In addition to the tax and securities law implications of offering restricted stock to employees located outside the U.S., there are many legal and administrative issues that must be considered when a restricted stock plan is extended overseas.

3.7.1 Cultural and Language Differences

It can generally be assumed that employees in the U.S. understand what stock is and how the stock market works; it can also usually be assumed that they have some experience with stock compensation. This may not always be true for employees located outside the U.S. While it is certainly true that in some countries, employees have an understanding of these concepts equaling that of U.S.-based employees, it is also likely that in some countries the concepts of stock and stock compensation are completely new to employees. Even in those countries where employees are familiar with these concepts, one may find that the forms of stock compensation they are familiar with differ from restricted stock. Often, the terminology used in reference to stock compensation, even in English-speaking countries, is different than the terminology used in the U.S. Where employees are not familiar with the concept of restricted stock, it is necessary to provide additional education to ensure that employees fully understand the arrangement and the restrictions associated with it. Where employees are required to pay for the stock, it is critical that they understand the risks associated with such purchases. It may be necessary to translate plan documents and other educational materials into local languages or dialects.

3.7.2 Labor Laws

Just like any other form of compensation, restricted stock can be subject to labor laws. These laws may provide specified rights to certain groups of employees (such as part-time employees or employees on leave of absence), create entitlements to future awards of stock, or provide certain entitlements and rights upon termination of employment. The restricted stock plan must be reviewed for compliance with local labor laws, and, in some cases, it may be advisable to include language in the plan relinquishing these rights.

3.7.3 Data Privacy Regulations

Many countries, especially countries that are members of the European Union, have regulations governing the collection and transmission of personnel data, such as name, address, compensation, and so on. Under these regulations, the U.S. is typically considered to provide inadequate privacy protections, causing the transmission of personnel data to the U.S. to be subject to special procedures. Unless the restricted stock plan is administered from an overseas office, administrating the restricted stock plan will most certainly require personnel data for overseas employees to be transmitted to the U.S. The company must ensure that the transmission of such data complies with any relevant data privacy regulations. In some cases, it may be necessary for employees to sign a release permitting the transmission of their personal data to the U.S.

3.7.4 Currency Exchange Controls

Where employees are required to pay for the restricted stock, the purchase may be subject to local currency exchange controls. These controls govern the transmission of funds into and out of the country. Where currency exchange controls limit the funds that can be transmitted to the U.S., it may be necessary to ensure that the purchase price does not exceed these limitations or to structure the purchase in a manner that is permissible under the exchange controls. In some cases, the currency exchange controls may prohibit the purchase altogether.

3.8 Administrative Matters

Many companies establish formal policies and procedures to facilitate the efficient administration of their restricted stock plan. Formal policies enhance the plan administrator's ability to operate the plan consistent with the company's objectives for the restricted stock purchase program. They also enable the plan administrator to resolve problems that arise during the course of operating the plan. Formal guidelines for processing restricted stock transactions can serve as an effective means for ensuring that all company procedures are properly followed.

A comprehensive restricted stock plan policy should address:

- How recipients are determined
- How the number of restricted shares offered to each employee is determined
- How often restricted stock is granted
- How the vesting schedule is determined
- The handling of restricted stock in special situations
- How applicable withholding taxes are calculated and collected
- The different treatment for directors and officers subject to Section 16 of the Securities Exchange Act of 1934 (applicable to publicly held companies only)

A written procedure should address:

- The company's internal approval process
- The tasks of the plan administrator
- The grant transaction recordation
- The purchase/award agreement preparation and completion process
- Transfer agent communications
- Inter-departmental communications

3.8.1 Internal Approval Process

Companies often find it beneficial to establish internal approval procedures for grants of restricted stock. These procedures should address such matters as who will be recommended for a restricted stock grant, what the size of the grant will be, and whether any special terms and conditions will be incorporated into the grant. The human resources department and/or other benefits personnel usually make these decisions, possibly with input from various management-level employees.

Following internal approval, all restricted stock arrangements—regardless of origin—are incorporated into a formal proposal and submitted to the company's board of directors for review and approval. If the board of directors has delegated responsibility for restricted stock arrangements to a subcommittee, such as a compensation committee, the recommendations are considered and approved. Alternatively, the committee may make its own recommendations that are submitted to the full board of directors for review and final approval. Restricted stock arrangements generally become effective as of the date of board action.

3.8.2 Restricted Stock Agreement

Most companies document a restricted stock arrangement by preparing a written agreement that sets out specific terms and conditions. The agreement typically contains:

- The correct name of the employee
- The effective date of the grant

- The number of shares of stock covered by the arrangement
- The price, if any
- The vesting schedule for the shares of stock covered by the arrangement
- The expiration date of the right, if any

In addition, the agreement usually sets out the permissible forms of payment (if payment is necessary) for the purchase price, and other related matters. Since the agreement usually also specifies the obligations of the employee and any restrictions imposed on the restricted shares, most companies require that the employee sign the agreement. A company should set a time limit within which employees must sign and return agreements, and address whether there is a penalty for failure to return an executed agreement.

When the restricted stock arrangement is formally approved, multiple copies (at least two) of the agreement are usually given to the employee for signature. One copy is retained by the employee for his or her records, and the plan administrator should include a copy in the employee's file. If desired, a third copy should be sent to the company's legal counsel.

3.8.3 Collateral Documents

In addition to the agreement, other documents may be provided to an employee in connection with a restricted stock arrangement. For purposes of compliance with applicable federal and/or state securities laws, it is customary for the company to provide each employee with a copy of the company's restricted stock plan or with a document that summarizes the principal terms and conditions of the plan, describes the tax consequences of participation, and advises employees where to obtain additional information about the company. This document is sometimes referred to as the plan "prospectus."

Other relevant documents may include investment representation letters or statements (in the event the restricted shares have not been registered with the Securities and Exchange Commission), escrow instructions, and a form of promissory note and security agreement. Many companies also prepare and distribute fact sheets and/or question-and-answer memoranda that address common questions asked by employees concerning their restricted stock arrangements.

3.8.4 Amendments

Generally, the agreement provides that the terms of the restricted stock arrangement can be amended or terminated by the board of directors at any time. To the extent that the amendment or termination has any adverse affect on the employee, however, the amendment or termination is not effective without the consent of the employee.

3.8.5 Purchase Procedures

If payment is required for the restricted shares, the employee must follow the procedures established by the company to purchase the stock. Typically, these procedures are set forth in the employee's restricted stock agreement. At a minimum, these procedures require that the employee provide written notice to the company stating his or her intention to purchase the restricted shares. This written notice may also contain other information, such as:

- Specific representations and/or statements by the employee deemed necessary by the company to ensure compliance with all required federal and/or state securities laws.
- Information relevant to the form of payment that the employee has selected to pay the total required purchase price for the number of restricted shares being purchased.
- Specific statements pertaining to the tax withholding obligations of the employee if any, arising in connection with the purchase and/or vesting of the restricted shares.
- Specific statements with respect to any restrictions and/or conditions imposed on the restricted shares.

Generally, the written notice must be submitted to the plan administrator or other designated representative of the company in person, or by registered or certified mail with return receipt requested, before the expiration date of the restricted stock purchase arrangement. The notice should be accompanied by full payment of the total purchase price for the number of restricted shares being purchased and any other required documents.

3.8.6 Filing of Section 83(b) Election

If the employee wishes to file a Section 83(b) election, it must be filed within 30 days of the purchase or award date. The election is filed with the IRS office where the employee files his or her tax return and must include the name, address and tax ID number of the employee, a description of the property for which the election is filed and the restrictions applicable to it, the date the stock was purchased or awarded, the fair market value of the stock on the purchase or award date, the amount paid for the stock, and a statement that all required copies of the election have been provided to the appropriate parties. A copy of the election must be provided to the company and the employee should also file a copy with his or her tax return for the year.

3.8.7 Withholding Taxes

Upon the vesting/distribution of the restricted shares (or the purchase or award, if a Section 83(b) election has been filed and the purchase or award price of the shares is less than the fair market value of the company's stock on the date of purchase or award), the company is obligated to withhold applicable federal and state income tax. In addition, withholding is required for purposes of the Medicare Insurance portion of FICA, and may be required for purposes of the Social Security portion of FICA to the extent that the employee has not already satisfied his or her annual obligation.

If the recipient is an employee of the company, arrangements must be made to satisfy any withholding tax obligations that arise in connection with the vesting (or purchase or award) of the restricted shares. In accordance with Section 83 of the Code, the applicable taxes will be calculated based on the fair market value of the company's stock on the vesting/distribution date (or the purchase or award date).

Most companies provide employees with notification of this tax liability in advance of the vesting/distribution date. In most cases it is not possible to accurately calculate the employee's tax liability until the vesting/distribution date, but the advance notice might estimate this liability based on the current fair market value of the company's stock and offer the employee several alternatives for paying the taxes. Subject to the terms of the restricted stock plan, these alternatives might include payment in cash (usually by check), additional withholding from the employee's paychecks before the vesting/distribution date, sale of the shares, loan, or tender of a portion of the shares vesting. As mentioned earlier, withholding sufficient shares to cover the employee's tax withholding liability is often the most expedient method of dispatching this obligation. Where feasible for the company from an administrative and cash-flow standpoint and where permissible under the terms of the plan, it may be advisable for the notice to provide that this method will be applied in the absence of any other election and to set a firm deadline for making a different election. In addition, the notice usually states the time period within which the company must receive the withholding tax payment, generally before or very shortly after the vest date. The company generally holds the certificate for the vested shares of stock until full payment of all amounts due is received. Where feasible and permissible, it may also be advisable to provide that if full payment is not received by the required deadline, a portion of the vested shares will be applied to the tax payment. This can alleviate a situation where employees procrastinate making the required tax payments and the company has no recourse but to continue holding the shares for an indefinite period.

3.8.8 Issuance of Shares

The plan administrator must provide instructions to the company's transfer agent for the preparation and issuance of a certificate for the restricted shares purchased or awarded for no consideration. The instructions should include the number of shares of stock to be issued, the number of certificates to be issued, the correct name under which the shares are to be registered, and appropriate mailing instructions. Generally, the transfer agent's instructions require the signature of an authorized company representative.

In anticipation of the initial purchase or award of restricted shares, the plan administrator should provide the company's transfer agent with a list of the relevant legends to be placed on certificates for the restricted shares. Transfer agents or legal counsel are usually able to assist with the drafting of these legends. Legends may be required by applicable federal and/or state securities laws to prevent transfers of the restricted shares that are not in compliance with such laws. In addition, where the restricted shares are subject to repurchase rights or transferability restrictions set forth in the restricted stock plan or imposed by the company, the certificates should include appropriate legends to notify potential grantees of these restrictions.

CHAPTER FOUR

Performance Award Plans

Helen H. Morrison
Kay Kemp
Joe Adams

Contents

A performance award plan rewards participants for the achievement of specified performance metrics. Under a typical performance award plan, participants receive a grant of a number of performance award units at the beginning of an award period, which entitles them to payment at the end of the award period to the extent the performance metrics were achieved. The award units may have a fixed value (e.g., a specified dollar amount) or a variable value (e.g., based on the value of the employer's stock). Award plans that use a fixed value are generally referred to as "performance unit" plans, while plans that are tied to the value of the underlying shares of stock (and sometimes pay out in shares of stock) are referred to as "performance share" plans. For the purpose of this chapter, we refer to both types as "performance award plans."

If the focus of this book is on equity-based programs, why do we have a chapter on performance award plans? Because, similar to equity-based programs, performance award plans are another form of long-term incentive compensation designed to motivate participants to increase shareholder value. The key difference between equity-based incentive compensation programs and performance awards is that the equity-based programs provide a benefit to the participant based on the value of the underlying company stock, while the benefits provided under a performance award plan do not necessarily depend on the employer's stock value.

Many employers acknowledge that their company stock price may not be the best indicator of an employee's performance. A performance award plan can be custom-designed to reward the participants for achievement of a specific financial or nonfinancial objective that may not correlate easily or immediately to an increase in the company's stock price. Although performance award plans take on many different forms, they all have the common aim of rewarding the participants for the achievement of a long-term goal that is objective, measurable, and generally within the participants' control.

This chapter discusses when a performance award plan is an appropriate long-term incentive compensation program, the design terms and conditions of such a plan, and the taxation issues.[1] (Accounting is covered in the chapter on accounting in this book.)

4.1 When Is a Performance Award Plan Appropriate?

4.1.1 What Type of Long-Term Incentive Plan Makes Sense?

The threshold question for any employer considering a performance award plan for executives or a broader group of employees is why this form of plan is more appropriate than another form of long-term program, such as an equity-based plan. Performance award plans are

---

1. See chapter 2 for a discussion of the ERISA and securities law issues related to long-term incentive compensation plans.

advisable when the employer's objective is to motivate the participants to achieve a specific financial or nonfinancial objective. Take, for example, a company that has experienced revenue growth consistently for a period of years but whose earnings have been flat or declining during that same period. In this case, a performance award plan that rewards the participants for the achievement of targeted earnings growth may be appropriate to focus the management's attention on growing the company's profitability.

The performance measures under the plan will depend on the employer's objectives. Is the intention of the plan to reward overall corporate performance, divisional performance, or individual performance? One of the advantages of a performance award plan as opposed to an equity compensation plan is that it may be custom-designed to meet the employer's specific goals. Typical financial measurements include revenue growth, EBITDA growth,[2] net income, return on equity, and return on assets. The targets may be company-wide or limited to a particular division. They may be stated in absolute terms or relative to a peer group or index. Peer group comparisons may be particularly effective because they eliminate the effect of general market conditions and enable the employer to reward superior performance even during a downturn in the market overall. Performance award plans may also include a component designed to focus the participants' attention on nonfinancial criteria such as staff development or retention.

When designing the appropriate metrics for the performance plan, the company probably will want to understand the metrics of any short-term (annual) incentive plan. Typically, companies do not want the performance plan to simply "double-up" rewards for the same type of performance rewarded in the annual incentive plan. Instead, the annual incentive plan might be designed to encourage one set of behaviors and metrics (e.g., growth in earnings per share (EPS)) while the performance plan might focus on different set (e.g., return on equity)

One way to think of a performance award plan is simply as a more complex form of profit sharing or gainsharing. In a typical profit sharing plan, employees get a payment based on the achievement of a target, usually over a period of one year or less. For instance, if the company

---

2. "EBITDA" means earnings before interest, taxes, depreciation, and amortization.

exceeds its earnings target, employees might get 20% of the excess. If a different measure is used, such as sales growth or quality control, employees get a payout based on a preset formula for each degree to which the goal is exceeded. A performance award plan simply extends the measurement and award period from one year or less to a few years or more. Unlike most profit or gainsharing programs, performance awards can be designed to be paid out in the form of shares instead of cash. Some public companies prefer to pay in shares to help employees meet applicable share ownership requirements; however, those companies will need to ensure that the shares ultimately delivered are authorized under a shareholder approved plan.

Before implementing a performance share plan, the employer must consider whether the plan is intended to retain employees as well to motivate better performance. If retention is important, the plan should be designed with an appropriate vesting schedule. Alternatively, the plan could be designed to provide annual grants that each have a specified vesting schedule (e.g., 3-year term). Under this design, the employee forfeits a portion of each grant upon termination at any time. Another variant of this approach is to provide that awards are earned based upon the performance over a specified period, and then at the end of that performance period the earned award (whether denominated in shares or cash) is automatically deferred for a certain period of time and subject to a vesting schedule.

4.1.2 Is a Performance Award Plan Affordable?

Whether a performance award plan is affordable depends on several factors: (1) the amount of the potential reward opportunity for each participant; (2) the number of participants; and (3) whether the financial targets strike the appropriate balance between motivating employees and increasing the company's ultimate value.

The company's compensation philosophy, its profitability, and its need to attract and retain key employees are all factors that must be considered to determine the level of reward. Another consideration is the level of long-term compensation provided by the company's peer group (or other companies outside the peer group that might be places company employees come from—or go to).

Eligibility is another critical issue to consider in determining whether any long-term incentive plan is affordable. A long-term plan is a particularly appropriate incentive for those management employees who are responsible for the company's strategic direction. As a general rule, long-term programs are offered only to senior management. At some level of employment, participation in a long-term program, if it means a reduction in short-term compensation, is counterproductive. Many employees are motivated exclusively by short-term compensation (e.g., base salary and annual bonus) and are less likely to focus on rewards based on the long-term performance of the company.

Finally, establishing the financial target is important to assure that the program provides a reward only for superior performance. Setting the right target level can be a delicate task. A target level that is too low may provide an excessive reward and result in shareholder dilution, while a target that is too great may seem unattainable and, therefore, de-motivating.

4.2 Performance Award Plan Design

4.2.1 Plan Administration

In a public company, the final determination on the form of long-term incentive compensation program, eligibility, and size of award typically will be made by the board of directors, as recommended by its independent compensation committee (particularly if payment will be made in the form of shares and/or if the plan is designed to provide compensation that is "performance-based" compensation for purposes of the exception to the $1 million limit on deductible compensation under Section 162(m) of the Internal Revenue Code (the "Code"). Private companies do not always have a compensation committee of the board of directors. Instead the president or CEO, with the approval of the board of directors, may determine the form of compensation programs.

4.2.2 Eligibility

Participation in the plan is generally limited to a select group of key employees who have a direct and measurable impact on the long-term financial success of the employer. The compensation committee of the employer's board of directors or its chief executive officer typically determines participation in the plan. The plan should make clear that participation may be determined on an annual basis; inclusion in one performance cycle does not guarantee an individual's continued participation in subsequent performance cycles.

4.2.3 Award Opportunity

A performance award plan may be designed as a promise to pay the participant a specified dollar amount at the end of a performance cycle, assuming the achievement of a pre-determined financial objective. The amount of the payment, if any, is typically based on the achievement of a threshold, target, or maximum financial objectives.

Alternatively, a performance award plan may provide for the grant of a specified number of performance units. The value of the performance units is determined at the end of the performance cycle based on the financial results.

In the plan design illustrated in table 4-1, the performance measures include a percentage increase in average revenue growth and average EBITDA growth during the performance cycle (e.g., a four-year period). The targeted value of each unit is $100. However, the ultimate unit value is based upon the actual results of revenue growth and EBITDA growth during the performance cycle. (Corporate results between performance levels may be interpolated on a linear basis.) If the participant's targeted award opportunity at the end of the performance cycle is $100,000, the employer will provide the participant with a grant of 1,000 performance units (1,000 units × $100 target = $100,000). If the company achieves average revenue growth of 7% and average EBITDA growth of 7% over the four-year performance cycle, the participant will be entitled to a payment of $100,000. If instead, the average revenue growth was 8% and the average EBITDA growth was 7%, the participant would be entitled to a performance award payment of $125,000 (1,000 performance units × $125). Note that the performance units have no value (participant will receive no payment) if performance is below a certain level (e.g., less than 6% average revenue growth, and less than 6.8% average EBITDA growth), and the maximum value is $150 per unit, which is achieved if

Table 4-1. Example of Performance Award Plan

Average EBITDA growth 2003–2006	Unit value					
	<6%	6.0%	6.5%	7.0%	7.5%	8.0%
7.20%	$0.00	$100.00	$112.50	$125.00	$137.50	$150.00
7.10%	$0.00	$87.50	$100.00	$112.50	$125.00	$137.50
7.00%	$0.00	$75.00	$87.50	**$100.00**	$112.50	$125.00
6.90%	$0.00	$62.50	$75.00	$87.50	$100.00	$112.50
6.80%	$0.00	$50.00	$62.50	$75.00	$87.50	$100.00
<6.80%	**$0.00**	**$0.00**	**$0.00**	**$0.00**	**$0.00**	**$0.00**

Average revenue growth 2003–2006

the average revenue growth is 8% or more and average EBITDA growth is 7.2% or more.

4.2.4 Performance Cycle

Each performance cycle is a specified period, generally three to five years. The value of the award typically is based on the cumulative financial performance during this period so as to distinguish the performance plan from a mere accumulated annual incentive plan. A new cycle of performance awards may be granted each year, although if there will be overlapping performance periods, care should be taken in establishing the payout amounts so that "one really good year" does not artificially inflate participants' payments for several performance cycles. At the end of each performance cycle, unit values are determined and paid out in cash unless the participant elects (in accordance with the deferred compensation rules under Code Section 409A) to defer receipt of the payment to some future date. Table 4-2 illustrates such a performance cycle.

4.2.5 Payout

Payments are made at the end of the performance cycle, typically as-suming the participant remains employed through that date. However, as discussed later in this chapter, some plan designs allow terminated participants to receive a pro rata payment if their employment terminated due to situations such as disability or death, retirement, termination without cause or a divestiture.

Payment may be made either in cash or in shares of company stock. If the performance award plan is paid in full within 2½ months after the end of the performance period, the award will be considered a "short-term deferral" under Section 409A of the Code.[3] As such, the award will be exempt from most requirements of Code Section 409A. If, on the other hand, the performance award plan permits a participant

---

3. As used in this chapter, the term "Code Section 409A" includes the applicable guidance issued by the IRS under that section of the Code, specifically Notice 2005-1 and proposed regulations issued in September 2005. See Prop. Treas. Reg. § 1.409A-1(b)(4) for the definition of "short-term deferral."

Table 4-2. Example of a Performance Cycle

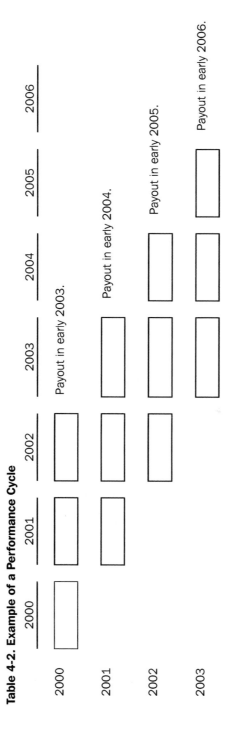

to defer the receipt of the performance award payment to a future date, then the plan will constitute a deferred compensation plan subject to Code Section 409A.

For amounts that are intended to be treated as short-term deferrals under Code Section 409A, the employer may choose either of the following approaches:

- The employer may specify in the plan document that payment is intended to be made within 2½ months after the end of the performance cycle. In this case, the employer will be deemed to have made payment within that 2½ month period as long as the payment is made by the end of the calendar year in which the payment date occurs.[4]

- If the applicable payment date is not specified in writing, then the payment will still qualify as a short-term deferral as long as it is made within 2½ months after the end of the performance cycle. However, that payment date may be extended only for administrative and economic impracticability.[5]

Obviously, use of a written plan document that specifies the payment date will provide the employer with more flexibility for making distributions. If the employer does not specify the payment date in writing and fails to make payment within 2½ months after the end of the performance cycle, then the payment would become deferred compensation without a specified payment date as required by Code Section 409A. That failure could cause a violation of Code Section 409A, resulting in immediate income inclusion in the year of vesting and a 20% income tax penalty. Interest is also payable, in an amount equal to the underpayment rate, plus one percentage point, imposed on the underpayments that would have occurred had the compensation been includible in income for the taxable year when first deferred, or if later, when not subject to a substantial risk of forfeiture. These penalties are assessed on the affected participant,[6] not the employer.

---

4.   Prop. Treas. Reg. § 1.409A-3(d).

5.   Prop. Treas. Reg. § 1.409A-1(b)(4)(ii).

6.   Section 409A applies to nonqualified deferred compensation arrangements

When the performance award plan permits a participant to elect to defer receipt of his or her award payment, the participant's election must be made in accordance with the requirements of Code Section 409A. The employer may adopt one of the following approaches for such deferrals:

- If the performance award constitutes performance-based pay under Code Section 409A,[7] the participant's deferral election can be made as late as six months before the end of the performance cycle, provided the performance cycle is at least twelve months long and the participant performs services continuously from the time the performance goals were established through the date of the deferral election. However, the deferral election cannot be made after the performance award amount has become both substantially certain to be paid and readily ascertainable. Thus, depending on the performance goals, a participant may be required to make his or her deferral election well before the date that is six months before the end of the performance cycle.

- If the performance award does not constitute performance-based pay, or if there is uncertainty as to whether a deferral election of performance-based pay could be made timely (as discussed above), the participant's deferral election may be made not later than twelve months before the end of the performance cycle. In this case, however, payment of the award must be deferred for a period of at least

---

involving common-law employees, as well as other service providers, such as independent contractors, consultants, and non-employee directors. Throughout this chapter, the term "employee" or "participant" should be understood to include all types of service providers when the requirements of Section 409A are being addressed.

7. In general, to be considered performance-based pay, the performance goals must be established in writing no later than 90 days after the beginning of the performance cycle. Subjective performance criteria may be used, provided they are related to the participant's performance or to the performance of the group that includes the participant, and the determination that the criteria are satisfied is not made by the participant, a member of the participant's family, or a person under the supervision of the participant or a member of the participant's family. See Prop. Treas. Reg. § 1.409A-1(e).

five years from the end of the performance cycle.[8] Payment may be made during the five-year deferral period only for death, disability, or a change as control (each as defined in Code Section 409A).

- If neither of the above approaches is adopted, then the participant's deferral election must be made before the beginning of the performance cycle.[9]

- Note that a special rule applies to newly eligible participants. Those individuals may make a deferral election even after the performance period has begun, provided they make the election within 30 days of their initial eligibility and at least 12 months before the award is no longer subject to risk of forfeiture.

A participant's deferral election must specify the date on which the deferred performance award will be paid, which date may be subsequently changed only if the following conditions are met: (1) the election to change the payment date is made at least 12 months in advance of the originally scheduled payment date, (2) the election does not become effective until 12 months after it is made, and (3) the payment is delayed for at least five years from the originally scheduled payment date.[10] In general, scheduled payment dates can only be further deferred; they may not be accelerated.

Note that the rules set forth in the preceding paragraph apply to changes in deferral elections made after December 31, 2007. Before that time, transition relief under Code Section 409A would allow payments to be further deferred without regard to the rules set forth above and would allow accelerations of distributions, provided that during the transition period, participants may not elect to move payments into or out of the year in which they make the election. For example, in 2007, a participant could change his or her distribution election with respect to amounts payable in 2010 to have those amounts payable in 2009 (i.e., no prohibition on acceleration) or in 2011 (i.e., no requirement to push out distributions five years). What the participant may *not* do is have the amounts paid to him or her in 2007 if the participant is mak-

---

8.   See Prop. Treas. Reg. § 1.409A-2(a)(3) and § 1.409A-2(b)(6), example 6.

9.   See Prop. Treas. Reg. § 1.409A-2(a)(2).

10.   See Prop. Treas. Reg. § 1.409A-2(b)(1).

ing the election in 2007; in that case, the closest the participant could come is to request a distribution as of January 1, 2008.

4.2.6 Service Requirements

Performance award plans are generally designed with a retention objective. In the event that a participant terminates employment before the last day of a performance cycle, he or she forfeits any value created in the award. In the case of overlapping performance cycles, as illustrated above, the participant forfeits a portion of the value built in the awards upon voluntary termination at any point.

4.2.6.1 *Termination Provisions: Death, Disability, and Retirement*

Termination of employment by reason of death, disability, or retirement before the completion of the performance cycle is a typical exception to the forfeiture provision.[11] In this case, the participant will typically receive a pro-rata distribution based upon actual corporate performance and the percentage of the performance cycle completed prior to termination.

4.2.6.2 *Change-in-Control Provisions*

A change-in-control provision is another typical exception to the forfeiture provisions. Typically, target performance is determined as of the change-in-control event and paid out as soon as administratively feasible.[12]

---

11. If the plan permits the deferral of performance awards, then the plan's definition of disability must comply with the requirements of Code § 409A(a)(2)(C) and Prop. Treas. Reg. § 1.409A-3(g)(4). In addition, if the company is a public company, payments after a participant's retirement will be subject to a six-month wait if the participant is a specified employee as defined in Prop. Treas. Reg. § 1.409A-1(i).

12. If the plan permits the deferral of performance awards, then the plan's definition of change-in-control must comply with the requirements of Notice 2005-1 (Q&A 11-14) and Prop. Treas. Reg. § 1.409A-3(g)(5).

4.3 Taxation of Performance Award Plans

The taxation of performance awards to the participants is relatively straightforward. Generally, participants are not subject to income taxation with respect to their performance award until payments of cash and/or stock are actually or constructively received.[13] The amount of cash and the fair market value of the stock paid under a performance award plan are taxable to the participant as ordinary income. In the unlikely event that the plan failed to satisfy the requirements of Code Section 409A (to the extent applicable), such failure could result in a 20% income tax penalty and interest payments, both imposed on the participant.[14]

The employer must withhold taxes from amounts paid to the employees as ordinary income.

The employer generally is entitled to take a tax deduction for any ordinary income recognized by employees. However, Code Section 162(m) precludes publicly traded corporations from taking a federal income tax deduction for certain compensation paid in excess of $1 million to the officers who are named in the corporation's proxy statement by reason of serving as an executive officer on the last day of the fiscal year.[15] Performance-based compensation is exempt from the $1 million limitation, as long as it is paid pursuant to a shareholder-approved plan that establishes the maximum amount that may be paid with respect to an executive and is administered by a committee consisting of at least two "outside directors."[16]

Many public companies design their performance award plans to constitute performance-based compensation for purposes of Code Sec-

---

13. Code §§ 409A, 451.

14. Under Code Section 409A, all "like" arrangements are generally treated as a single arrangement. The IRS has established four categories of arrangements: account-based arrangements, non-account-based arrangements, separation pay arrangements, and "other" types of arrangements (generally including SARs and other forms of equity-based arrangements). If a failure occurs with respect to an arrangement in one of these categories, then all other arrangements in that same category are deemed to have failed as well, so that the aforementioned penalties would apply to all arrangements in that category.

15. Code § 162(m)(1)-(3).

16. Treas. Reg. § 162(m)(4)(C)-(D).

tion 162(m). However, in 2003 and 2004 the IRS conducted a pilot audit program of 25 large companies' compliance with executive compensation rules and identified many violations of the performance-based exception to Section 162(m). As a result, the IRS updated its "audit package" to make Section 162(m) compliance a required examination item on any IRS audit of any large or mid-sized business. Given this enhanced IRS focus on Section 162(m), if a plan is designed to comply with Section 162(m), care should be taken to ensure that the plan meets all of the Section 162(m) requirements—i.e., the outside directors establish the goals at the beginning of the performance period, the goals are not changed (in the employee's favor) during the performance period, and at the end of the performance period the outside directors certify whether the performance goals have been satisfied.

The timing of an employer's tax deduction is also relevant. Under a common performance award plan, the participant is entitled to payment only if he or she is employed on the last day of the performance cycle, which is typically the last day of the year. Payments are made sometime thereafter, generally within 2½ months after the end of the year. The general rule is that the employer is entitled to the tax deduction only in the taxable year in which (or with which) ends the taxable year that the employees included the compensation in income. Applying this rule, the employer's deduction would be deferred to the year following the year in which the performance cycle ended.

In TAM 199923045, the Internal Revenue Service concluded that the "all events" and "economic performance" tests under Code Section 461 were satisfied as of the close of the taxable year when the performance units vested and, consequently, the employer was entitled to the tax deduction in that year.[17] For example, assume that an employee has the right to receive a performance bonus payment earned as of December 31, 2006, the last day of the performance period, provided that the employee is still employed on that date. If the employee terminates before that date, he or she will forfeit the bonus. On December 31, 2006, the employee is still employed and has earned the right to receive a bonus.

---

17. This ruling follows the permissible timing for annual bonuses that are paid within 2½ months into the next taxable year, rather than the rule for deferred compensation under Code § 404(a)(5) and Treas. Reg. § 1.404(b)-1T.

If the employer pays the bonus by March 15, 2007, the employer may deduct the accrued bonus in its 2006 tax year.

In the current climate of restatements of company financials, some companies are consciously not paying bonuses to some or all employees within the 2½-month period because they want to wait until the company's financial performance has been certified by the company's outside auditors. Additionally, it is becoming a corporate governance best practice to insert a "clawback" provision pursuant to which performance-based awards are required to be repaid to the company if the company's financial statements are later restated and the restated numbers suggest that a lesser amount would have been payable under the performance plan. Sarbanes-Oxley permits a similar type of clawback from the CEO and the CFO in the event of a restatement, but ambiguities about the precise contours of the Sarbanes-Oxley clawback and a desire to apply the clawback to additional executives have led many companies to incorporate a clawback provision directly in their plan documents.

CHAPTER FIVE

Direct Stock Purchases in Closely Held Companies

David R. Johanson

Contents

Sometimes a closely held company that wishes to permit employees to purchase company stock may desire greater flexibility and discretion than is allowed under a government-endorsed ("statutory") stock ownership program. This chapter explores alternative forms of motivating employees to improve a company's productivity and profitability through incentives that involve the direct purchase of company stock in closely held companies by employees outside of the traditional methods provided under Sections 422 (incentive stock option plans) and 423 (qualified employee stock purchase plans) of the Internal Revenue Code of 1986, as amended (the "Code"). It also discusses restricted stock concepts as they relate to such direct stock purchases, and it briefly addresses bonuses of company stock to employees. The direct purchase of company stock by an employee is typically based on the discounted and/or book value of a company's capital stock. This alternative is examined from the following fundamental perspectives: (1) valuation, (2) design and structure, (3) tax implications to the sponsoring company and its employees, (4) financing and/or funding, and (5) securities laws. Please note that although this chapter focuses on stock-based programs, the same concepts generally apply to limited liability companies in which membership interests are granted in lieu of company stock.

5.1 Direct Stock Purchase Programs

Direct stock purchase programs typically permit executives and other key employees to purchase company stock at a purchase price that is discounted for minority interest and/or lack of marketability purposes. This does not mean that such stock purchase programs provide for the bargain purchase of company stock, as this could result in unintended tax consequences to the employees making the purchases. Many company stock purchases are properly discounted for minority interest and/lack of marketability purposes, and such discounted value constitutes fair market value with respect to the purchasers. Some employers also use book value for purposes of establishing the purchase price for company stock under such a direct stock purchase program. These types of direct stock purchase programs are most popular with closely held corporations. While these programs are most often made available to executives or other key employees, they can be made available more broadly. The broader use of such plans, however, may entail more complex planning, documentation, and securities law requirements.

5.1.1 Valuation Considerations

Establishing an appropriate purchase price for shares of company stock is one of the most important decisions that a company will make about a direct stock purchase program. This decision requires thorough analysis and advice.

5.1.1.1 *Enterprise Value*

In this approach, the company must first establish the purchase price for the entire enterprise, including all cash and assets minus debt and preferred stock (the "enterprise value"). The starting point for establishing the purchase price is typically the company's enterprise value, as based upon an independent appraisal or a pre-established formula (most commonly a multiple of earnings or sales). This value indicates what the company would be worth if it were sold in its entirety to a single purchaser. When divided by the number of outstanding shares of company stock, a per-share price is established

Next, the per-share price of the company stock must be discounted to address the negative impact that the minority interest or a lack of marketability has on company stock value. When one or more parties owns less than 50% of the shares of stock in the corporation, the value of his or her ownership may be reduced for (1) not having a controlling interest (the "minority discount"), or (2) not having a ready market for the shares of company stock due to the corporation's status as a closely held company (the "marketability discount"). These discounts can be substantial, often ranging from 20% to 50% of the purchase price for one share of company stock if it had both control rights (the ability to direct the use of company assets) and marketability (the ability to sell at any time at an undiscounted price).

5.1.1.2 *Book Value*

Book value as established by a corporation's audited, reviewed, or compiled financial statements also can be used to establish the purchase price for a direct stock purchase program. Book value is set at a corporation's common stock equity, i.e., total assets minus liabilities, preferred stock, and intangible assets such as goodwill. The book value method is commonly used to value closely held companies that are expected to grow and generate profits. Book value is readily determinable and provides price stability (which may not be present under formula prices based on earnings multiples or comparisons with prices of comparable publicly traded companies). Because the employee knows that the value of his or her shares of company stock will increase in an amount equal to the corporation's earnings per share less dividends, a book value direct stock purchase plan provides a direct link between performance and the payoff to the employee who decides to purchase company stock. On the other hand, a book value direct stock purchase plan may provide employees with an incentive not to increase, or possibly even to reduce, dividends in order to increase the corporation's book value. Book value also usually understates the real value of a corporation because it is, by definition, a less than fair market measure of accumulated net assets, whereas the real value of a company is driven more by its potential for future earnings. A growing company, therefore, is almost always worth more, and often considerably more, than book value. This relationship could make an executive more conservative in managing assets to assure high current net asset book value rather than taking risks on investments for future growth. If book value is used for purposes of a stock purchase program, there also is a concern that the Internal Revenue Service (IRS) may conclude that an executive will be purchasing company stock at less than fair market value and that this difference between fair market value and the actual purchase price could constitute ordinary compensation income and be subject to taxation to the executive. Please see the discussions of tax consequences in sections 5.1.2 and 5.1.3 below, as this may not always be cause for concern.

5.1.1.3 *Fair Market Value for ESOP Purposes*

Where the majority of a closely held company's capital stock is owned by an employee stock ownership plan (ESOP), the fair market value of the corporation must be established on an annual basis by an independent, outside appraisal. This independent appraisal will almost always include the lack of marketability discount (albeit a lesser lack of marketability discount than the discount that would be applicable for less than a controlling interest in the company). If the price of an ESOP corporation's capital stock is established on a marketable-minority interest basis (i.e., the ESOP does not own a controlling interest but a price can be set by reference to actual public market pricing for stock in companies comparable to the closely held company without the need to adjust for the lack of an active market in the subject company's stock), an additional discount for minority interest purposes is necessary. If the corporation does not maintain an ESOP, the minority interest discount, plus a typically larger discount for lack of marketability than the discount used for ESOP purposes, can be applied to fair market value to establish the purchase price for a direct stock purchase of company stock. A company should focus on the fairness of the stock purchase price in such a stock purchase program relative to the ESOP fair market value so as to be fair to the ESOP from a financial perspective. It also is generally advisable for a corporation that establishes a stock purchase program of a certain magnitude to engage an executive compensation consultant to provide an opinion as to the reasonableness of compensation contemplated by a particular stock purchase program design as it applies to various executives.

5.1.1.4 *EBITDA Value*

Where an ESOP does not exist, a closely held company's board of directors could determine its earnings before income, taxes, depreciation, and amortization (EBITDA) and then apply a multiple to such EBITDA for purposes of establishing the overall fair market value of its capital stock. Discounts for minority interest and lack of marketability purposes can then be applied to establish the purchase price for purposes of a direct stock purchase of company stock. The appropriate multiples of earnings and discounts for minority interest and lack of marketability should be obtained either from an independent appraiser and/or from empirical data. Furthermore, outstanding long-term debt and excess cash also should be considered in establishing the purchase price for company stock in a direct stock purchase program. This applies under all circumstances. Ultimately, it is advisable to obtain an independent appraisal of company stock; however, this may not be financially feasible in every case.

Regardless of how a corporation establishes the purchase price for purposes of a direct stock purchase program, it should be consistent from year to year in how the formula works. Furthermore, the corporation should carefully and repeatedly communicate the formula in simple terms to the employees who participate in making the direct stock purchases.

5.1.2 Purchase and Sale of Company Stock

Shares of company stock under a direct stock purchase program may be purchased for cash or with secured and/or unsecured promissory notes (preferably recourse as opposed to non-recourse debt for tax purposes), or they may be issued as stock bonuses. As with other types of equity incentive plans, the employer generally imposes vesting restrictions on the company stock that an employee purchases. For example, an employer may retain the right to repurchase the company stock at the initial purchase price paid for the stock in the event of termination of employment before a specified date, the employee's voluntary termination of employment with the corporation without "good reason" (as defined in the stock purchase agreement, a form of which appears as an appendix to this book) or termination by the corporation with "cause" (as defined in the stock purchase agreement). One common reason that a corporation might require that any shares of company stock be repurchased at the initial purchase price is that an employee may go to work for a competitor or set up a competing business upon termination of employment. Corporations imposing this restriction should attempt to require employees to sign non-compete agreements specifying these terms if the jurisdiction allows such agreements. Because the requirements for and enforceability of these agreements vary from state to state, non-competition agreements, as well as the definitive stock purchase agreement, should be crafted only with the advice of qualified legal counsel. Corporations that allow employees to purchase company stock pursuant to a direct stock purchase program also should require them to sign proprietary rights, confidentiality, and non-disclosure agreements to protect against competitors who may later hire such employees (again, as allowed by the applicable jurisdiction).

Direct stock purchase programs for company stock that are subject to a non-lapse restriction for income tax purposes are typically referred to as formula price or "delta" stock purchase programs. A non-lapse restriction normally requires the employee to resell the company stock at the stock's formula price or book value to the corporation upon termination of employment or at other times that are specified in the stock purchase agreement, and it prohibits any other transfer of the company stock by the employee. Such a restriction generally reduces the fair market value of the company stock to its formula price or book value (as opposed to whatever market value the stock might obtain) for income tax purposes. Upon the sale of the company as a result of a change in control, however, the sale price is typically adjusted to be consistent with the (usually higher) purchase price established by the terms of the sale to the third party. The employer also has the discretion to design the direct stock purchase program to give dividend and voting rights to and/or withhold such rights from the employee purchaser.

Direct stock purchases of company stock other than common stock can be structured so that the stock may be convertible into regular common stock of the corporation at a conversion ratio equal to the original purchase price per share of the company stock divided by the fair market value per share of the regular common stock on the date that the company stock was purchased by the employee. Although this also can be accomplished with the change in control feature described above, this conversion feature allows the employee to participate in the future appreciation of the corporation's common stock with minimal downside economic risk. This is because the typical structure of such preferred stock would provide that the employer would repurchase the stock from the employee at either the initial purchase price or a formula or book price unless the stock is converted to common stock. This conversion feature may create income tax problems for the employee if economic value is created without cost to the employee upon conversion of the company stock. This potential taxation is discussed under the heading "Non-Lapse Restriction Considerations" below.

5.1.3 Tax Considerations

5.1.3.1 *Restricted Stock Issues*

Restricted stock is stock that is purchased by or granted to an employee that is subject to specified restrictions, such as a vesting schedule or meeting performance targets. Generally, restricted shares of company stock. whether purchased or granted as a bonus through a direct stock purchase or bonus program, and whether or not subject to a non-lapse restriction (i.e., a permanent formula or book value repurchase formula), constitute "property" subject to the rules of Section 83 of the Code. The purchase of company stock by an employee, or grant by an employer, should in most cases constitute a transfer for purposes of Section 83 of the Code. Section 83(a) of the Code provides that an employee receiving properly restricted stock under a direct stock purchase or stock bonus program will realize no income for Federal income tax purposes at the time of the purchase or bonus (unless he or she files an election pursuant to Section 83(b) of the Code). Rather, he or she will realize income when the restriction or forfeiture provisions lapse in an amount equal to the then per share fair market value multiplied by the applicable number of shares of company stock. [1] The company issuing the shares of capital stock will be entitled to a compensation deduction at that time equal to the amount taken into income by the employee to the extent that the amount constitutes reasonable compensation to the employee. Upon the employee's subsequent sale of the shares of capital stock to the corporation, the employee also will realize gain or loss, as the case may be.

Because Section 83 of the Code generally applies to the purchase or bonus of restricted company stock under a direct stock purchase or bonus program, the excess, if any, of the fair market value of the company stock purchased pursuant to such a program (i.e., the formula or book value price if a non-lapse restriction is used) over the purchase price paid by the employee will be compensation, and thus, ordinary income to the employee upon receipt of the company stock. This assumes the stock is vested (see below for a discussion of vesting) at the time of purchase or a Section 83(b) election is filed with the IRS. The ultimate sale of the company stock should result in a capital gain (taxed at the maximum rate for ordinary income thereafter) or loss measured by the difference between the sale proceeds and the original value of

---

1. Section 83 of the Code, and the technical requirements applicable to restricted stock plans, including the pros and cons of making an election under Section 83(b) of the Code, are more fully described in the chapter "Restricted Stock Plans" elsewhere in this book.

the company stock at the time of the initial purchase by the employee. The employee can usually avoid this ordinary income tax treatment on the subsequent sale of the corporation by making an election under Section 83(b) of the Code to close the ordinary income tax element of the transaction at the time of the initial purchase.

In a Section 83(b) election, the employee elects to pay taxes at the time of purchase or grant of the company stock. In that case, the employee would pay ordinary income tax on the difference between the purchase price (if any) and the fair market value of the shares of company stock. No further taxes would be due until the shares of company stock are sold (not, as without a Section 83(b) election, when the restrictions lapse), and then the tax would be capital gains, not ordinary income tax. If the restrictions do not lapse (such as where the employee leaves before vesting), then the employee cannot claim any credit for taxes previously paid.

Vesting typically refers to certain restrictions on the company stock purchased or granted pursuant to a direct stock purchase or bonus program. Such restrictions may serve to make the company stock subject to a substantial risk of forfeiture upon certain conditions and establish other restrictions upon an individual's or entity's ability to freely transfer the company stock to other parties. If the forfeiture and nontransferability conditions are fully enforced, the employee may not receive anything as a result of the initial purchase of company stock, even if there is a difference between the fair market value of such company stock and the initial purchase price. This probably will not be present in a properly constructed direct stock purchase program (i.e., one in which the company stock is repurchased at the formula or book value purchase price upon a subsequent triggering event). Therefore, if the risk of forfeiture is substantial, and the company stock is not freely transferable, no tax is generally imposed upon the direct purchase of company stock. It is only when the restrictions lapse at a later date that tax consequences may ensue.

Under a direct stock purchase or bonus program, an employee may purchase or be granted shares of capital stock of the issuing corporation that are subject to a substantial risk of forfeiture and transfer restrictions that will lapse only if he or she remains in the employ of the corporation for a specified period after such receipt and/or if certain corporate or individual performance objectives have been achieved. If the employee terminates employment before the expiration of the restriction period or before satisfaction of any performance objectives, he or she may forfeit the shares of company stock to the company and will receive only the original purchase price (if any) back at such time. If the employee remains employed by the corporation until the end of the restriction period, the forfeiture provisions will lapse and the employee will own the company stock, assuming required performance objectives have been achieved.

5.1.3.2 *Non-Lapse Restriction Considerations*

If the company stock purchased under a direct stock purchase program is subject to a non-lapse restriction that sets a price for the resale of the stock in advance (i.e., the repurchase of the company stock at a formula price or book value) and the sponsoring corporation at some time later cancels the restriction, the employee will realize ordinary income upon such cancellation equal to the excess of (1) the fair market value of the regular common stock at that time over (2) the book value of the company stock immediately before the cancellation, unless the employee can prove that the cancellation is not compensatory and that the corporation will treat it as non-compensatory by not taking a deduction that it would be entitled to if the cancellation were compensatory. (Non-lapse provisions would typically not apply to bonus shares of company stock.)

Whether a cancellation is compensatory depends on the facts and circumstances of each case and is covered in detail in applicable Treasury Regulations under Section 83 of the Code. Ordinarily, if an employee is required to perform additional services or if the employee's salary is adjusted to take the cancellation into account, then the cancellation has a compensatory purpose. An example of a noncompensatory cancellation is if the cancellation is made solely because the original purpose of the restriction no longer exists. The regulations indicate that a cancellation in connection with a public offering of company stock generally may be non-compensatory and, therefore, will be tax-free to the employee. It is not clear, however, whether a direct stock purchase program may provide in advance for automatic cancellation of the formula or book value repurchase restriction upon a public offering or another change in control. In theory, at least, the time at which the restriction is lifted (i.e., whether in advance by the terms of the stock purchase agreement or by a decision made concurrently with the public offering or change in control) should be immaterial if in fact the motive for the cancellation is non-compensatory (i.e., to remove the restriction that was originally imposed to create a market for capital stock rather than to increase or defer compensation).

The tax consequences of adding a conversion feature to the terms of the direct stock purchase program (i.e., giving the holder of the restricted company stock the right to convert that stock into regular common stock) are uncertain. First, the conversion privilege adds value to the restricted company stock at the outset, and the employee may have to pay more than the formula price or book value for the company stock to avoid recognizing compensation income upon the purchase of the company stock. Second, unlike the case of a convertible debenture, it is not clear that the actual conversion into regular common stock will be tax-free to the employee. There is little or no regulatory and/or case law authority with respect to this issue. In the case of restricted company stock subject to a non-lapse restriction, the IRS may assert that the conversion is in fact a compensatory cancellation of the company's right to repurchase the company stock for the formula price or at book value, resulting in ordinary income to the employee at the time of conversion. Alternatively, the existence of the conversion feature may turn the non-lapse restriction into a lapse restriction from the outset because the conversion feature negates the permanent nature of the formula price and/or book value repurchase restriction. Under these circumstances, the employee will be liable for tax on the excess of (1) the fair market value of the regular common stock over (2) the purchase price for the company stock at the time of the original purchase. Any subsequent conversion into regular common stock should then be tax-free.

Although the IRS has considered this issue only in a publicly traded company context, a brief discussion of one such ruling may be instructive here. The IRS has concluded that in a formula price direct stock purchase plan where a publicly traded company discounted its stock from the fair market value by 60%, a non-lapse restriction was not present because upon an executive's termination of employment he was obligated for only five days to sell the company stock back to the employer at the discounted formula price. Following the five-day period, the executive could sell the company stock to anyone at full fair market value. The IRS stated that the executive's five-day right of first refusal was not a permanent restriction as required by applicable U.S. Treasury regulations. The IRS also pointed out that the purpose of the non-lapse restriction is to provide a method for valuing the company stock of a closely held corporation where it is difficult to establish fair market value. (Without a non-lapse restriction, the fair market value of the company stock on the date of purchase less the purchase price is typically ordinary income to the employee.) It is unclear whether this IRS guidance means that the non-lapse restrictions will not work for formula price direct stock purchase plans of publicly traded companies or that they will work for both closely held and publicly traded companies where the valuation procedure is not an arbitrary discount from fair market value and the right of first refusal period is extended.

5.1.3.3 *Section 409A Considerations*

Finally, it is worth noting that Section 409A of the Code, added in October 2004 by the American Jobs Creation Act, applies only to nonqualified deferred compensation plans. Nonqualified direct stock purchase programs in which the stock purchase is not deferred are not governed by Section 409A.

Section 409A of the Code provides that all amounts deferred under a nonqualified deferred compensation plan (generally beyond March 15 of the year following the date of grant) must be currently included in gross income to the extent they are not subject to a substantial risk of forfeiture and not previously included in gross income unless certain requirements are met:

- Compensation may not be distributed earlier than the participant's separation from service, disability, death, or a change in control of the corporation, or an unforeseeable emergency causing severe financial hardship to the participant.

- The receipt of benefits may not be accelerated beyond the time or schedule of payments set forth in the plan unless allowed by government regulation.

- A participant must make his or her initial decision to defer compensation before the end of the preceding taxable year or as provided by regulation. In the case of performance-based compensation based on services performed over 12 months or more, the participant's election must be made at least 6 months before the end of the period.

- Any changes in time and form of distribution must not take place until at least 12 months after the date the election is made.

- An election related to a payment made for reasons other than death, permanent disability, or an unforeseeable emergency must be deferred for at least five years from the date the payment would otherwise have been made.

- An election related to a payment made at a time specified under the plan must be made at least 12 months before the date of the first scheduled payment under the plan.

On October 4, 2006, the U.S. Department of Treasury (the "Treasury Department") released IRS Notice 2006-79 ("Notice 2006-79"), which provides transition relief associated with certain discounted stock rights and payment elections and extends the 409A compliance deadline. The IRS originally issued proposed regulations under Section 409A and transitional guidelines in IRS Notice 2005-1 on December 20, 2004, with an effective date for the final regulations of January 1, 2007. Commentators expressed concern that the period between the publication of the final regulations and the effective date of January 1, 2007, would not be long enough to analyze and comply with the final guidelines. Accordingly, the IRS and the Treasury Department changed the effective date of the final regulations to January 1, 2008, and provided further transition relief through December 31, 2007.

Under Notice 2006-79, a deferred compensation plan (including a stock purchase program) implemented before or on December 31, 2007, will not deemed in violation of Section 409A of the Code before January 1, 2008, provided that the plan is operated through December 31, 2007, in "reasonable, good faith compliance" with the provisions of Section 409A of the Code, IRS Notice 2005-1, and any other applicable regulations published with an effective date before January 1, 2008, and the plan is amended in conformity with the final regulations on or before December 31, 2007. Compliance with the proposed Section 409A regulations and the final regulations before their effective dates is evidence of "reasonable, good faith compliance"; however, compliance with the proposed and final Section 409A regulations before their effective dates is not required. A plan will not satisfy the "reasonable, good faith compliance" requirement if "discretion provided under the terms of the plan is exercised in a manner that causes the plan to fail to meet the requirements of section 409A."

With respect to changes in payment elections or conditions of amounts subject to Section 409A of the Code prior to January 1, 2008, Section 3.02 of Notice 2006-79 provides that as long as the plan amendment and elections are made on or before December 31, 2007, such amendment and elections will not be deemed a change in the time or form of payment under Section 409A(a)(4) of the Code or an acceleration of a payment under Section 409A(a)(3) of the Code. Furthermore, such election or amendment may apply only to amounts that would not otherwise be payable in 2006 or 2007, in the respective calendar years, and may not cause an amount to be paid in 2006 or 2007 that would not otherwise be payable in 2006 or 2007, respectively. The transition relief provisions under Section 3.02 of Notice 2006-79 apply to elections and amendments by a service provider, a service recipient, or both. Multiple elections and amendments are permitted as long as each amendment or change complies with the requirements of Section 3.02 of Notice 2006-79. Notice 2006-79 provides similar guidelines for amendments to discounted stock rights.

Section 3.03 of Notice 2006-79 extends through 2007 the ability to link a payment under a nonqualified deferred compensation plan to a qualified plan; it also adds employer plans to the list of qualified plans that payments may be linked to, including Section 403(b) annuities, Section 457(b) eligible plans, and certain foreign broad-based plans. With respect to stock options and stock appreciation rights, IRS Notice 2005-1 stated that the cancellation and reissuance of certain stock options or stock appreciation rights would not be considered a material modification provided that the cancellation and reissuance occurred on or before December 31, 2005. IRS Notice 2006-79 extends this period to on or before December 31, 2007.

The transition relief provided in IRS Notice 2006-79 does not extend to the following stock options or stock appreciation rights: (1) those granted with respect to the stock of publicly traded companies; (2) those granted to a person who was subject to the disclosure requirements of Section 16(a) of the Securities Exchange Act of 1934; and (3) those granted with related expenses that were not "timely reported on financial statements or reports for the period in which the related expense should have been reported under generally accepted accounting principles."

Nonqualified deferred compensation plans maintained pursuant to at least one collectively bargaining agreement in effect on October 3, 2004, must be in compliance with Section 409A of the Code and the final Section 409A regulations on or before the earlier of December 31, 2009, or the latest termination date of the collective bargaining agreements, irrespective of any extensions of such agreement(s) after October 3, 2004. The plan amendment deadline has been extended to December 31, 2007. Taxpayers still have the burden, however, of demonstrating that the deferral election was made by the March 15, 2005, deadline.

5.1.4 Comparison of Direct Stock Purchase Programs to Stock Option Plans

Under a direct stock purchase plan, an employee generally must pay (or obligate himself or herself to pay) full formula price or book value for the shares of company stock that he or she purchases. In a stock option plan, an employee is not obligated to expend funds until a gain on his or her investment is reasonably assured. Furthermore, under a direct stock purchase plan, the employee's upside potential for gain on the appreciation of the market value of the corporation's common stock is limited by a formula price or by book value, except possibly in the case of a cancellation of the formula price or book value repurchase restrictions in connection with the public offering, a conversion of the shares of company stock to regular common stock, or a change in control. Stock options could have these features built in as well, however (other than a change in control provision), normally do not; the option usually is simply for the purchase of common stock. The principal disadvantages of a direct stock purchase program as compared to a stock option plan, however, are the uncertain federal income tax consequences involved with the use of non-lapse restrictions and the possible adverse tax treatment for programs with conversion features. Stock option programs have recently lost some of the favorable accounting treatment they previously enjoyed. In December 2004, the accounting standards for stock-based compensation changed. When a corporation changes the price of an employee stock option or otherwise alters the option terms so as to increase the intrinsic value of the stock option, the corporation is now required to recognize any difference in fair market value between the option immediately before and after the change. The new standard ameliorates the impact of this change by permitting corporations to increase the value placed on the "before" option, thereby providing more replacement value to employees without incurring an additional earnings charge. Adverse changes in tax treatment of stock options anticipated to occur have not come to pass. In particular, the IRS formerly argued that employers should withhold taxes on incentive stock options (ISOs) and Section 423 employee stock purchase plans (ESPPs); however, it put its plans to require this on indefinite hold, and then in 2004 the American Jobs Creation Act was enacted, providing in relevant part that ISOs and ESPPs are not subject to payroll tax withholding.

5.1.5 Loans to Employees

In some cases, corporations may want to loan employees the money or extend credit to employees to fund the purchase shares of company stock. The IRS will be concerned that such loans should be considered a form of disguised compensation. These loans are subject to the same rules as with any loan to an employee. If the loan interest terms are more favorable than an equivalent arms-length transaction, Section 7872 of the Code provides that the difference in interest charged and the interest that would accrue under the applicable federal rate ("imputed interest income") is generally taxable to the employee and is treated as part of the employee's gross income. Loan programs, therefore, need to be established with appropriate legal, tax, and accounting advice. Loans between employer and employee that do not, in the aggregate, exceed $10,000 are generally exempt from imputed interest under a de minimis exception; however, if one of the principal purposes of the loan is to avoid paying tax, then the de minimis exception does not apply. For various tax purposes (e.g., in order to qualify an employee for tax-deferral under Section 1042 of the Code), recourse loans are advisable as compared to non-recourse loans.

In addition, personal loans to officers and directors of publicly traded companies are now banned under the Sarbanes-Oxley Act of 2002. Personal loans made by closely held companies are not subject to the Sarbanes-Oxley Act; therefore, this restriction does not apply.

5.2 Stock Bonus Plans

Under a stock bonus plan, an employee's bonus is typically contingent upon the issuing corporation's earnings exceeding a stated level for a specified period, although this is not a requirement. Corporations could simply issue shares of company stock to employees as a bonus regardless of company or individual performance. If the company stock is given as a bonus to employees, corporations would typically require the shares of company stock to be forfeited if not fully vested before termination of employment. A stock bonus plan allows a corporation great flexibility and creativity in compensating its employees. For example, such a plan can provide that if the corporation's earnings rise above a certain minimum level, the bonus amounts also will increase. This type of incentive provides the corporation's employees who receive these stock bonuses with an incentive to achieve maximum earnings. The bonuses may be paid in the form of the corporation's capital stock or cash or a combination of both. Again, if a corporation chooses to fund the benefit that is earned with respect to the grant of stock bonuses by distributing company stock to employees, the stock that is distributed may be restricted so that it may be sold only to the corporation, the corporation has a right of first refusal with respect to the future sale and purchase of such stock, and/or the stock must be sold to the corporation when the employee's employment terminates, at a price equal to the fair market value per share at the time of the sale.

An employee receiving shares of capital stock under a stock bonus plan does not realize income for federal income tax purposes until the amount of his or her stock bonus is determined and issued. At that point, he or she will realize ordinary income in an amount equal to the fair market value per share multiplied by the number of shares of company stock that he or she receives plus the amount of any cash that he or she receives. The sponsoring corporation is entitled to a compensation deduction equal to the amount that the employee(s) recognize as ordinary income to the extent that such amount constitutes reasonable compensation to the employee(s). When the employee sells the capital stock back to the company, he or she realizes gain or loss, as the case may be.

Stock bonus plans may be more appropriate when a corporation wants to provide stock to a broad group of employees, rather than just key executives. In most (but certainly not all) corporations, employees generally do not have the discretionary income, or risk tolerance, to buy shares of company stock. It is important to recognize, however, that when employees are given company stock, they typically incur a tax obligation even though they only have pieces of paper that cannot be sold for some time. In some cases, this may be demotivating to employees unless the corporation also provides a cash bonus to pay the taxes.

5.3 Providing a Market for the Company Stock

Whatever kind of plan a corporation establishes, it is essential that consideration be given to how the shares of company stock can be sold. In too many cases, the plan is simply that the shares of company stock will have value when the corporation goes public or is sold in a sale to a third party. While the dramatic stock market decline at the turn of the 21st century dampened enthusiasm for going public, even at its boom, very few relatively small closely held companies succeeded in completing an initial public offering (IPO). At most, there were only about 800 IPOs in a year, and 200–300 is more typical. Many of these are spin-offs of larger companies or large closely held companies that decide to go public. In 1999, *Inc.* magazine found that 109 of the fastest growing closely held companies planned to go public that year; only nine succeeded. In 2004, 233 companies went public, an increase of 195% over the number of companies to go public in 2003; this was, however, well below the crest of the IPO wave a few years before.

Selling to another company or an investor group is more common; however, here too expectations many times may outrun reality. Merger and acquisitions markets run hot and cold, however, and finding the right buyer, even in good times, can be difficult.

There are other alternatives, however. Corporations can repurchase the stock directly (note that such repurchases are not deductible) or set up an ESOP (employee stock ownership plan) to do so (in which case they are deductible and, in certain cases, may allow the selling employee to take a tax deferral). They can also informally connect employees who want to buy additional shares of company stock with employees willing to sell. Finally, corporations may be able to attract outside investors to buy stock, although this may be the most difficult of any of the alternatives described here. Whatever approach is taken, there needs to be a "Plan A" and a backup plan. Allowing employees to purchase company stock, or even just giving them company stock, with no realistic liquidity process in mind is substituting wishful thinking for solid business planning.

5.4 Securities Law Considerations

Securities laws exist at the state and federal level. Each state has its own rules, although there are broad similarities among states. Securities law is a large and complex subject; however, the two key elements are registration and disclosure. Registration means the filing of documents with the state and/or federal securities agencies concerning the employer whose stock is being sold. There are registration procedures for small offerings of company stock (under $1 million or $5 million, depending on the procedure) that can be accomplished for relatively small legal fees; however, larger offerings require a lot of complex paperwork, and fees often exceed $100,000. Registration requires the filing of audited financial statements and continuing reporting obligations to the Securities and Exchange Commission (SEC) and appropriate state agencies.

Disclosure refers to providing information to purchasers about what they are getting, similar to but frequently less detailed than what would be included in a prospectus. At times, there are specific state and federal rules about what needs to be included in these documents (i.e., objective discussions of risks, the financial condition of the company, officers' and directors' salaries, and other information). In the absence of requirements for the registration of the securities, disclosure is intended to satisfy the anti-fraud requirements of federal and state securities laws.

5.4.1 Federal Securities Law

5.4.1.1 *Registration and Disclosure*

Generally, offers to sell securities (stocks, bonds, etc.) require registration of those securities unless there is a specific exemption. Direct stock purchases of company stock would fall under this definition. Furthermore, while not necessarily applicable to the direct stock purchase programs maintained by closely held companies that this chapter addresses, corporations with more than 500 shareholders and more than $10 million in assets are considered publicly traded companies under federal law and must comply with the reporting requirements of the 1934 Act even if they do not have to register under the Securities Act of 1933 (the "1933 Act").

There are a number of exemptions from these rules listed below. These are exemptions from registration; any time company stock is offered for sale, it should include appropriate financial disclosure to satisfy anti-fraud rules. The principal exemptions under federal law are:

- Offers to a corporation's employees, directors, general partners, trustees, officers, or consultants can be made under a written compensation agreement. Under SEC Rule 701, the maximum dollar amount of stock that may be sold to these people in a year without registration is the greatest of: (1) $1 million, (2) 15% of the issuer's total assets, or (3) 15% of the issuer's outstanding class of stock being sold. The 15% ceiling would not apply if the offering is under $1 million. The offer itself does not count for purposes of the available exempted amount. If more than $5 million of securities are being sold, however, the issuer is required to disclose risk factors to potential buyers and deliver financial statements in accordance with Form 1-A of Regulation A.

- Another exemption is available under Section 4(2) of the Securities Act of 1933, which has been interpreted to allow for exemptions from federal registrations of offerings of stock to a limited number of investors who have access to the same information normally provided in a public offering and who are accredited investors or sophisticated enough both to assess and to bear the risks. This exemption has been interpreted in different ways by the courts. Whether it allows such approaches as offering stock to more than just a company's key employees is unclear. It does probably work for many direct stock purchase programs to selected management employees.

- Another set of exemptions is available under the SEC's Regulation D, which provides three exemptions for small offerings, Rules 504, 505, and 506. Rule 504 exempts offerings up to $1 million to an unlimited number of people, with no limits of their being sophisticated or accredited. Rule 505 provides an exemption for offerings of up to a total of $5 million to as many as 35 non-accredited investors and an unlimited number of accredited investors in any 12-month period. Rule 506 exempts offerings of any size made to as many as 35 sophisticated investors and an unlimited number of accredited investors.

  "Accredited investors" include directors, partners, or executives of the issuing company; anyone with a net worth (including that of their spouses) of over $1 million; and anyone with an income over $200,000 (or whose joint income with a spouse is more than $300,000) who has made that amount for the preceding two years and is likely to continue to make it; and financial institutions, business development companies, or other companies with total assets exceeding $5 million. "Sophisticated investors" are people who, on their own or with the aid of a representative such as an accountant, are able to judge the risks, merits, and disadvantages of a particular investment.

- Offerings that are made only to residents of the state in which the offering is made are generally exempt if the offeror has its principal office in that state, gets 80% of its gross revenue from business conducted in the state, and has 80% of its assets in the state.

5.4.1.2 *Anti-fraud Provisions*

To comply with the anti-fraud provisions of federal securities laws, disclosure of certain corporate information to employees under a direct stock plan is advisable. The disclosure standard for registration statements filed under the 1933 Act may be used as a guideline for the type of information that needs to be disclosed. The following is a list of information that generally must be disclosed in registration statements:

- Description of business.
- Description of property.
- Description of any legal proceedings.
- Market price of and dividends on the company's shares.
- Recent financial statements.
- Other pertinent financial data.
- Management's discussion and analysis of financial condition and results of operations.
- Changes in and disagreements with accountants on accounting and financial disclosure.
- Names of directors and executive officers.
- Executive compensation.
- Security ownership of certain beneficial owners and management.
- Certain relationships and related transactions.
- General plans for the company's future.

It is important to note that meeting the disclosure standard for registration statements filed under the 1933 Act is not a requirement for closely held companies that implement a stock option plan; rather, the disclosure would be helpful in responding to anti-fraud claims by the employees against the company and its board of directors for transactions arising under a stock option plan.

5.4.2 State Securities Laws: The California Example[2]

State laws generally require that any offer or sale of securities in the state by an issuer must either be qualified by the department of corporations or secretary of state or be exempt from such qualification requirements. In this respect, the California securities laws will be used as an example. California law requires that any offer or sale of securities in the state by an issuer must either be qualified by the California Department of Corporations or be exempt from the qualification requirements. Company stock purchased by an employee pursuant to a direct stock purchase program is a security and an employer issuing company stock is considered an issuer. Thus, an employer's direct stock purchase program must comply with California securities laws in addition to any federal requirements that must be met. Given the considerable effort and expense involved in qualifying securities issuable under a direct stock purchase program, finding an exemption to the qualification requirement can be important.

5.4.2.1 *Exemptions from Qualification*

If an employer offers direct stock purchases only to key employees, it may rely on the exemption found in Section 25102(f) of the California Corporations Code. The exemption is generally limited to sales to no more than 35 people (excluding certain sophisticated purchasers) who have a preexisting personal or business relationship with the offeror or its directors, officers and managers. If an employer wants to expand the direct stock purchase program to reach other than key employees, it may find that the 35-person limit is unduly restrictive.

Recognizing this, the California legislature enacted an exemption to the qualification requirements in 1996. Section 25102(o) of the California Corporations Code exempts offers and sales of securities in connection with stock purchase or stock option plans or agreements without limiting the number of persons eligible, where the securities involved are exempt from federal registration requirements under

---

2. For a broader discussion of this issue, see Matthew Topham, "State Securities Law Considerations for Equity Compensation Plans," in the NCEO's book *Selected Issues in Equity Compensation.*

Rule 701 of the 1933 Act. The transaction must, however, meet several other requirements promulgated by the state Corporations Commissioner. Those include:

- A plan must specify the number of shares available for issuance and the persons eligible to receive options or purchase stock.

- The exercise price of options for the company stock cannot be less than 85% of the stock's fair value at the time of the grant, unless the recipient already owns more than 10% of the issuer's total voting stock, in which case the exercise price must be 110% of fair value. The conditions for purchase plans are the same except that the price must be 100% of fair value for 10% owners. This purchase price restriction may present a problem for a company that desires to allow all of its employees to participate in a direct stock purchase program of the type discussed in this chapter. In other words, the company may have to qualify the securities that are being issued or may have to limit the number of employees that participate in the program in order to satisfy the requirements of the exemption from the qualification requirements under Section 25102(f) of the California Corporations Code.

- The options or purchase rights are not transferable except by will or the laws of descent.

- The plan must be approved by the company's stockholders and must terminate no later than 10 years after the date of adoption or stockholder approval, whichever is earlier.

- Options must be exercisable at a rate of at least 20% per year over five years from the date of grant. The right to exercise in the event of termination of employment, to the extent the optionee is entitled to exercise on the date of termination, must continue for at least 30 days from the date of termination of employment. The plan may allow for an issuer's repurchase upon termination.

- The number of shares issuable upon exercise of all outstanding options and any direct stock purchase plan (except for a direct stock purchase plan that provides that all shares of company stock will have a purchase price of 100% of fair value) cannot exceed 30% of the then outstanding shares.

- The employees participating in an option or direct stock purchase plan must receive annual financial statements unless the issuance of the security is limited to key employees who have access to such information as a result of their job duties.

5.5 Closing Remarks

Direct stock purchase programs, and even stock bonus plans (other than tax-qualified stock bonus plans, not described here) typically are not designed to provide equity incentives on a broad basis to all or a large number of a closely held company's employees. They typically work best to motivate certain key employees to improve a corporation's productivity and profitability and, in turn, the corporation's fair market value. A direct stock purchase program or stock bonus program is an excellent supplement to a broad-based stock option plan and/or an ESOP. One important exception to this is for very small corporations with just a few or several regular employees. These corporations may find direct stock purchase or bonus programs the only practical way to share company stock with most or all of their employees, although, as this article makes clear, there still will be significant legal, tax, financial and securities laws issues to consider. A handful of larger corporations may want to use these approaches for broader plans as well, although the tax and securities law advantages of the kinds of qualified plans or stock option plans described in the penultimate chapter of this book, such as ESOPs and 401(k) plans, make them more appealing to most companies in such circumstances.

If a direct stock purchase program or stock bonus program is created and used together with the design, implementation, and continued maintenance of an appropriate ownership and participation program and a broad-based employee stock ownership plan and/or equity incentive plan, empirical evidence and years of experience have demonstrated that the sponsoring employer should achieve enhanced productivity and profitability and that, ultimately, the fair market value of its capital stock should increase over time.

CHAPTER SIX

Accounting Issues

Corey Rosen
Helen H. Morrison

Contents

The accounting treatment of a long-term incentive compensation program is a critical consideration (some would argue the *most* critical consideration) in determining what type of program is appropriate and how it should be structured. As of this writing, accounting rules have been in a transitional mode. As noted at various points in this book, however, the accounting treatment for restricted stock, phantom stock, SARs, and similar plans is much like it has been, with the notable exception of performance-vested awards. This chapter discusses accounting standards that were in effect through 2005 (APB 25 and FAS 123), as well as the accounting standard (FAS 123(R)) that became effective in 2006.

Under Accounting Principles Board Opinion No. 25 ("APB 25"), stock option grants were reported based on the intrinsic value method. Consequently, stock options that were awarded with an exercise price equal to the fair market value of the stock on the date of grant had no

The authors thank Dan Coleman, a senior manager in the financial advisory services practice of Deloitte & Touche LLP, for his assistance with this chapter.

intrinsic value and were not reported as a compensation expense.[1] As a result of this favorable accounting treatment, "plain vanilla" stock option programs became the primary long-term compensation program for employees and directors of most public and many private employers. In April 2003, the Financial Standards Accounting Board (FASB) announced that it would modify generally accepted accounting principles (GAAP) to require stock options to be expensed under Statement of Financial Accounting Standards No. 123 (revised 2004) ("FAS 123(R)"). The equity-based accounting rules of FAS 123(R), which include the requirement to expense stock option awards, became effective for public companies in the first fiscal year beginning after June 15, 2005, and for private companies after December 15, 2005.

The accounting rules applicable to the long-term incentive compensation programs addressed in this book—SARs, phantom stock, restricted stock, and performance award plans—have always required the reporting of a compensation expense on the employer's income statement. The change in the stock option accounting rules under FAS 123(R) places these types of long-term programs on a more even playing field with stock options and, consequently, may make them more attractive to employers.

Service-vested SARs, phantom stock, restricted stock, and performance award plans are accounted for in essentially the same manner as cash bonuses that are paid out over a period of time and whose value could vary. The intrinsic value of these types of awards is determined when the award is granted and recognized as an expense over the period of service associated with the award. In some cases, this expense is then "marked to market" until the award is actually paid out. This process is explained in further detail below.

---

1.   Accounting Principles Board Opinion No. 25 ("APB 25"), *Accounting for Stock Issued to Employees,* issued in 1972, was the accounting standard used by most companies to account for stock compensation to employees and nonemployee directors. Companies could instead elect to account for these plans on their income statements under FASB Statement of Financial Accounting Standards No. 123 ("FAS 123"), *Accounting for Stock-Based Compensation.* However, most waited until FAS 123(R) became mandatory to shift away from APB 25. In this chapter, we note the differences in accounting treatment for stock appreciation rights and restricted stock under these two standards as well as the new standard, and we also discuss the accounting treatment of performance award plans.

Performance-vested awards receive a different treatment under APB 25 and FAS 123(R). Under APB 25, performance vesting triggered variable plan accounting; under FAS 123(R), the expense per share is fixed at the time of grant. Although the expense is still adjusted for forfeitures in most cases, it is not for subsequent changes in stock price, as it would have been under APB 25. Under APB 25, no expense was recognized if the award was forfeited (any previously recorded expense was reversed). FAS 123(R) differentiates between market conditions and other performance conditions. Market conditions are those that relate to the company's stock price, such as a target stock price, performance relative to the market, or shareholder return. Where the arrangement vests based on a market condition, expense is still recognized even if the condition is not met, resulting in a forfeiture.

It is important to note that the accounting treatment and tax treatment of SARs, phantom stock, restricted stock, and performance award plans are not always equivalent. For instance, a company often recognizes a charge to earnings on its income statement for the portion of an award that vests in a given year, even though it will not actually pay out the award and become entitled to claim a tax deduction for the compensation expense until years later.

This discussion of accounting rules covers only the basic considerations for typical plan structures. It is essential that companies obtain advice from qualified accountants knowledgeable about these specific rules to complete their financial reporting.

6.1 SARs and Phantom Stock

As explained in chapter 2, a stock appreciation right (SAR) is an award that entitles the employee to receive cash, stock, or a combination of cash and stock in an amount equivalent to the excess of the fair market value of the underlying stock over a stated price for a stated number of shares. The stated price is generally the fair market value of the underlying stock on the date of grant. Phantom stock awards are designed to provide the employees with the right to participate in the employer's stock performance generally without issuing additional shares of stock (or options). Under a phantom stock plan, as we have defined it in chapter 2, the employee has a deferred compensation arrangement generally denominated as a stated number of stock units on a memorandum basis, which have a value equal to the underlying stock value.

For accounting purposes, SARs and phantom stock awards are governed by the same accounting rules and are treated somewhat similarly.[2] These plans are treated essentially like deferred cash bonuses (variable plan accounting). For SARs, the amount of compensation expense is equal to the increase in the fair market value since the grant date, multiplied by the number of SAR units granted. The amount of compensation expense for phantom stock grants is determined in the same manner, with the exception that the compensation amount includes the underlying value of the stock. Even though the employee pays no taxes when the SAR or phantom stock award is granted, and the company takes no tax deduction until the payment is made, the company still must recognize a compensation expense on its income statement over the period the award is outstanding.

The calculation of the amount of the compensation expense inherent in a cash-settled SAR or phantom stock grant is relatively straightforward. The more complicated accounting matter is the appropriate periods in which to recognize the compensation expense. In addition, the accounting rules vary under APB 25 and FAS 123(R) if the award is paid only in shares of company stock or is performance vested.

Before it was superseded by FAS 123(R), FASB Interpretation No. 28 ("FIN 28") provided that the measurement of the compensation expense for service-based, cash-settled awards should be made at the end of each reporting period based on the current fair market value of the stock. The compensation expense was assumed over the vesting period of the SAR or phantom stock award. Significant differences resulted for "cliff" vesting and graded vesting schedules. These differences are best explained with examples.

Assume that an employer granted SARs to employees based on 1,000 shares at a stated price of $10, which was equal to the current fair market value of the underlying stock. The SARs became 100% vested at the end of the fifth year and were zero percent vested before that date

---

2.   APB 25 and various interpretations thereof, e.g., FASB Interpretation No. 28, *Accounting for Stock Appreciation Rights and Other Variable Stock Option or Award Plans*, or FAS 123 governed the accounting for SARs and phantom stock awards. Now FAS 123(R) does.

("cliff" vesting). In this example, the SARs could only be exercised for cash. The accounting rules provided that the measurement date occurred when the SARs were exercised, because that was the date that the amount to be settled in cash was known. However, to determine the amount of expense recognition before exercise, the vesting provisions had to be considered. For awards that had a cliff vesting provision, the compensation expense was reported equally over the vesting period. In this example, for instance, one-fifth of the amount of the compensation expense would have been taken each year. In the first year, one-fifth of the compensation computed to that date would have been recognized as an expense. Similarly, the expense for the next year would have been two-fifths of the compensation measured to date, less the cumulative expense recognized in the prior year, and continuing on for each year thereafter. Table 6-1 illustrates the accounting treatment.

This treatment assumed that the employee actually exercised the SARs at the vesting date. It is possible that the employee would not have exercised the SAR when fully vested, either for tax reasons or because of the expectation that share prices would appreciate. In that case, additional expense (or income) needed to be recognized based on changes in the stock price until the award was exercised.

The accounting treatment was more complicated if the SARs vested gradually (as opposed to "cliff" vesting). In this case, FIN 28 provided that each vesting tranche of the award was treated as a separate award. Appreciation was allocated to each award pro-rata during the time over which it was earned, with the result that the compensation expense was front-loaded.

Assume in the example above that the employee received an award of 1,000 SARs, and that this award vested at 20% per year. Under FIN 28, it was as though the employee had received five separate grants that would have been accounted for at the end of year 1 as follows:

1. The first tranche of 200 shares was 100% vested. The gain was worth $2, so the company took a charge of 200 shares at $2 per share ($400).

2. The second tranche (200 shares vesting over a two-year period) was considered 50% earned, so a charge was taken for 100 shares at $2 ($200).

Table 6-1. SAR Accounting Treatment Under FIN 28

(1,000 SARs granted at $10 per share, 100% vesting after five years)

	Year				
	Year 1	Year 2	Year 3	Year 4	Year 5
Exercise price per SAR	$10.00	$10.00	$10.00	$10.00	$10.00
Market value of underlying stock	12.00	13.00	8.00	14.00	15.00
Spread	$2.00	$3.00	$0.00	$4.00	$5.00
Total shares	1,000	1,000	1,000	1,000	1,000
Aggregate compensation expense	$2,000	$3,000	$0	$4,000	$5,000
Cumulative percentage accrued	20.0%	40.0%	60.0%	80.0%	100.0%
Cumulative compensation expense	$400	$1,200	$0	$3,200	$5,000
Expense previously recognized	0	400	1,200	0	3,200
Expense (income) for current year	$400	$800	($1,200)	$3,200	$1,800

3. The third tranche (200 shares vesting over three years) was considered 33.3% earned, so a charge was taken for 66.7 shares at $2 ($133).

4. The fourth tranche (200 shares vesting over four years) was considered 25% earned, so a charge was taken for 50 shares at $2 per share ($100).

5. The fifth tranche (200 shares vesting over five years) was considered 20% earned, so a charge was taken for 40 shares at $2 per share ($80).

6. Overall, for year 1, the company took a charge of $913.

Table 6-2 illustrates this vesting percentage and the "front-loaded" accounting treatment.

As noted in chapter 2, if the SAR award is paid in stock rather than cash, the accounting treatment under APB 25 and FAS 123(R) is different. APB 25 was similar to the example above. The company had to use variable accounting (taking a compensation charge as the award was earned, making adjustments for changes in the value of the award) up until the time the award was exercised.

Under FAS 123(R), SAR awards that are paid only in stock are accounted for in the same way as stock options. The value of the SARs is determined as of their grant date using a stock option pricing model, such as the Black-Scholes model or the binomial model. This value is then recognized as a compensation expense over the vesting period of the SARs, either using the method for cliff-vested awards or the method for ratably vested awards described above. In the case of performance-vesting SAR awards, the expense amount is recognized over the expected vesting period based on projections of whether and when the performance goals will be achieved.[3]

If phantom stock awards are made rather than SARs, i.e., the employee is entitled not only to the appreciation in the stock but also its underlying value, then the accounting (assuming five-year graded vesting) over the five-year period would be as in table 6-3.

---

3. See chapter 2 for a further explanation of the accounting treatment of stock SARs.

Table 6-2. SAR Accounting Treatment When Vesting Is Graded Under FIN 28

Vesting tranche	Percentage recognized in:					Total
	Year 1	Year 2	Year 3	Year 4	Year 5	
Tranche one	20.0%					20.0%
Tranche two	10.0%	10.0%				20.0%
Tranche three	6.67%	6.67%	6.67%			20.0%
Tranche four	5.0%	5.0%	5.0%	5.0%		20.0%
Tranche five	4.0%	4.0%	4.0%	4.0%	4.0%	20.0%
Percentage recognized per year	45.67%	25.67%	15.67%	9.0%	4.0%	100.0%
Cumulative percentage accrued	45.67%	71.33%	87.00%	96.0%	100.0%	

Table 6-3. Phantom Stock Accounting Treatment

(1,000 phantom shares granted at $10 per share, vesting at 20% per year for five years)

	Year 1	Year 2	Year 3	Year 4	Year 5
			Year		
Market value of underlying stock	$12.00	$13.00	$8.00	$14.00	$15.00
Number of phantom shares	1,000	1,000	1,000	1,000	1,000
Aggregate compensation expense	$12,000	$13,000	$8,000	$14,000	$15,000
Cumulative percentage accrued	45.67%	71.33%	87.0%	96.0%	100.0%
Cumulative compensation expense	$5,480	$9,273	$6,960	$13,440	$15,000
Expense previously recognized	0	5,480	9,273	6,960	13,440
Expense (income) for current year	$5,480	$3,793	($2,313)	$6,480	$1,560

6.1.1 Balance Sheet Treatment

For phantom stock and SARs that must be settled in cash, the accrued compensation is recorded as a liability, with an offsetting credit when the payment is made. Of course, the cash assets of the company are reduced upon payment. For SAR awards that are settled only in stock or may be settled in stock at the company's election, the accrued compensation is reported as additional paid-in capital.

6.2 Restricted Stock

As explained in chapter 3, restricted stock is a transfer of stock to an employee subject to a risk of forfeiture and transfer restrictions. The stock may be transferred to the employee at no cost or sold for a specified price. Under a typical restricted stock grant, the employee's right to the stock is conditioned on future performance of service (time-vested) or the achievement of a financial target (performance-vested). If the employee terminates employment before the vesting date or the company fails to meet the specified financial target, the employee forfeits the shares.

The financial accounting treatment of time-vested restricted stock is the same under APB 25 and FAS 123(R). Under APB 25, time-vested restricted stock was accounted for as a fixed plan since the number of shares that a participant would be entitled to receive, provided the participant continued to provide service until the vesting date, was known on the date of grant. Under FAS 123 and the fixed plan accounting provisions of APB 25, the difference between the purchase price (if any) and the aggregate market price was recognized as compensation expense and was amortized in a systematic and rational manner over the vesting period. If the plan had "cliff" vesting, the compensation expense was amortized on a straight-line basis over the vesting period. If the plan had a graded vesting schedule, FIN 28 required each vesting tranche of the award to be treated as a separate award, similar to the accounting for SARs and phantom stock described above. FAS 123(R) does not change this treatment.

The next example assumes that in Year 1, 10 employees are each awarded 2,500 shares of time-vested restricted stock. The value of the stock on the date of grant was $40 per share, and the shares cliff vest

Table 6-4. Time-Vested Restricted Stock Award Accounting

		Year		
	Year 1	Year 2	Year 3	Year 4
Number of restricted shares outstanding	25,000	25,000	22,500	22,500
Fair market value of shares on date of grant	$40.00	$40.00	$40.00	$40.00
Grant date value of restricted stock (aggregate compensation expense)	$1,000,000	$1,000,000	$900,000	$900,000
Percentage of vesting period completed at year-end	25%	50%	75%	100%
Cumulative compensation expense	$250,000	$500,000	$675,000	$900,000
Expense previously recognized	0	250,000	500,000	675,000
Expense (income) for current year	$250,000	$250,000	$175,000	$225,000

after four years. It further assumes that during Year 3, one of the participants terminates employment and forfeits the 2,500 shares. Table 6-4 outlines the expense recognition patterns under both APB 25 and FAS 123(R).

The financial accounting treatment of performance-vested restricted stock is different under APB 25 than under FAS 123(R). As with a performance award plan, under APB 25 performance-vested restricted stock resulted in variable plan accounting because the number of shares that a participant was entitled to receive was not known until the performance measurement period was complete. Under FAS 123 and 123(R), the grant date value of the shares that ultimately vest is recognized over the performance measurement period. Under both APB 25 and FAS 123 methods, no compensation expense is recognized for shares that do not vest as a result of failure to attain a non-market-based performance goal.[4] Performance vesting tied to a market condition (something related to stock price) does not allow a reversal of charges, however. The amount of compensation expense recognized each year during the performance measurement period is dependent on management's estimate of the number of shares that will vest based on its assessment of the probability that the performance goals will be attained.

If this type of award is accounted for under FAS 123(R), the value of the award is not marked to market as the expense is recognized over the vesting period. The expense amount is fixed at the value of the shares on the grant date, less any amount paid for them by the employee. This expense is then recognized over the estimated vesting period based on projections of whether the performance goals will be achieved.

The next example highlights the difference in the accounting treatment of non-market-condition, performance-vested restricted stock under APB 25 and FAS 123(R). Once again assume that in Year 1, at a time when the stock had a fair value of $40 per share, 10 employees were each awarded 2,500 shares of restricted stock. In this example, however, the awards will vest only if certain average annual profit margin and revenue growth goals are achieved over the four-year performance

---

4. The one exception to this rule is that if the performance condition is a target stock price, compensation expense is recognized for awards to employees who remain in service for the requisite period regardless of whether the target stock price is reached. See ¶ 26 of FAS 123.

period from Year 1 through Year 4. The average annual profit margin and revenue growth were above target during Year 1, at target after Year 2, below target after Year 3, and at target at the completion of the performance measurement period after Year 4. Also, assume once again that during Year 3, one of the participants terminates employment and forfeits the 2,500 shares.

Tables 6-5 and 6-6 illustrate the expense recognition differences under APB 25 and FAS 123(R). Table 6-7 summarizes the difference in the expense recognition between APB 25 and FAS 123(R).

6.3 Earnings per Share Treatment

Public companies will also need to report the effect of these awards on earnings per share (EPS). Public companies need to report EPS in the conventional sense of the earnings reported on the income statement divided by the number of shares. In addition, companies need to report diluted EPS, which adds the number of common stock equivalents to the denominator (a calculation known as the "treasury stock method"). So if awards have been granted in shares (as with restricted stock) or settled in shares (as might happen with SARs), then the number of shares goes up. This includes the number of shares outstanding under all SARs (here, the share equivalent of the value of SARs), restricted stock, and stock options. In calculating EPS, companies can take a credit for any proceeds from the awards, including any consideration paid for the shares (e.g., the exercise price for stock options), tax benefits, and any unamortized expenses associated with the awards.

6.4 Performance Award Plans

A performance award plan must be accounted for as a variable plan because the amount of the cash award (or number of shares if payment is made in company stock) is not known until the performance period has been completed. The general guideline is that compensation expense (and income) should be recognized on a systematic and rational basis.

More specifically, under a performance award plan where compensation is earned based on attaining one or more particular goals over

Table 6-5. Performance-Vested Restricted Stock Award Accounting Under APB 25

	Year			
	Year 1	Year 2	Year 3	Year 4
Number of restricted shares outstanding	25,000	25,000	22,500	22,500
Management's estimate of the probability that the shares will vest	100%	100%	70%	100%
Probability-weighted number of shares	25,000	25,000	15,750	22,500
Fair market value of stock at year end	$44.00	$43.00	$46.00	$48.00
Value of restricted stock	$1,100,000	$1,075,000	$724,500	$1,080,000
Percentage of vesting period completed at year-end	25%	50%	75%	100%
Cumulative compensation expense	$275,000	$537,500	$543,375	$1,080,000
Expense previously recognized	0	275,000	537,500	543,375
Expense (income) for current year	$275,000	$262,500	$5,875	$536,625

Table 6-6. Performance-Vested Restricted Stock Award Accounting Under FAS123(R)

	Year			
	Year 1	Year 2	Year 3	Year 4
Number of restricted shares outstanding	25,000	25,000	22,500	22,500
Management's estimate of the probability that the shares will vest	100%	100%	70%	100%
Probability-weighted number of shares	25,000	25,000	15,750	22,500
Fair market value of stock on date of grant	$40.00	$40.00	$40.00	$40.00
Value of restricted stock	$1,000,000	$1,000,000	$630,000	$900,000
Percentage of vesting period completed at year-end	25%	50%	75%	100%
Cumulative compensation expense	$250,000	$500,000	$472,500	$900,000
Expense previously recognized	0	250,000	500,000	472,500
Expense (income) for current year	$250,000	$250,000	($27,500)	$427,500

Table 6-7. Difference in Expense Recognition Under APB 25 and FAS 123 or FAS 123(R)

| | Year | | | | |
	Year 1	Year 2	Year 3	Year 4	Total
Expense recognized under APB 25	$275,000	$262,500	$5,875	$536,625	$1,080,000
Expense recognized under FAS 123R	250,000	250,000	(27,500)	427,500	900,000
Difference (decrease under FAS 123(R))	$25,000	$12,500	$33,375	$109,125	$180,000

a period of time, compensation should be accrued over the period in relation to the results achieved to date. Also, to the extent results previously estimated or determined to have been achieved prove not to be sustainable, then compensation expense is reversed.

The accounting is best explained in an example. Using the Unit Value matrix from chapter 4 and assuming that (1) 10 employees were each awarded 1,000 performance units for a total of 10,000 units (or a targeted payment of $1 million) and (2) performance was at target after one year, above target during years 2 and 3, but ended up below target at the end of year 4 (2006 was a tough year and adversely affected aggregate performance), the annual expense (and income) would be as in table 6-8.

The above example also assumes that there are no forfeitures. To the extent any employee's employment is terminated before the end of Year 4 (2006), cumulative compensation expense with respect to that employee is reversed.

Finally, the accounting is the same for performance awards under both APB 25 and FAS 123(R) if the award is paid in cash, as described in this chapter. If paid in stock, the measurement date for performance awards occurs at grant under FAS 123(R), but it occurs at vest under APB 25.

Table 6-8. Performance Award Accounting

	Year			
	Year 1	Year 2	Year 3	Year 4
Margin and revenue results achieved to date (expressed in terms of unit values)	$100.00	$112.50	$112.50	$75.00
Number of units outstanding	10,000	10,000	10,000	10,000
Aggregate compensation expense	$1,000,000	$1,125,000	$1,125,000	$750,000
Cumulative percentage accrued	25%	50%	75%	100%
Cumulative compensation expense	$250,000	$562,500	$843,750	$750,000
Expense previously recognized	0	250,000	562,500	843,750
Expense (income) for current year	$250,000	$312,500	$281,250	($93,750)

ESOPs, ESPPs, 401(k) Plans, and Stock Options: When the Old Standbys Still Make Sense

Corey Rosen

Contents

Clearly, there are many advantages to setting up a phantom stock, restricted stock, direct stock purchase, performance award, or stock appreciation rights (SAR) plan (for simplicity, I will call these plans "alternative equity plans" in this chapter). These plans are simple, they do not require any actual stock to be distributed, and they are supremely flexible in how they are designed. But there are some potentially serious disadvantages that need to be considered as well. In particular, these plans:

- Can raise regulatory issues unless properly designed;
- Have accounting disadvantages;
- Can leave employees skeptical that actual benefits will be distributed;
- Have less favorable tax consequences than other kinds of employee ownership plans;
- May, if they require employees to buy stock, make ownership riskier and available mostly to higher-paid people with sufficient discretionary income; and
- Fail to create a way for people who own stock to provide for business continuity.

But even if a company decides it wants one of these plans, that does not preclude it from using one or more of the plans that have been the mainstays of broad-based employee ownership for years: employee stock ownership plans (ESOPs), stock options, employee stock purchase plans (ESPPs), and, in some cases, 401(k) plans.

This chapter looks at each of the potential disadvantages to the plans discussed in this book. These disadvantages may mean that these plans might not be appropriate at all or might need to be used in combination with the more standard kinds of plans mentioned in the paragraph above. This is followed by a very brief discussion of some of the other kinds of plans that may deserve consideration. First, though, we need to discuss a key reason people set up these plans in the first place: to avoid losing control.

7.1 The Specter of Losing Control: Why It Is Not a Key Issue

First, it's useful to consider one of the principal reasons why employers often think they specifically need a phantom stock plan or stock appreciation rights plan instead of a more traditional equity plan (discussed below): they don't want to risk losing control. This is rarely as important an issue as it seems. The issue comes up almost entirely in closely held companies; actual share ownership by employees in public companies is almost never substantial enough to provide any meaningful control. In almost any variation on the plans described in this book, it would be rare for there to be more than a small minority of shares held by any one employee or even a group of employees at any one time. If companies are concerned that employees might sell their shares to outsiders, companies can require the shares be sold back to the company or retain a right of first refusal. If state securities law allow, they could also provide that awards are for non-voting shares, although this should lower the per-share value of shares acquired.

If ownership is through a employee benefit plan qualified under ERISA (the Employee Retirement Income Security Act of 1974), such as an ESOP (described below), the risk of losing control is similarly small. In an ESOP, the trustee is considered the legal owner of record. The trustee actually votes the shares. While many closely held ESOP companies allow employees to direct the trustee as to the voting of the shares, most do not. Instead, the trustee either uses independent judgment or is instructed by a third party, often the board of directors. Employees must be able to direct the trustee, however, on a few "mandatory" issues, the most important of which are sale of all or substantially all the assets (but not on sale of the stock), liquidation, reclassification (such as going public), and mergers. These issues rarely, if ever, come up. More important, we do not know of a single case where employees have been able to prevent management from doing something it wanted to do based solely on their ability to vote on these required issues. Where management does not want employees to have effective control, the board appoints the trustee, and the trustee votes for the board, an entirely circular arrangement. While many, and perhaps now even most, ESOPs voluntarily allow at least some employee input (if not actual voting control) into corporate-level decisions, it is not legally required.

A more serious issue with ESOPs is that the fiduciary responsibilities of the trustee are to operate the plan for the benefit of plan participants. This can place some, if not many, limits on management behavior. For instance, a trustee of the Delta Star Company successfully sued the company's CEO when he paid himself a salary of $3 million, which was what the company earned that year. Because the trustee can be an appointee of management, however, trustees very rarely sue management. Instead, what normally happens is that employees sue the trustee for failing to follow fiduciary standards. The most frequent causes of action are the ESOP paying too much for the shares and the plan's failing to make distributions according to its own rules or the law. All but a few of these cases involve what most observes would agree is egregious behavior by management. Plans that are run in conventional ways with sound legal advice almost never are sued. So while owners give up some control with an ESOP, they don't have to give up much, and if the ESOP owns a minority of the shares, they give up virtually no control.

This is even truer in profit sharing or 401(k) arrangements in which the plan invests in company stock. There are no voting requirements in these plans. Only fiduciary rules impose any constraints on management control. Because both qualified ERISA plans and stock option plans have much better tax treatment than phantom stock and similar plans, if losing control is the only reason for avoiding these more favored plans, then the decision should probably be reconsidered.

7.2 Risks and Disadvantages of Alternative Equity Plans

As discussed earlier, one of the issues in setting up a broad-based phantom stock plan or stock appreciation rights plan is that their terms may make them a *de facto* retirement plan subject to regulation under the Employee Retirement Income Security Act (ERISA). It is, of course, possible to avoid this by limiting the design of the plan so that it covers only key people or, if broad-based, it makes periodic payouts rather than waiting until separation or retirement. But many companies want to structure their plans as both broad-based and with long-deferred payouts. Deferring the payouts conserves cash, at least in the short run, and gives employees more of an incentive to stick around. Giving up these features may not be worth the advantages of a phantom stock or stock appreciation rights plan. Restricted stock and direct purchase plans should not run the regulatory risks of being covered under ERISA, and some kinds of equity plans can be structured to allow deferrals past the vesting date. However, deferring compensation under some of these plans can subject the participant to punitive taxes under Section 409A of the Internal Revenue Code (the "Code"). See the relevant chapters in this book for details on whether and how Section 409A affects individual plans such as phantom stock.

A second issue is accounting treatment. As the chapter on accounting in this book notes, individual equity compensation plans (such as stock options, phantom stock, restricted stock, and SAR plans) require that companies determine their cost at the time the awards are granted, based on their current fair value, and recognize that cost over the service period for the award. For public companies, this can be an important issue. Many of these companies have gone to some lengths to minimize the costs of stock awards as current charges to income because they fear the public will view their earnings more negatively. For closely held companies, the issue is less cut and dried. Pre-IPO companies generally care a great deal about what their income statements look like. So do many companies seeking an acquirer. For companies not in these situations, their income statements are of most concern to their bankers and other creditors. If they have a good relationship with these entities, the accounting issues can usually be explained. Companies can honestly point out that they could have set up a plan with more favorable accounting rules, but that the real effect on cash and on shareholder equity would be much the same. Research and experience indicate that shareholders will "look through" accounting conventions to gauge companies on the real economic value delivered. Because of that, I have strongly argued that companies should choose equity plans based on their economic costs and benefits, not their accounting impact.

With an ESOP, the value of shares allocated to employee accounts already incurs a compensation charge on the income statement, and has since 1992, at which point the plans lost favor in public companies. But now that the accounting playing field is leveled, ESOPs deserve another look because their tax benefits are substantially greater than those of other plans.

A third issue is taxes. Phantom stock, restricted stock, RSUs, and SARs really have no significant tax benefits for companies, and, for restricted stock, only a very limited tax benefit for employees. Like any other kind of compensation, employees must pay tax when they acquire a nonforfeitable right to a benefit, even if they do not actually receive it. For restricted stock (but not restricted stock units), employees can choose Section 83(b) treatment, but this means the employee may risk paying taxes on a benefit the employee may never receive (and the taxes will not be credited back). Once paid, the employee cannot avoid paying ordinary income tax. The employer, meanwhile, takes no deduction for the award until paid, even though the expected future cost of an award will show up on the company's income statement when the award is granted. Direct stock purchase plans require employees to buy stock with after-tax money.

In contrast, incentive stock options allow employees to take capital gains treatment on their awards. Moreover, no tax is due until sale of the stock (employers cannot take a tax deduction, however, if employees who have these kinds of options keep them for the full tax holding period). In an ESOP or other qualified ERISA plan, employers get a deduction *at the time the time the contribution is made*, but employees do not pay any tax until they actually receive the stock or its cash value years later. Qualified ERISA plans such as ESOPs are the only kind of compensation where the normal tax rule that companies can only take a deduction at the time the employee incurs a tax obligation does not apply. Qualified ERISA plans, unlike all other kinds of equity compensation, also allow the employee to further defer taxation by rolling over amounts into other defined contribution plans or into IRAs. Employers and sellers get additional tax benefits as well, as described below. Moreover, companies with an ESOP can deduct dividends paid on ESOP shares that are used to repay an ESOP loan (a loan to the ESOP to acquire company shares, repaid with company contributions and/or dividends), are passed through to employees, or are voluntarily reinvested by employees in company stock.

A fourth issue is that phantom plans and SARs cannot create a market for an owner's shares. Many owners of closely held companies want to use employee ownership as a means for providing business continuity. Phantom plans and SARs simply give away bonuses based on equity value; they do nothing to provide a market for owners' shares.

With direct stock purchase plans, two significant problems can arise. First, because employees are using their own money to buy stock, they are taking considerably more risk than in other plans. That means they will probably expect more (often including some say in how the company is run), be more discouraged if the company does not do well, and be more likely to sue if things go very badly. Second, ownership will be available only to those with the means to buy it. For companies wanting to get a broad distribution of ownership to employees, this will be a significant problem.

Finally, and often most importantly, employees may not respond as positively to phantom plans or SARs as other kinds of plans. In part, this may just be familiarity. Many employees know about stock options, ESOPs, 401(k) plans, and profit sharing plans. Restricted stock lies somewhere in between; it is real stock, with specific rules about its use, but it is less familiar (so far) to employees than other plans. That familiarity may breed greater confidence that the plans really will pay off. Moreover, these plans have various rules they must follow; the plans described in this book have rules the company determines entirely on its own. Moreover, where employees get something based on what the company says is its equity value, employees may be skeptical about how this is measured, at least in closely held companies. Employees may also be skeptical about whether the plan really will make payouts or the stock will be liquid, although that concern can be lessened over time as the company builds a history on this. One result of these concerns is that companies with the kinds of plans described here, ironically, may need to be *more* open about their books, their strategies, and their appraisal methods than companies with other plans if they are to make the plans believable. However, these same concerns would apply to ESOPs, stock options, 401(k) plans, and profit sharing plans used to acquire stock in private companies as well.

This recital of problems does not mean these plans do not have substantial advantages, as the rest of this book describes. It does mean that companies should at least consider other alternatives.

7.3 Plan Types

There are a number of other kinds of employee ownership plans companies should at least consider. In this section, we will look at four of the principal vehicles: ESOPs (employee stock ownership plans), 401(k) plans, stock options, and qualified stock purchase plans.

7.3.1 ESOPs

An ESOP is a kind of employee benefit plan. Governed by ERISA, ESOPs were given a specific statutory framework in 1974. In the ensuing years, they were given a number of other tax benefits. Like other qualified deferred compensation plans governed by ERISA, they must not discriminate in their operations in favor of highly compensated employees, officers, and owners. To assure that these rules are met, ESOPs must appoint a trustee to act as the plan fiduciary. This can be anyone, although larger companies tend to appoint an outside trust institution, while smaller companies typically appoint a manager or create an ESOP trust committee.

The most sophisticated use of an ESOP is to borrow money. In this approach, the company sets up a trust. The trust then borrows money from a lender. The company repays the loan by making tax-deductible contributions to the trust, which the trust gives to the lender. The loan must be to acquire stock in the company. Proceeds from the loan can be used for any legitimate business purpose. The stock is put into a "suspense account," where it is released to employee accounts as the loan is repaid. After employees leave the company or retire, the company buys back the stock purchased on their behalf. In practice, banks often require a second step in the loan transaction of making the loan to the company instead of the trust, with the company reloaning the proceeds to the ESOP.

In return for agreeing to funnel the loan through the ESOP, the company gets a number of tax benefits, provided it follows the rules to assure employees are treated fairly. First, the company can deduct the entire loan contribution it makes to the ESOP, within certain payroll-based limits described below. That means the company, in effect, can deduct interest and principal on the loan, not just interest. Second, the company can deduct dividends paid on the shares acquired with the proceeds of the loan that are used to repay the loan itself (in other words, the earnings of the stock being acquired help pay for stock itself). Reasonable dividends passed through to employees or voluntarily reinvested in the company's stock (including through putting the dividends into a 401(k) plan offering company shares). Again, there are limits, as described below in sections on the rules of the loan and contribution limits. Finally, if the company is an S corporation, then the share of corporate earnings attributable to the ESOP are not subject to corporate income tax. Note, however, that rules designed to prevent abuses of this extraordinary tax benefit generally make it impractical for an S corporation ESOP to have fewer than 10 participants or be limited primarily to management.

The ESOP can also be funded directly by discretionary corporate contributions of cash to buy existing shares or simply by the contribution of shares. These contributions are tax-deductible up to 25% of pay.

7.3.1.1 *ESOP Applications*

The ESOP can buy both new and existing shares, for a variety of purposes.

- The most common application for an ESOP is *to buy the shares of a departing owner of a closely held company*. Owners in closely held C corporations (but not S) who have owned the stock for at least three years can defer tax on the gain they have made from the sale to an ESOP if the ESOP holds 30% or more of the company's stock once the purchase is completed. Any subsequent sales also qualify for the tax deferral. To qualify for the deferral, owners must reinvest the sale proceeds in stocks and bonds of U.S. corporations not receiving more than 25% of their income from passive investment. Sellers have 12 months after the sale to select the replacement property. The tax break is a deferral; when the replacement investments are sold, capital gains taxes are due going back to the original basis on the closely held company's stock. Moreover, the purchase can be made in pretax corporate dollars.

- ESOPs can *buy newly issued shares in the company, with the borrowed funds being used to buy new capital*. The company can, in effect, finance growth or acquisitions in pretax dollars while these same dollars create an employee benefit plan. ESOPs can also be used this way to fund a match to a 401(k) plan.

- The above uses generally involve borrowing money through the ESOP, but a company can simply contribute new shares of stock to an ESOP, or cash to buy existing shares, *as a means to create an employee benefit plan.* As more and more companies want to find ways to tie employee and corporate interests, this is becoming a more popular application. In public companies especially, an ESOP contribution is often used as part or all of a match to employee deferrals to a 401(k) plan.

7.3.1.2 *Basic ESOP Rules*

Shares in the ESOP trust are allocated to individual employee accounts. Although there are some exceptions, generally all full-time employees over 21 participate in the plan. Allocations are made either on the basis of relative pay or some more equal formula. As employees accumulate seniority with the company, they acquire an increasing right to the shares in their account, a process known as vesting. Employees must be 100% vested within five to seven years.

When employees leave the company, they receive their stock, which the company must buy back from them at its fair market value (unless there is a public market for the shares). Private companies must have an annual outside valuation to determine the price of their shares. In private companies, employees must be able to vote their allocated shares on major issues, such as closing or relocating, but the company can choose whether to pass through voting rights (such as for the board of directors) on other issues. In public companies, employees must be able to vote all issues.

There are a number of other rules and benefits of ESOPs that are beyond the scope of this brief summary. The NCEO publishes a number of detailed books on this subject. For most companies considering an equity-equivalent plan, the decision on whether to do an ESOP instead usually comes down to a few key points:

1. ESOPs are more complicated and require extensive and expensive legal, appraisal, and administrative costs; a leveraged ESOP generally costs at least $40,000 to set up and $15,000 per year to operate.

2. ESOPs must follow specific rules about how stock is allocated and distributed, rules that do not allow for individual discretion as to who gets what when.

3. ESOPs provide substantial tax benefits, particularly for business continuity.

4. ESOPs can only buy shares at an appraised value or less; if sellers are convinced their stock is worth more, an ESOP may not work.

7.3.2 Section 401(k) Plans

Section 401(k) plans allow employees to defer part of their pay on a pretax basis into an investment fund set up by the company. The company usually offers at least four alternative investment vehicles. Because the law requires that participation in the plans not be too heavily skewed toward more highly paid people, companies generally offer a partial match to encourage broad participation in these voluntary plans. This match can be in any investment vehicle the company chooses, including company stock. There is a limit of 25% of taxable pay that the company can contribute to the plan. This limit is reduced by other company contributions to other defined contribution plans, such as ESOPs or profit sharing plans. Employees can annually defer up to $15,500 on a pretax basis into the plan (as of 2007; this amount is indexed annually for inflation). However, the sum of employee deferrals and employer contributions to all defined contribution plans cannot exceed the lesser of $45,000 or 100% of pay (as of 2007). The $45,000 figure is also indexed for inflation.

There are several factors that favor the use of a 401(k) plan as a vehicle for employee ownership. In public companies, company stock may be one of the most cost-effective means of matching employee contributions. If there are existing treasury shares or the company prints new shares, contributing them to the 401(k) plan may impose no immediate cash cost on the company; in fact, it would provide a tax deduction. Other shareholders would suffer a dilution, of course. If the company has to buy shares to fund the match, at least the dollars being used are used to invest in itself rather than other investments. From the employee standpoint, company stock is the investment the employee knows best and so may be attractive to people who either do not want to spend the time to learn about alternatives or have a strong belief in their own company.

Public companies also often use an ESOP to provide the match to the employees' deferrals into 401(k) plans. This technique allows the

company to deduct dividends paid to the ESOP that are used to repay
an ESOP loan, that are passed though to employees, or that employees
voluntarily reinvest in company stock. Balanced against these advantages,
of course, must be an appreciation on both the part of the employee
and the company that a failure to diversify a retirement portfolio is very
risky. This gained considerable attention in 2001 and 2002 with the
Enron bankruptcy, as well as similar debacles for employee retirement
accounts at Global Crossing, Lucent, Rite-Aid, and other large companies.
In 2006, Congress passed the Pension Protection Act, which requires
that 401(k) plans in public companies (including plans integrated with
an ESOP) allow employees to choose to diversify any investments in
company stock at any time; shares contributed by the company must
be diversifiable after three years in the plan. For shares contributed by
the company before plan years beginning in 2007, the rules are phased
in at 33% in 2007, 66% in 2008, and 100% in 2009 (except for certain
older participants, who do not have to wait to diversify 100%). These
rules do not apply to stand-alone ESOPs, or to 401(k) plans or ESOPs
in closely held companies.

For closely held companies, 401(k) plans are less appealing as an
employee ownership vehicle, although very appropriate in some cases.
If employees are given an option to buy company stock, this can often
trigger securities law issues most private firms want to avoid. Employer
matches make more sense, but require the company to either dilute
ownership or reacquire shares from selling shareholders. In many closely
held businesses, the first may not be desirable for control reasons and
the second because there may not be sellers. Moreover, the 401(k) approach does not provide the "rollover" tax benefit that selling to an ESOP
does, and the maximum amount that can be contributed is a function
of how much employees put into savings. That will limit how much
an employer can actually buy from a seller through a 401(k) plan to a
fraction of what the ESOP can buy.

Despite these limitations, 401(k) plans, and their new, simpler
cousins, SIMPLE plans (plans for employers under 100 employees that
are much like 401(k) plans but with stricter rules and easier administration), are attractive as ownership vehicles in cases where a company
wants employees to become owners, but has no need to buy out existing
owners or use the borrowing features of an ESOP. A company can match

employee deferrals with company stock or make a straight percentage of pay contribution to all employees eligible to be in the plan in the form of company stock. Companies do need to be cautious, however, to assure that employees have enough diversified investments in their accounts so that if the company fails, their retirement is not at risk.

As noted above, 401(k) plans and ESOPs can be combined, with the ESOP contribution being used as the 401(k) match. This can work on either a nonleveraged or leveraged basis. In the nonleveraged case, the company simply characterizes its match as an ESOP. That adds some set-up and administrative costs, but allows the company to reap the additional tax benefits of an ESOP. In a leveraged case, the company estimates how much it will need to match employee contributions each year, then borrows an amount of money such that the loan repayment will be close to that amount. If it is not as much as the promised matching amount, the company can either just define that as its match anyway, make up the difference with additional shares or cash (if the loan payment is lower), or pay the loan faster. If the amount is larger, the employees get a windfall. Combination plans must meet complex rules for testing to determine if they discriminate too heavily in favor of more highly paid people.

7.3.3 Stock Options

As noted above, ESOPs are qualified under ERISA, meaning they must meet federal rules to assure that participation in them does not excessively favor more highly compensated people. Not every company wants to abide by these rules, nor does every company want the additional tax benefits they can offer. Moreover, some companies believe ownership means more if employees have to put something up to get it. Some growing companies find that contributing or purchasing existing stock is too much of a strain on either their capital structure or their finances, or both. They would prefer to give employees a right to future ownership. Even if they do have the means to contribute stock or pay cash awards through a SAR or phantom plan, companies may prefer stock options because they do not impose an unpredictable future cash expense. Options, in effect, impose a shareholder expense rather than a cash expense, unless the company chooses to settle the option by buying back shares. Many growing private companies do not pay taxes, so the tax benefits of an ESOP may not be attractive, making the greater flexibility of options more appealing.

For companies persuaded by one or more of these arguments, stock options may make an attractive choice. In the past, options were granted primarily to highly paid executives. In recent years, however, more and more companies have decided to grant options to most or all employees. We at the NCEO estimate that 12% of public companies do this, and that a majority of these companies are outside the technology sector. An NCEO analysis in 2001 found that 77% of pre-IPO technology companies granted options to all employees as well. Of course, many companies, including companies with other employee ownership plans, also grant options just to a limited number of people.

7.3.3.1 *What Is a Stock Option?*

A stock option gives an employee the right to buy shares at a price fixed today (usually the market price, but sometimes lower) for a defined number of years into the future. The options might be granted on a percentage of pay basis, a merit formula, an equal basis, or any other formula the company chooses. Most plans provide grants regularly (every one to three years), either on the basis of the passage of time (every year, for instance) or an event (a promotion, meeting certain corporate or group targets, or a performance appraisal, for instance). The options are typically subject to three- to five-year vesting, meaning that if someone is 20% vested, he or she can exercise only 20% of the options. An employee can usually exercise vested options at any time. Most options have a 10-year life, meaning the employee can choose to buy the shares at the grant price at any time they are vested for up to 10 years. The option life, however, can be any amount (except in the case of incentive stock options, as described below). The difference between the grant price and the exercise price is called the "spread."

Most public companies offer a "cashless exercise" alternative in which the employee exercises the option, and the company gives the employee an amount of cash equal to the difference between the grant price and the exercise price, minus any taxes that are due. Options also can be exercised with cash, although employees must have enough to pay for the shares and taxes (if any), by exchanging existing shares employee own, or by selling just enough of the shares acquired through the options to pay the costs and taxes, then keeping the remaining shares.

In closely held firms, employees usually have to wait until the company is sold or goes public to sell their shares, although some companies have arrangements to purchase the shares themselves or help facilitate buying and selling between employees. When an employee exercises an option, however, this constitutes an investment decision subject to securities laws. At a minimum, these require "anti-fraud financial disclosure statements" and, in some cases, will require securities registration as well. For this reason, stock options are used most frequently in closely held firms when the intention is to sell or go public.

7.3.3.2 *Nonqualified Options*

Nonqualified stock options are options that do not qualify for any special tax consideration. Anyone, employees or non-employees, can be given a nonqualified option on any basis the company chooses. When a nonqualified option is exercised, the employee must pay ordinary income tax on the "spread" between the grant and exercise price; the company can deduct that amount.

For example, say that Chip Salter, a mechanic at PepsiCo's Frito-Lay division, makes $20,000 per year. Under PepsiCo's plan, Chip gets options worth 10% of pay each year, which vest at 20% per year over five years. Ten years down the road, Chip has fully vested options worth $10,000 at the grant price. For convenience, we'll say it is $100 per share for each year. Thanks to the efforts of Chip and his colleagues, PepsiCo stock is now worth $200 per share. Chip now has the right to buy $20,000 worth of stock for the $10,000. He can borrow the money (a bank might be willing to make the loan given that he's going to get $20,000 in a very liquid investment), or perhaps he has savings to use, so that he can buy the stock and keep it in the hopes it will go higher. He must pay ordinary income tax on $10,000 gain. Alternatively, he can have PepsiCo buy the shares for him, pay his tax, and give him what is left, probably about $7,000.

Nonqualified options can be issued at fair market value or a discount, but if they are issued at a discount, they are subject to the deferred compensation tax rules under Section 409A of the Code, meaning that unless recipients choose well in advance when to exercise the award, the award would be subject to heavy current taxation to the company and employee. Discounted options, therefore, are likely to disappear as a plan choice.

7.3.3.3 Incentive Stock Options

With an incentive stock option (ISO), a company grants the employee an option to purchase stock at some time in the future at a specified price. With an ISO, there are restrictions on how the option is to be structured and when the option stock can be transferred. The employee does not recognize ordinary income at option grant or exercise (although the spread between the option price and the option stock's fair market value may be taxed under something called the alternative minimum tax, or AMT), and the company cannot deduct the related compensation expense. The employee is taxed only upon the *disposition* of the option stock. The gain is all capital gain for a qualifying disposition. For a disqualifying disposition (i.e., one not meeting the rules specified below for a qualifying disposition), the employee will recognize ordinary income as well as capital gain based on the lower of (1) the difference between the exercise price and grant price at exercise ("the spread") or (2) the difference between the grant price and the sale price. However, the spread is a "preference item" for AMT purposes, meaning people who exercise must add back the spread as a taxable item to calculate their AMT obligation and see whether they must pay this tax. ISOs are not subject to the deferred compensation rules under Section 409A of the Code.

For a stock option to qualify as an ISO and thus receive special tax treatment under Section 421(a) of the Code, it must meet the requirements of Section 422 of the Code when granted and at all times beginning from the grant until its exercise. The requirements include:

- The option may be granted only to an employee (grants to non-employee directors or independent contractors are not permitted), who must exercise the option while an employee or no later than three months after termination of employment (unless the optionee is disabled, in which case this three-month period is extended to one year).

- The option must be granted under a written plan document specifying the total number of shares that may be issued and the employees who are eligible to receive the options. The plan must be approved by the stockholders within 12 months before or after plan adoption.

- Each option must be granted under an ISO agreement, which must be written and must list the restrictions placed on exercising the ISO. Each option must set forth an offer to sell the stock at the option price and the period of time during which the option will remain open.

- The option must be granted within 10 years of the earlier of adoption or shareholder approval, and the option must be exercisable only within 10 years of grant.

- The option exercise price must equal or exceed the fair market value of the underlying stock at the time of grant.

- The employee must not, at the time of the grant, own stock representing more than 10% of the voting power of all stock outstanding, unless the option exercise price is at least 110% of the fair market value and the option is not exercisable more than five years from the time of the grant.

- The ISO agreement must specifically state that the ISO cannot be transferred by the option holder other than by will or by the laws of descent and that the option cannot be exercised by anyone other than the option holder.

- The aggregate fair market value (determined as of the grant date) of stock bought by exercising ISOs that are exercisable for the first time cannot exceed $100,000 in a calendar year. To the extent it does, Code Section 422(d) provides that such options are treated as nonqualified options.

Closely held companies must have an acceptable way to determine fair market value at grant, such as an appraisal or a formula acceptable to the IRS.

Stock options require a charge to income based on a present value calculation for grants. To calculate this, companies must use a formula such as Black-Scholes or a binomial model. Such formulas factor in stock volatility, dividends, the term of the option, and other factors to determine what an option would be worth if sold before exercise.

7.3.4 Employee Stock Purchase Plans

Finally, millions of employees become owners in their companies through employee stock purchase plans (ESPPs). Many of these plans are organized under Section 423 of the Code and thus are often called "Section 423" plans. Other ESPPs are "nonqualified" plans, meaning they do not have to meet the special rules of Section 423 and do not get any of the special tax treatment. Most of these plans, however, are very similar in structure. In addition to these broad-based stock purchase plans, companies can simply sell stock to selected employees on terms determined by the company.

Because of the need to comply with securities laws, broad-based stock purchase plans are almost exclusively found in public companies or, to a lesser extent, closely held companies planning on an IPO in the next year. The most tax-favored plan is a Section 423 plan. In these plans, companies must allow all employees to participate (except for 5%-or-more shareholders, who must be excluded), but they can exclude those with less than two years' tenure, part-time employees, and highly compensated employees. All employees must have the same rights and privileges under the plan, although companies can allow purchase limits to vary with relative compensation (most do not do this, however). Plans can limit how much employees can buy, and the law limits it to $25,000 per year.

Section 423 plans, like all ESPPs, operate by allowing employees to have deductions taken out of their pay on an after-tax basis. These deductions accumulate over an "offering period." At a specified time or times, employees can choose to use these accumulated deductions to purchase shares or they can get the money back. Plans can offer discounts of up to 15% on the price of the stock. Most plans allow this discount to be taken based on *either* the price at the beginning or end of the offering period (this is called a "look-back" feature). The offering period can last up to five years if the price employees pay for their stock is based on the share price at the end of the period, or 27 months if it can be determined at an earlier point.

Plan design can vary in a number of ways. For instance, a company might allow employees a 15% discount on the price at the end of the offering period but no discount if they buy shares based on the price at the beginning of the period. Some companies offer employees interim opportunities to buy shares during the offering period. Others provide smaller discounts. Offering periods also vary in length. NCEO studies, however, show that the majority of plans have a look-back feature and provide 15% discounts off the share price at the beginning or end of the offering period. Most of the plans have a 6-month or 12-month offering period, with three months the next most common.

In a typical plan, then, our friend Chip Salter might start participating in an ESPP plan when the shares are worth $40. He puts aside $20 per week for 52 pay periods, accumulating $1,040. The offering period ends in the 52nd week, and Chip decides to buy shares. The current price is $45. Chip will obviously choose to buy shares at 15% off the price at the beginning of the offering period, meaning he can purchase shares at $34. For his $34, he gets shares now worth $45. If the share price had dropped to $38 at the end of the offering period, Chip could buy shares instead at 15% off $38.

The tax treatment of a 423 plan is somewhat similar to that of an incentive stock option. If Chip holds the shares for at least two years after grant and one year after purchase, he pays ordinary income tax on the lesser of (1) the discount as of the time of grant (i.e., the fair market value at the date of grant minus the discount percentage), and (2) the actual gain (the difference between the purchase price and the sale price). He pays capital gains taxes on all additional gain, i.e., the amount of the difference between the purchase price and the sale price that has not been taxed as ordinary income (or, if the sale price is less than the purchase price, there is no ordinary income and he recognizes a capital loss). The company gets no tax deduction, even on the 15% discount.

In our example, suppose that Chip, having bought the shares for $34 (a 15% discount from the $40 value at the date of grant), holds them for at least two years after grant and one year after purchase and sells them for $48 per share. In that case, he will pay ordinary income tax on $6 per share (the lesser of the 15% discount at the date of grant, i.e., $6, and his actual gain of $14). He will pay capital gains tax on the remaining gain, $8 per share ($48 sale price - $34 purchase price - $6 taxed as ordinary income). If Chip does not meet the holding period rules because he sells earlier, then he will pay ordinary income tax on $11 per share, the entire difference between the purchase price ($34) and the market value at purchase ($45). Any increase or decrease in value between the market value at purchase and the sale price is a capital gain or loss. The company gets a tax deduction for the amount recognized as ordinary income ($11 per share in this case).

Nonqualified ESPPs usually work much the same way, but there are no rules for how they must be structured and no special tax benefits; in fact, nonqualified ESPPs that offer discounts are subject to the deferred compensation rules of Code Section 409A, which effectively means the employee would have to choose a payout date in advance or pay steep penalty taxes.

ESPPs are found almost exclusively in public companies because the offering of stock to employees requires compliance with costly and complex securities laws. Closely held companies can, and sometimes do, have these plans, however. Offerings of stock only to employees can qualify for an exemption from securities registration requirements at the federal level, although they will have to comply with anti-fraud disclosure rules and, possibly, state securities laws as well. If they do offer stock in a stock purchase plan, it is highly advisable they obtain at least an annual appraisal.

As with options, companies must show the cost of an ESPP as a charge to income, based on a present value calculation of the value of the discount plus any look-back feature. Discounts of 5% of less with no look-back feature, however, are not covered by this requirement.

7.4 Making the Choice

Deciding on what kind of equity award plan to have requires careful consideration of several factors, most prominently:

- Is there a substantive reason for not giving out shares to employees, such as a legitimate concern about losing control or a corporate structure that does not provide for shares (such as an LLC or partnership, or the company is an operating unit of a foreign corporation that cannot or does not want to make its share available)?

- Is the company willing to forego the tax benefits of other kinds of ownership plans in return for the greater flexibility of a phantom stock, restricted stock, or SAR plan?

- Does the owner of a closely held company either not want to sell or not need or care about the tax benefits offered by an ESOP?

- Is there a strong philosophical commitment to employees actually buying shares, but qualified plan approaches to this look too cumbersome or restricted?

- Is the company too small to make the legal costs of a more formal plan practical?

- Is the employer-employee relationship strong enough so that employees will believe that stock appreciation rights or phantom shares are "real?"

- Does the employer have other plans already in place (such as a 100% ESOP or an S corporation with close to 75 shareholders) that may preclude providing options or other share plans to a selected group of employees it wants to reward?

If the company does not fall into one of these categories, then the four plans described in this section (ESOPs, stock options, 401(k) plans, and ESPPs) at least deserve a careful look.

CHAPTER EIGHT

A Tiered Approach to Equity Design with Multiple Equity Compensation Vehicles

Martin Staubus
Blair Jones
Daniel Janich
Clare Hatfield

Contents

There was a time, not so very long ago, when equity compensation was simple. With technology companies leading the way, employers who wanted to give their people a stake in the growth of the company turned to a single, "no-brainer" solution: stock options. And who could argue with that strategy? After all, stock options are unrivalled in the linkage they create between employee compensation and growth in a company's stock price. Even better for the employers of that era, those options were free—free in terms of cash costs, free in terms of financial reporting, and free of taxation to the employees (at least until exercise).

My, how things have changed. In the years since the technology-led "bubble economy" burst, changing economic conditions have brought the limitations of stock options sharply into focus. Companies have learned that while stock options perform admirably when equity prices are rising, they lose their luster when growth slows, and blow up in your face when stock prices fall. And options are no longer free. Today's accounting standards now require that stock options be expensed on corporate financial statements, thereby taking an uncomfortable bite out of the reported bottom line.

As the significant limitations of stock options have become apparent, many companies have turned to other equity compensation vehicles, with restricted stock having received the most acclaim as the "true successor" to stock options for twenty-first century equity compensation design. While that vehicle—and variations on the theme such as restricted stock units—has been implemented by a good number of companies, there is a notable absence of consensus that it is indeed the "chosen one," the worthy successor to stock options as "the" answer to every company's equity compensation needs.

Indeed, an undeniable truth is that there simply is no "true successor" to stock options in equity compensation—no single, universally embraced approach of the "one size fits all" variety. Instead, the picture that is emerging as the business cycle moves through a new round of growth has two notable features. First, companies are no longer acting in lockstep, all using essentially the same approach, as they did during the dot-com era. Instead, companies have come to recognize that each must evaluate for itself its own unique needs and circumstances to fashion an equity program that works well for it, and that the program that is right for one company may be quite different from the one being implemented by competitors down the street. Second, few companies are finding the perfect and complete answer in a single equity compensation vehicle. As outlined in table 8-1, there is a range of vehicles that companies can draw on in fashioning their equity plans that extends well beyond options and restricted stock. Instead of relying upon just one equity compensation vehicle, effective equity compensation programs are increasingly composed of a combination of vehicles, uniquely blended at each company to achieve a range of business objectives, and with each element offsetting the potential vulnerabilities of the others.

There is nothing new per se in having multiple equity compensation plans. Public companies especially have frequently employed a mix of equity vehicles, typically including stock options, ESPPs, 401(k) matches, and more. However, companies both public and private often lack a well-developed strategy for coordinating their multiple equity plans and integrating those diverse vehicles into a comprehensive employee ownership program.

We present here just such a strategy, which we call a "tiered" approach to equity program design. This approach can help a company harness the advantages of multiple equity vehicles with an eye toward the big picture to achieve coordinated, comprehensive results. For companies that have only a single equity plan, this chapter will show the benefit of using multiple equity plans. For companies that already have multiple equity plans, this chapter will discuss how they may be organized to work more effectively together. Also included are examples of how individual companies are applying the tiered approach to equity compensation design. Finally, we illustrate how a private company can use an ESOP to make a market for shares that employees acquire through the other equity vehicles in the company's tiered program—an important consideration where there is no existing market for the shares.

8.1 Preliminary Considerations

When companies restructure their equity compensation programs, whether to attract and retain talent, motivate individuals to achieve key goals, build a team-oriented culture, or achieve something else, they will be required to address a host of critical issues that relate to the continuing appropriateness of their equity compensation designs. The following four considerations will serve as guideposts when going through this process.

Table 8-1. Tax and Accounting Impacts of Different Equity Vehicles

| Vehicle | Tax | | Accounting |
	Company[a]	Employee	
Stock options	Spread deductible at exercise	Spread taxable at exercise	Fair value of options expensed
Performance-based stock options/shares	Spread deductible at exercise/full value deductible when earned	Spread deductible at exercise/full value deductible when earned	Full value of option shares earned expensed over performance period
Cash-settled SARs	Spread deductible at exercise	Spread taxable at exercise	Treated as a liability
Stock-settled SARs	Spread deductible at exercise	Spread taxable at exercise	Treated like a stock option
Stock grants	Full value deductible at grant	Full value taxed at grant	Full value expensed
Restricted stock/ restricted stock units	Full value deductible at vesting/issuance	Full shares taxable at vesting/issuance	Full value expensed over vesting period
ESOPs	Contributions and dividends deductible when made	Taxed when benefits are received	Interest and cost of allocated shares expensed
Qualified (423) stock purchase plans	No deduction	Taxed at sale (ordinary income/ capital gain)	Fair value expensed if discount is greater than 5%
Nonqualified stock purchase plans	Spread and discount deductible at exercise	Spread and discount taxable at exercise	Fair value is expensed
401(k)	Pretax contributions deductible when made	Taxed when benefits are received	Contributions expensed
Qualified and nonqualified deferred compensation	Deductible when benefits paid	Taxed when benefits are received	Expensed and carried as a liability

[a] Subject to Section 162(m) or applicable tax qualification rules, as the case may be.

8.1.1 Think Deeply about Why You Want to Share Company Equity and How It Will Lead to Improved Business Performance

As wise heads have long pointed out, "If you don't know where you're going, any road will get you there." And indeed, in their rush to "benchmark" and keep up with what everyone else was doing, many companies in the past plunged into equity compensation without a carefully developed idea of how (i.e., by what mechanisms) such a program would improve the performance of the company. During the technology boom, many companies certainly didn't need a profound analysis. The reality they encountered, very simply, was that they couldn't hire the people they needed unless they offered stock options. Understandably, that was all the reason they needed to implement an equity plan.

With labor markets less overheated today, there is room for deeper reflection on the question of whether and how a company might improve corporate results by giving employees an equity stake in the business. In general, approaches to employee stock ownership tend to fall into two camps:

- The "compensation" camp cleaves to a traditional model of the business organization, seeing employees as people who are hired to work in an enterprise that is ultimately operated for the benefit of others (outside shareholders). With little inherent interest in their employer's success, these individuals need incentives—incentives to come to work for the employer and, once there, incentives to perform diligently. For adherents to the compensation camp, equity serves as a useful addition to the array of incentives that are available to organizations to foster effective performance by employees.

- The "ownership" camp seeks to redefine traditional employee roles and relationships, using shared equity as the foundation for a new approach in which the people at all levels of the organization see themselves as partners in a team united by, and focused on, a common financial stake in the success of the business. While traditional companies typically feature an "us" and "them" culture that divides management from the rest, companies in the ownership camp seek to create an organization in which there is only "us"—co-owners with a shared commitment to company success.

Fundamental to a company's reexamination of equity compensation strategies and programs, then, is an assessment of where it wants to be along the spectrum of organizational models—whether it wants to "incent" employees who are otherwise seen as lacking an intrinsic reason to perform, to build an organizational culture in which employees are "co-owners" and central stakeholders in their own right, or whether it wants to design equity programs to achieve both of these goals.

8.1.2 Look More Broadly than Stock Options

There is a diverse range of equity compensation vehicles from which companies can choose in fashioning programs to share ownership and create long-term incentives. These include grants of stock (usually "restricted" by a vesting requirement), stock purchase programs, qualified retirement programs such as 401(k) plans and ESOPs, deferred compensation, synthetic equity (SARs and phantom stock) and a host of variations on these basic themes.

Determining which of these many choices may be right for a given company will involve an assessment of that company's business situation. Selecting the right equity vehicle(s) for a given company will be influenced by:

- The current growth stage of the business (i.e., start-up, growth, or maturing).

- The long-term strategic goals (i.e., is the goal to push for maximum short-term growth and then sell the company, or is the goal to create a company that is "built to last"?).

- The specific purposes that the plan is intended to achieve (e.g., attraction and retention of good employees, motivating employees to improve performance, building a nest egg for retirement, or repositioning employees as central stakeholders).

- The accounting impact (see table 8-1) and economic impact—i.e., what is affordable for the company in terms of impact on cash flow, dilution, and unwanted turnover.

8.1.3 Do Not Assume a Single Vehicle Will Emerge as the Clear Choice for Every Company

It was, and remains, too much to expect any single equity vehicle to be "all things to all companies." Bottom line, the vehicles that work for one company may not be appropriate for another company or even for the same company at a later stage in its development. For example, many commentators have suggested that Microsoft chose to move from stock options to restricted stock units in recognition of its transition from a company experiencing rapid growth to one that is more mature and focused upon longer-range goals. The creation of an effective equity compensation program, therefore, requires that it be designed to fit the company's present situation with an understanding that its elements will likely change with the company's circumstances.

8.1.4 Employ a Combination of Vehicles for Maximum Impact

Each equity vehicle has both strong points and weak points. When a company attempts to rely on just one vehicle, the danger is that the weaknesses inherent in that particular vehicle may cripple the program and result in its falling short of ideal effectiveness. As an alternative, companies may find that if they assemble an equity-sharing program that employs more than one equity vehicle, the weaknesses inherent in any one vehicle may be offset to some degree by strengths in one or more other vehicles. Like investors who diversify their investments among several different stocks so that weak performance by one can be offset by strengths in others, companies are likely to find that they will create the most effective equity compensation program by combining several equity compensation vehicles into a multi-tiered program.

8.2 Building Effective Equity Programs by Combining Vehicles: A Tiered Approach to Equity Design

As discussed above, the choices on the equity compensation menu are many: stock options, restricted stock, ESPPs, ESOPs, 401(k) plans, synthetic equity, stock-settled SARs and more. How does one go about selecting from these diverse choices to produce an effective employee ownership program? Do you just throw them at the wall to see what sticks? Or can there be a method to this madness?

To get a handle on the effective design of equity programs, it may be effective to think about a company's program as having three tiers, as illustrated in table 8-2.

Table 8-2. A Tiered Approach to Multiple Equity Vehicle Programs

Tier	Purpose	Example equity vehicles
Investment tier	• Encourages employees who are committed to the company to invest their own money in the business • At a private company especially, this can be a special privilege that outsiders do not have	• ESPP • Nonqualified compensation deferral • 401(k) employee investment
Performance tier	• Awards more ownership to individuals who contribute more to the growth of the company	• Stock options • Restricted stock
Base tier	• Assures that every employee will have at least a basic financial stake in the future success of the company	• ESOP • 401(k) employer match

Each tier is focused on achieving different objectives for the business:

- A *base tier* is used to create broadly shared, long-term employee ownership, ensuring that every employee has a stake in the company's success. It sends the message that "we're all in this together, we all have a stake in the fortunes of this company." In most large organizations, this would likely be in the form of a highly tax-efficient vehicle such as an employee stock ownership plan (ESOP) or 401(k) employer-matching contributions.

- The *performance tier* is designed to offer additional ownership to incent and reward those employees who make special contributions to the growth of the company. This will typically be done through such vehicles as stock options or restricted stock awards. In this tier, awards are tied to individual performance, and payouts should be clearly linked to the creation of shareholder value.

- The *investment tier* allows employees who are committed to the company to invest their own money in the business. Public companies can take advantage of the ESPP vehicle for this purpose, while private companies can offer direct share purchase opportunities.

This tiered approach to equity compensation design allows a company to use equity in various ways to motivate and reward behaviors of different groups of employees that are required to drive the company's success. While most companies will have elements relevant to each tier, different emphasis may be placed on different tiers, and different designs may be used to accomplish objectives in the three tiers. These differences might depend upon whether the company is public or private.

8.3 ESPPs After FAS 123(R)

In addition to requiring companies to recognize the fair value of stock options as an expense on their financial statements, the new accounting standard under FAS 123(R), effective for reporting periods of large public companies that start after June 15, 2005, and for fiscal years of small public companies (with revenues of less than $25 million annually) and nonpublic companies that begin after December 15, 2005, has also affected the recognition of expense relating to ESPP awards by requiring such awards to be treated for accounting purposes as the grant of a stock option when the offering period commences, unless three conditions are satisfied that would allow such awards to receive "noncompensatory" treatment. These three conditions require the plan to: (1) offer a discount that does not exceed the cost of offering shares through an underwriter; (2) be broad-based; and (3) have no option-like features such as look-backs, which allow the purchase price to be set using the lower of the stock price on the first or last day of the offering period.

Although the new accounting rules allow companies to assume that their underwriting costs are at least 5%, thus allowing for a 5% discount without triggering compensatory accounting treatment, the failure of the conditions for "noncompensatory" treatment to allow either a look-back period or a greater discount akin to the 15% discount allowed before the adoption of the new accounting rules has caused some companies to conclude that perhaps the days of ESPPs are over. Early surveys, however, have shown that ESPPs may in fact be here to stay as companies in greater numbers recognize the value that ESPPs provide in promoting an ownership culture and have come to realize that the accounting expense may be manageable. Consequently, companies with ESPPs and those considering one are placing a greater focus upon controlling the accounting expense associated with maintaining an ESPP through creative plan design.

The earnings charge—and thus the "on-the-books-cost" of maintaining an ESPP—that FAS 123(R) now requires to be recognized may be reduced in one or more of the following ways: by reducing the maximum amount employees can invest; by reducing the employee purchase discount; or by eliminating or reducing the look-back. The most effective of these plan design changes will attempt to balance the impact that such change will have upon the earnings charge against any adverse impact that the change will have upon the plan's continuing employee participation levels. Recent studies suggest that reduction—rather than elimination—of the look-back period will likely provide the greatest reduction in earnings charge without a significant risk of reducing plan participation. Thus, at the very least we should expect to see ESPPs with much shorter offering periods than what was common in the recent past.

Although the new accounting standards certainly will cause companies to reexamine the future role that ESPPs will be expected to play in overall equity compensation strategy, a newer version of ESPPs that effectively controls the accounting expense will continue to find a place in the mix of equity compensation programs from which employers may choose in designing their multi-tiered program.

8.4 Six Benefits of Using Multiple Equity Vehicles in a Tiered Approach

Companies may find a number of appealing advantages to using multiple equity vehicles in a tiered approach to equity design, including:

1. *Achieves multiple objectives:* Using more than one equity vehicle can allow a company to achieve multiple objectives. For example, a company may wish to build an organizational culture that focuses company-wide attention on business performance and encourages conscientious job performance through a base tier that is built on

a longer-term focused vehicle (such as an ESOP or equity grants at hire). At the same time, the company may want to focus top management and other key contributors on building intermediate and longer-term shareholder wealth through a tier of performance-based restricted stock, stock options, or annual incentives that pay out in stock or restricted stock. Selected individuals could also have the opportunity to invest further in the company through a nonqualified deferred compensation plan with company stock as an investment alternative. In this way, the company uses multiple equity vehicles to achieve multiple objectives, where one vehicle standing alone may end up "just missing" on all objectives.

2. *Maximizes tax efficiency while retaining flexibility:* While ESOPs and 401(k) plans offer tremendous tax benefits—giving the company a deduction for the full value of any equity contributed to the plan while imposing no current tax liability on the employees who receive that equity—these tax-qualified vehicles come with rules that significantly limit the company's ability to determine which employees will get how much of the total equity pie. By using a tax-qualified plan as the base tier while "topping off" as needed with a second vehicle that is not restricted by federal income tax nondiscrimination rules (but at the cost of the favorable tax treatment), a company can capture most of the tax benefits that could be obtained by relying exclusively on a qualified plan while gaining the flexibility to create incentives and rewards for those who earn them.

3. *Protects against unintended consequences within a tier:* Multiple equity vehicles within a tier can be structured to complement each other to achieve the right objectives in the right way. For example, stock options alone allow holders to realize gains based on absolute stock price appreciation. However, complementing stock options with restricted stock that vests based on relative total shareholder return can create a powerful combination that sends the message that the real focus is sustained above-average wealth creation for shareholders.

4. *Provides a balance between long-term and short-term equity interests:* Another advantage of combining vehicles is that it enables a company to provide part of its equity awards in a form that gives the

employee-shareholder the freedom to control when he or she will liquidate the equity while providing other equity that must be held for the long term. If employees cannot cash in their equity except at retirement, many will see a very limited value in that equity. At the same time, if employees can, and do, sell off their equity within a short time after receiving it, the linkage between company performance and the employee's financial well-being will come to an end. ESOPs and 401(k) plans, for example, are retirement programs that pay out only after the employee leaves the company (except for certain exceptions such as dividends on ESOP-held stock paid directly to employees), while gains on vested stock options and the value of restricted stock (once vested) may be realized whenever the employee chooses. Providing a balance of long-term and short-term equity interests will likely produce the optimal outcome.

5. *Manages dilution:* Companies also need to be cognizant of the fact that different vehicles tend to lead to different levels of dilution. By using vehicles with different dilutive impacts, companies can manage dilution. For example, a company that has in the past relied solely on stock options (a highly dilutive vehicle) could reduce dilution by substituting another, less dilutive, vehicle (such as performance-restricted stock) in place of at least some of the erstwhile option awards.

6. *Manages predictability of payout:* Different equity vehicles also provide distinct future gain opportunities. While future stock option gains may be difficult to predict, restricted stock values operate within a more certain range. Therefore, companies can gauge the level of predictability required for their equity compensation program by adjusting grant patterns of different vehicles to balance near-term pay delivery needs with longer-term opportunities.

8.5 Risks to Be Managed When Combining Multiple Vehicles

Despite the advantages that companies might realize by combining equity vehicles, a number of risks exist that also need to be managed when designing a multi-vehicle equity compensation program. These risks include:

1. *Too many vehicles can become too complex:* From a practical design perspective, the idea is not to use multiple vehicles for multiple vehicles' sake but to use multiple vehicles in pursuit of a stronger program than would exist using one vehicle. This means every vehicle needs to have a specific role to play, and to the extent the design of the vehicle can make its purpose transparent, all the better. Well-designed communications can also ease concerns about complexity and greatly enhance the effectiveness of a given design.

2. *The performance tier may have inadequate leverage:* Many companies have responded to the reduced appeal of stock options by replacing some, or all, of their performance tier stock option opportunity with another equity vehicle. These companies must be mindful that replacing stock options with a vehicle that has less potential upside for employees could dampen the entrepreneurial drive that this tier of the equity program is intended to foster.

3. *The equity design may become all about pay delivery:* A multi-tiered design would be misused if it were seen solely as a way of delivering immediate pay to employees. Companies must make sure that the overarching focus of its equity program is not so much on what the equity is worth at grant but on what the employees, through their performance, can make it worth in the future. If a grant of $10,000 of equity is seen simply as $10,000 of pay, it loses its power to incent employees to build shareholder value or to promote a culture in which employees are seen, and behave, as owners themselves.

8.6 Public Companies: Emerging Practices

Most activity among public companies appears to be in the performance tier, where companies are diversifying the vehicles they are using to address the current environment and stock options' shortfalls. A few companies are sticking steadfastly with stock options as their vehicle of choice in the performance tier, they are likely to be in the minority. These tend to be companies that have historically exceeded peer group performance levels and have strong communication to help employees understand how their jobs impact stock price performance.

Initially, diversification focused primarily on the replacement of options with service-vested restricted stock. To drive greater performance in the performance tier, this trend has evolved to include a high prevalence of performance restrictions, which ultimately might prove to be a powerful adjunct to stock options, linking vesting to achievement of strategic business results. Another interesting variation in the restricted stock arena is to allow executives to voluntarily defer bonus payments to buy discounted restricted stock, typically with cliff vesting provisions (e.g., at HCA).

Common to all of these practices, the desire on the part of investors that senior executives in particular have some "skin in the game" is as strong as ever, given the continuing corporate scandals that have fueled regulatory and legislative changes. This has raised interest at some companies in new investment tier alternatives. In many cases, the vehicles now fulfilling the objectives of the investment tier are simpler than their earlier counterparts but no less powerful in the messages that they send. One of the more popular methods currently in practice is to mandate executives to defer a portion of their bonuses into company stock, often with ownership requirements attached. First coming to prominence in the early 1990s, ownership guidelines, which require executives to hold a certain level of stock (often expressed as multiples of salary) are making a return in aligning executive and shareholder interests.

Tables 8-3 and 8-4 illustrate what two public companies are doing at this time with multi-tier equity programs.

Table 8-3. Public Company Example A:
Multi-Billion Dollar Pharmaceutical Company

Investment tier	A nonqualified bonus deferral program allows a select group of senior management to defer portions of their salaries and bonuses, with company stock as one investment option.
Performance tier	Stock options combined with performance shares earned based on financial performance focus executives on intermediate drivers of business value in addition to longer-term stock price appreciation.
Base tier	Company-wide stock option grants every two years provide lots of opportunity for all employees to build ownership in their company and a 401(k) investment option in company stock.

Table 8-4. Public Company Example B:
Multi-Billion Dollar Hospital Management Company

Investment tier	A nonqualified stock purchase plan allows members of the executive team to defer their bonuses to purchase restricted stock at a 25% discount to fair market value. The restricted stock cliff-vests after three years and is coupled with stringent ownership expectations to ensure significant long-term ownership levels.
Performance tier	Stock options, combined with earned annual equity, reinforce short- and longer-term performance achievement. Earned annual equity is restricted stock that is earned based on achievement of annual performance objectives within individuals' control. Once earned, the restricted stock vests over two years. This approach reinforces employee ownership and complements stock options by providing a vehicle with higher "line-of-sight" because the basis for earning awards is within employees' control.
Base tier	An ESOP ensures all employees have some stake in the company.

8.7 Private Companies: Emerging Practices

Private companies may have more latitude, especially in the investment tier, because their stock will generally be unavailable for purchase unless specially offered by the company. Our first example is one of the growing legends in the world of employee stock ownership, Springfield ReManufacturing Corporation (SRC) and its remarkable CEO, Jack Stack (author of "The Great Game of Business" and "A Stake in the Outcome"). From its beginnings in the mid-1980s as a management buyout of a grimy little diesel engine rebuilding plant from an old and dying International Harvester, SRC has used its employee stock ownership programs as the foundation for an operation philosophy that has seen its stock price climb from $1 a share at the time of the buyout to more than $900 a share currently.

SRC's employee stock ownership system consists of three tiers. At its base is an ESOP, which assures a solid, long-term ownership stake for all employees on highly tax-advantaged terms (for both the company and the employees). The ESOP holds about one-third of the equity in the SRC employee stock ownership system. To combat any tendency toward complacency, the company also issues stock options to anyone in the organization who is in a position to be a key driver of growth for the organization. The outstanding stock options represent another one-third of the equity in the program. The final third of the employee-owned stock is represented by shares of stock that employees have purchased for their own investment.

Tables 8-5 and 8-6 illustrate how two other private firms—an engineering firm and a management consulting firm respectively—have structured their multi-tier equity programs.

**Table 8-5. Private Company Example B:
150-Employee Engineering Firm**

Investment tier	Annual cash profit-sharing bonuses may be invested in company stock, with employee-investors receiving a "free" stock option for every two shares purchased.
Performance tier	Stock options granted to reward actions that are anticipated to produce revenue in the future. Restricted stock granted to reward current revenue production.
Base tier	Employee stock ownership plan (ESOP) that purchases shares from founding shareholders to hold for all permanent, full-time employees.

**Table 8-6. Private Company Example C:
100-Employee Management Consulting Firm**

Investment tier	Purchase opportunities granted to newly hired consultants to give them the ability to increase their ownership stake early on.
Performance tier	Restricted stock granted to reward current revenue production.
Base tier	Employee stock ownership plan (ESOP) that purchases shares from founding partners and from employees who want to sell shares they acquired through the other tiers of the equity program.

8.7.1 The ESOP as a Market for Shares Owned by Employees in Private Companies

Note that in example C (table 8-6), the company is using the ESOP not only as the base tier of its equity ownership program *but also as a market for stock that employees acquire through the other tiers*. This creative method of gaining multiple benefits from diverse equity vehicles offers tremendous power to private companies, who otherwise inevitably struggle with the difficulty of providing liquidity to shareholders, including employees who acquire company equity.

Generally, money that a company spends on redeeming stock from a shareholder is not deductible; it is an after-tax expenditure. A company with an ESOP, however, can channel the money that it has earmarked for stock redemptions through the ESOP, making every penny of that money deductible for corporate income tax purposes. With companies in most states paying a combined federal and state tax bill in excess of 40%, a company that provides liquidity to employee-shareholders via its ESOP is in effect getting the IRS and the state to provide 40% of the funding for such redemptions. These redemptions by the ESOP in turn provide a continuing source of shares to feed into the "base tier" so that new employees can participate and all employees can build their equity interests over time as they remain with the company. The result is a dynamic system of employee stock ownership in which equity can be acquired by employees through multiple, flexible vehicles while providing a financially efficient mechanism for shareholder liquidity and a continuous renewal of the program.

8.8 Conclusion

Many companies are reconsidering their use of stock options. That does not mean that they will abandon employee stock ownership. A truly effective equity plan starts with a soul-searching evaluation of what the company wants to get out of it. By fashioning a set of complementary equity vehicles into a multi-tiered program, a company can tailor its equity program to fit its individual needs. Don't be disheartened by the end of the glory days for stock options. There are plenty of other equity vehicles out there, and more than one is likely to be suitable as an adjunct to, or substitute for, stock options.

Using the
Model Plan Documents

This part of the book provides model documents for the various plans discussed in this book. These documents are included on the CD attached to the inside back cover. At various points, optional provisions and comments to the book's readers have been inserted in square brackets. In some of the plans, endnotes comment on various provisions.

Please note that these model agreements contain common features found in these types of plans but are drafted to provide general terms only. The terms of any actual plan, however, should be tailored to the needs and situation of a particular company. For example, state securities laws vary and may affect the drafting of a plan.

The model plans and agreements have been prepared for use by stock corporations. With appropriate modifications, they may be used by limited liability companies (LLCs). If a limited liability company intends to grant restricted securities to its employees, it should also consult with its legal and financial advisors regarding the possible treatment of employee owners for employment tax purposes.

Although the authors have attempted to identify common legal or accounting issues relating to common provisions in these types of plans, by publishing these documents, neither the NCEO nor the authors and their firms shall be deemed to be providing legal advice. Before using any of the model documents, a company should consult with its own legal and accounting advisors.

Contents of the CD

The CD is organized as follows: Each appendix (Appendix A, etc.) is represented by a directory (folder) named after it. Within each directory, there are different files for each document in that appendix. Each document is provided in both Microsoft Word format and, in case your word processor cannot open the Word file, Rich Text Format.

Phantom Stock Plan Documents

Robin Struve
Kay Kemp

The following documents are included on the CD-ROM that accompanies this book. These are sample documents that must be customized before being used. A company should consult with its own legal and accounting advisors before implementing any equity (or equity-equivalent) compensation plan. Before working with these documents, please read appendix A of this book for more information and important disclaimers.

ABC CORPORATION PHANTOM STOCK PLAN

1. PURPOSE OF THE PLAN

ABC Corporation (the "Company"), a corporation organized under the laws of the State of _____, hereby adopts this Phantom Stock Plan (the "Plan"). The purposes of the Plan are:

(a) To promote the long-term financial interests and growth of the Company and its Subsidiaries (as defined below) by attracting and retaining management and personnel with the training, experience, and ability to enable them to make a substantial contribution to the success of the business of the Company and its Subsidiaries;

(b) To motivate personnel by means of growth-related incentives to achieve long range goals;

(c) To further the identity of interests of participants with those of the Company's stockholders (as defined below) through opportunities for equity-based ownership in the Company; and

(d) To allow each participant to share in the increase in value of the Company following the date such participant is granted Phantom Stock (as defined below) in accordance with the terms of the Plan.

2.   DEFINITIONS

(a)   "Administrator" means the Board of Directors or a committee of the Board of Directors appointed to serve as the administrator of the Plan.

(b)   "Award" means a grant of Phantom Stock.

(c)   "Award Agreement" an agreement entered into between the Company and the Participant evidencing the terms of Phantom Stock.

(d)   "Board" or "Board of Directors" means the Board of Directors of the Company as it may be constituted from time to time.

(e)   [¹"Change in Control" means the occurrence of any of the following events:

(i)   the acquisition, directly or indirectly, by any "person" or "group" (as those terms are defined in Sections 3(a)(9), 13(d), and 14(d) of the Exchange Act and the rules thereunder) of "beneficial ownership" (as determined pursuant to Rule 13d-3 under the Exchange Act) of securities entitled to vote generally in the election of directors ("voting securities")² of the Company that represent [20%]³ or more of the

---

1.   Include only if Change in Control (CIC) is one of the Vesting Date or payment date triggers. The following definition is generally more relevant for a public company. However, it can be tailored to fit a private company sale also. Because this Plan must comply with Internal Revenue Code ("Code") Section 409A, this definition must conform to the requirements of that section, and the definition of Change in Control must be consistent with the definition in Treas. Dept. Prop. Reg. § 1.409A-3(a)(5).

2.   The Company should consider whether this prong of the definition should be limited to the acquisition of *voting* securities or should apply to outstanding equity securities in general. If the latter, references to "voting securities" and "combined voting power" should be conformed throughout the definition.

3.   The appropriate percentage will depend on a number of factors, including the Company's capital structure, whether there are shareholders that own a significant percentage of stock, whether the Company has a "poison pill" (and if so, what percentage will trigger the pill), and whether the Company uses its stock as currency in significant acquisitions or joint ventures. The range is typically between 15% and 50%.

combined voting power of the Company's[4] then outstanding voting securities, other than:

(A) an acquisition by a trustee or other fiduciary holding securities under any employee benefit plan (or related trust) sponsored or maintained by the Company or any person controlled by the Company or by any employee benefit plan (or related trust) sponsored or maintained by the Company or any person controlled by the Company,

(B) an acquisition of voting securities by the Company or a corporation owned, directly or indirectly, by the stockholders of the Company in substantially the same proportions as their ownership of the stock of the Company,[5] or

(C) an acquisition of voting securities pursuant to a transaction described in clause (iii) below that would not be a Change in Control under clause (iii).[6]

---

4. It is important to make sure that the "Company" as defined in the Plan is the appropriate entity to trigger the CIC. For example, an employment agreement or equity plan at the subsidiary level may define "Company" as the subsidiary entity, and a transaction involving the parent would not necessarily trigger a CIC. Consideration must therefore be given to whether the CIC should be triggered at the parent level, subsidiary level, or both.

5. An additional carve-out that the Company may want to consider here is "any acquisition of [voting securities or equity securities] directly from the Company." The rationale behind this carve-out is that a CIC should not be triggered if the Board or the Company, knowing that the acquisition will result in significant share ownership by the acquiring person, agrees to directly sell the shares to that person in a friendly transaction. Such a carve-out may be important to a company that uses its stock as currency in connection with joint ventures and other business acquisitions. Note that the inclusion of this carve-out should make it easier for the Company to agree to a lower percentage CIC threshold. Consideration should also be given to excepting acquisitions by persons who currently own a significant percentage of the Company's stock, especially if the Company's poison pill contains a similar carve-out for such persons.

6. When drafting a CIC definition, it is important to make sure that all subparts of the definition work together so that a transaction which is excepted from one prong does not unintentionally constitute a CIC under another less obvi-

Notwithstanding the foregoing, neither of the following events shall constitute an "acquisition" by any person or group for purposes of this clause (i): [(x) a change in the voting power of the Company's voting securities based on the relative trading values of the Company's then outstanding securities as determined pursuant to the Company's Articles of Incorporation,[7] or (y)] an acquisition of the Company's securities by the Company that[, either alone or in combination only with the other event,] causes the Company's voting securities beneficially owned by a person or group to represent [20%] or more of the combined voting power of the Company's then outstanding voting securities; *provided, however,* that if a person or group shall become the beneficial owner of [20%] or more of the combined voting power of the Company's then outstanding voting securities by reason of share acquisitions by the Company as described above and shall, after such share acquisitions by the Company, become the beneficial owner of any additional voting securities of the Company, then such acquisition shall constitute a Change in Control.

(ii)   individuals who, as of the date hereof, constitute the Board (the "Incumbent Board") cease for any reason to constitute at least a majority of the Board; *provided, however,* that any individual becoming a director subsequent to the date hereof whose election, or nomination for election by the Company's shareholders, was approved by a vote of at least a majority of the directors then comprising the Incumbent Board shall

---

ous prong. For example, a reverse triangular merger of equals or a "butterfly" merger that would not constitute a CIC under prong (iii) should not trigger a CIC under prong (i) by virtue of the acquisition of [20%] of the Company's voting securities (which would necessarily occur pursuant to such a merger).

7.   Clause (x) is intended to carve out instances where the voting power of the Company's securities could change based on the relative values of different series or classes of those securities (*e.g.,* in the case of a tracking stock). If applicable, consideration should also be given to including a carve-out relating to an acquisition of voting securities that results from the exchange or conversion of other securities.

be considered as though such individual were a member of the Incumbent Board, but excluding, for this purpose, any such individual whose initial assumption of office occurs as a result of an actual or threatened election contest with respect to the election or removal of directors or other actual or threatened solicitation of proxies or consents by or on behalf of a person other than the Board;

(iii) the consummation[8] by the Company (whether directly involving the Company or indirectly involving the Company through one or more intermediaries) of (x) a merger, consolidation, reorganization, or business combination or (y) a sale or other disposition of all or substantially all of the Company's assets or (z) the acquisition of assets or stock of another entity,[9] in each case, other than a transaction:

(A) that results in the Company's voting securities outstanding immediately before the transaction continuing to represent (either by remaining outstanding or by being converted into voting securities of the Company or the person that, as a result of the transaction, controls, directly or indirectly, the Company or owns, directly or indirectly, all or substantially all of the Company's assets or otherwise succeeds to the business of the Company (the Company or such person, the "Successor Entity")) directly or indirectly, at least [50%][10] of the combined voting power of the Successor Entity's

---

8. Note that the *consummation* of the transaction (rather than shareholder approval) is a more appropriate trigger. In several recent high-profile cases (including one involving Sprint and one involving Northrop Grumman), shareholders have sued the company where a CIC was triggered by shareholder approval of a transaction that was never consummated.

9. Clause (z) is intended to address transactions (such as joint ventures) in which the Company uses its stock as currency.

10. This carve-out is intended to except a "merger of equals" or a combination in which the Company's shareholders retain control. The percentage should generally be in the 40% to 60% range. A percentage at the lower end of this range might be appropriate where other components of the carve-out provide the Company with additional protection against the loss of control (such as a

outstanding voting securities immediately after the transaction, and

[(B)   after which more than 50% of the members of the board of directors of the Successor Entity were members of the Incumbent Board at the time of the Board's approval of the agreement providing for the transaction or other action of the Board approving the transaction,[11] and]

(C)   after which no person or group beneficially owns voting securities representing [20%][12] or more of the combined voting power of the Successor Entity; *provided, however,* that no person or group shall be treated for purposes of this clause (C) as beneficially owning [20%] or more of combined voting power of the Successor Entity solely as a result of the voting power held in the Company [and the other entity][13] prior to the consummation of the transaction, or

(iv)   a liquidation or dissolution of the Company.[14]

For purposes of clause (i) above, the calculation of voting power shall be made as if the date of the acquisition were a record date for a vote of the Company's shareholders, and for purposes of clause (iii) above, the calculation of voting power shall be made as if the date of the consummation of the transaction were a record date for a vote of the Company's shareholders.]

(f)   "Code" means the Internal Revenue Code of 1986, as amended.

---

requirement that the Company's directors constitute a majority of the Board of the surviving entity).

11.   The appropriateness of this type of provision will depend on the percentage used in the preceding clause (A). A less common provision might require that the Company's CEO be the CEO of the surviving entity following the CIC.

12.   This percentage should generally be the same as the percentage in prong (i) of the definition. See notes 3 and 6 above.

13.   Consider whether it would be appropriate to also exclude stock ownership by a person who also owns securities of the other entity.

14.   In the case of a liquidation or dissolution, it might be more appropriate for the CIC to be triggered upon shareholder approval of the event.

(g) "Common Stock" means (i) the common stock of the Company, par value $_____ per share, as adjusted as provided in Section 7, or (ii) if there is a merger or consolidation and the Company is not the surviving corporation, the capital stock of the surviving corporation given in exchange for such common stock of the Company.

(h) "Company" means ABC Corporation, a _____ corporation.

(i) ["Disability" means a Participant is, by reason of any medically determinable physical or mental impairment that can be expected to result in death or can be expected to last for a continuous period of at least 12 months, receiving disability benefits for a period of at least three months under the Company's long-term disability programs as in effect from time to time.][15]

(j) "Dividend Equivalent" means the right to receive in cash an amount equal to the dividends that would be paid on a share of Phantom Stock if such Phantom Stock were shares of Common Stock held by the Participant[; provided that, a Dividend Equivalent shall not include any distribution to the Company's shareholders that is intended to allow the members to satisfy their tax obligations due on allocable income of the Company][16].

(k) "Employee" shall mean any officer or other employee (as defined in accordance with Section 3401(c) of the Code) of the Company, or of any corporation which is a Subsidiary.

(l) "Exchange Act" means the Securities Exchange Act of 1934, as amended, and any successor statutes or regulations of similar purpose or effect.

(m) "Fair Market Value" of a share of Common Stock as of a given date shall be (i) the closing price of a share of Common Stock on the principal exchange on which shares of Common Stock are then trading, if any (or as reported on any composite index which includes such principal exchange), on the trading day

---

15. Include if Disability is a vesting or settlement trigger under the Plan.

16. Include if the Company is an S corporation and the Plan provides for payment of Dividend Equivalents to Participants.

previous to such date, or, if shares were not traded on the trading day previous to such date, then on the next preceding date on which a trade occurred, (ii) if Common Stock is not traded on an exchange but is quoted on Nasdaq or a successor quotation system, the mean between the closing representative bid and asked prices for the Common Stock on the trading day previous to such date as reported by Nasdaq or such successor quotation system, or (iii) if Common Stock is not publicly traded on an exchange and not quoted on Nasdaq or a successor quotation system, the Fair Market Value of a share of Common Stock as established by the Administrator acting in good faith.[17]

(n) "Grant Date" means the date an Award is granted to a Participant.

(o) ["Liquidity Event" means any of the following:

    (i)   A Qualifying IPO;

    (ii) The dissolution, liquidation or sale of all or substantially all of the business, properties and assets of the Company; or

    (iii) any acquisition by any person or group (as defined in Section 13(d) of the Exchange Act) of beneficial ownership of more than 90% of the Company's then outstanding shares of common stock, whether by a reorganization, merger, consolidation, sale, or exchange of securities of the Company or otherwise, unless such a transaction is solely between the Company and any affiliate or affiliates of the Company or between any two (2) or more affiliates of the Company.][18]

(p) "Participant" means an Employee who has received an Award that has not been settled, cancelled or forfeited [and which has not expired].[19]

---

17. A private company may establish a formula price for determining Fair Market Value (e.g., book value or multiple of EBITDA). If formula price is being used, the plan or the Award Agreement should specify the formula. Also consider tying Fair Market Value to the price received per share of Common Stock in a Change in Control, Liquidity Event, or Qualifying IPO if any of those events are used as settlement triggers.

18. Liquidity Event is more applicable to a private company and should be tailored to the individual company's situation, depending upon share ownership.

19. Include only if Phantom Stock has an expiration date that could occur prior to Settlement Date.

(q) "Phantom Stock" means a contractual right to receive the Fair Market Value of a share of Common Stock on the Exercise Date and, to the extent provided in the Award Agreement, to receive Dividend Equivalents on and after the Grant Date on each share of Phantom Stock subject to such Award.

(r) "Plan" means the ABC Corporation Phantom Stock Plan, as may be amended from time to time.

(s) ["Qualifying IPO" means a sale of shares of Common Stock pursuant to an effective registration statement of the Company filed by the Company pursuant to the Securities Act in which the gross selling price of the shares of Common Stock is at least $_____ million provided, however, that a Qualifying IPO shall not include (i) a sale of shares of Common Stock pursuant to an effective registration statement of the Company filed by the Company under the Act if such shares of Common Stock were issued in connection with a transaction the primary purpose of which is the issuance and sale of any debt securities of the Company or issued in satisfaction of any interest or other obligations pursuant to the terms of any debt securities of the Company, or (ii) if such sale does not result in shares of Common Stock being held by less than 300 holders.][20]

(t) "Securities Act" means the Securities Act of 1933, as amended, and any successor statutes or regulations of similar purpose or effect.

(u) "Settlement Date" means the date set forth in Section 6 pursuant to which a Participant becomes entitled to payment for his Phantom Stock.

(v) "Subsidiary" means (i) any corporation the majority of the voting power of all classes of stock entitled to vote or the majority of the total value of shares of all classes of stock of which is owned, directly or indirectly, by the Company, or (ii) any trade, business, or other entity other than a corporation of which the majority of the profits interest, capital interest, or actuarial interest is owned, directly or indirectly, by the Company.

---

20. This provision is applicable to private company and should be tailored to expected IPO proceeds.

(w) ["Vesting Date" means the date on which the Participant becomes vested in his Award as provided in Section 5.][21]

3. ADMINISTRATION OF THE PLAN

(a) *Duties and Powers of the Administrator.* The Plan will be administered by the Administrator. The Administrator may adopt its own rules of procedure, and the action of a majority of the Board or committee, as applicable, taken at a meeting or, to the extent permitted by law, taken without a meeting by a writing signed by such majority (or by all or such greater proportion of the members thereof if required by law), shall constitute action by the Administrator. The Administrator shall have the power, authority, and discretion to administer, construe, and interpret the Plan and Award Agreements, including, without limitation, the discretion to determine which Employees shall be Participants and the terms and conditions, subject to the Plan, of the individual Award Agreements. The decisions and interpretations of the Administrator with respect to any matter concerning the Plan shall be final, conclusive, and binding on all parties who have an interest in the Plan. Any such interpretations, rules, and administration shall be consistent with the basic purposes of the Plan.

(b) *Delegation.* In its absolute discretion, the Administrator may delegate to the Chief Executive Officer or other senior officers of the Company its duties under the Plan subject to any conditions and limitations as the Administrator shall prescribe.

(c) *Expenses; Professional Assistance; Good Faith Actions.* All expenses and liabilities incurred by the Administrator in connection with the administration of the Plan shall be borne by the Company. The Administrator may employ attorneys, consultants, accountants, appraisers, brokers, or other persons. The Administrator, the Company and its Subsidiaries, and the officers and directors of the Company and its Subsidiaries shall be entitled to rely upon the advice, opinions, or valuations of any such persons. All

---

21. Include only if Phantom Stock is subject to vesting as well as payment triggers.

actions taken and all interpretations and determinations made by the Administrator in good faith shall be final and binding upon all Participants, the Company and its Subsidiaries, and all other interested persons. No member of the Administrator shall be personally liable for any action, determination or interpretation made in good faith with respect to the Plan or the Awards, and all members of the Administrator shall be fully protected by the Company with respect to any such action, determination, or interpretation.

4. INDIVIDUAL GRANTS; ELIGIBILITY; UNITS

(a) *Eligibility.* Participants will be chosen by the Administrator, in its sole discretion, from Employees who, in the Administrator's judgment, have a significant opportunity to influence the growth of the Company or whose outstanding performance or potential merit further incentive and reward for continued employment and accomplishment.

(b) *Phantom Stock.* The maximum number of shares of Phantom Stock available for Awards under this Plan shall be _____, subject to adjustment as provided in Section 7.

5. AWARDS

(a) *Grant of Awards.* The Administrator may, in its sole discretion, at any time and from time to time grant shares of Phantom Stock to any eligible Employee. Each Award will be evidenced by an Award Agreement containing such terms and conditions, not inconsistent with the Plan, as the Administrator will approve. An Award will become effective upon the execution by the Participant of an Award Agreement, acknowledging the terms and conditions of the Award.

(b) *Unit Accounts.* Any shares of Phantom Stock awarded to a Participant shall be credited to a Phantom Stock account to be maintained on behalf of such Participant. Such account shall be debited by the number of shares of Phantom Stock with respect to which any payments are made pursuant to Section 6.

(c) [*Vesting.* Each Award shall vest on the Vesting Date as specified by the Administrator in the Award Agreement.][22]

[Include vesting terms, if applicable.]

[Any Award, or portion thereof, not vested upon the date of a Participant's termination of employment with the Company and all Subsidiaries will be forfeited, and no payment will be made thereon. If a Participant's employment is terminated for Cause, the Participant shall forfeit any Award, or portion thereof, outstanding as of the date of such termination of employment.][23]

[Notwithstanding the foregoing, each Award shall become fully vested on the Settlement Date.][24]

(d) [*Term.* The term of each Award will be 10 years from Grant Date, unless otherwise specified by the Administrator in the Award Agreement].[25]

6. SETTLEMENT OF PHANTOM STOCK

(a) *Settlement Date.* Each vested Award shall become payable upon the earliest to occur of:[26]

---

22. Include only if Phantom Stock is subject to vesting as well as payment triggers. If all Phantom Stock Awards are to have identical vesting terms, the vesting schedule may be included in the Plan.

23. Consider whether the forfeiture of the Award is appropriate upon termination for Cause. Cause should be defined and consistent with any other definition of Cause that may exist in an Employee's employment agreement.

24. Include only if Settlement Date triggers are to fully vest the Award.

25. Consider whether the Award should have a term limit before the Settlement Date. If the Award has a term limit, then the end of the term will be a settlement trigger under the Plan.

26. Under Code Section 409A, a scheduled payment cannot be accelerated, except in limited circumstances. If desired, this section could provide for the following accelerations: (1) payment of a de minimum amount (under $10,000) could be made immediately upon separation from service (if otherwise a settlement trigger under the Plan); (2) payment could be made to comply with a qualified domestic relations order, or (3) if the Plan is maintained by an S corporation owned all or in part by an ESOP, payment could be made to avoid a nonallocation year under Code Section 409(p).

[Include relevant payment triggers such as a specified payment date,[27] Change in Control, Liquidity Event, Qualifying IPO, death, Disability, separation from service,[28] or other thresholds.][29]

(b) *Settlement of Award.* On the Settlement Date, each Participant shall be entitled to receive an amount in cash[30] for each share of Phan-

---

Conversely, a schedule payment cannot be delayed without violating Code Section 409A, except as follows: (a) to preserve a deduction under Code Section 162(m); (b) if payment would violate a loan covenant or securities laws, (c) if a bona fide dispute exists over the Participant's right to payment, or (d) if immediate payment is administratively or economically impractical. In these cases, distribution must be made as soon as practicable after the obstacle has been removed. Note, however, that payments may not be delayed for any of the aforementioned reasons with respect to amounts that are treated as short-term deferrals under Code Section 409A.

27. The specified payment date would be the last day of the Award term if a term limit is set forth in Section 5(d). Alternatively, the Plan could permit participants to elect a fixed payment date, which election would be specified in the Award Agreement.

28. Separation from service is not often a trigger event, as it could encourage participants to quit in order to receive payment.

29. If the Plan provides for deferral of payment of an Award beyond the year in which the Award vests, then the Plan must comply with the requirements of Code Section 409A, including the following: (1) the definitions of "separation from service" and "change in control" must conform to the applicable definitions prescribed by Code Section 409A; (2) if the company is a public company, then payments made on the separation from service of a specified employee (as defined in Prop. Treas. Reg. § 1.409A-1(i)) will be subject to a six-month wait; and (3) Liquidity Events and Qualifying IPO will not be permissible distribution events unless they can be defined in a manner that conforms to the definition of "change in control" under Code Section 409A. On the other hand, if the Plan were designed to make all payments within 2½ months after the end of the year in which the Award vests (presumably at the expiration of the Award's term), then vesting and payment could be accelerated for specified events (e.g., Liquidity Event, Qualifying IPO, change in control, death, or disability) without violating Code Section 409A.

30. Awards may also settle in stock. However, if Awards are settled in stock, then the Awards will be considered "securities" for Federal and state securities law purposes, and either the Awards and the shares subject to the Awards will need to be registered under the Securities Act of 1933 (the "Securities Act"), or they must satisfy an exemption from registration such as Rule 701 of the Securities

tom Stock awarded to such Participant equal to the Fair Market Value of a share of Common Stock on the Settlement Date, less any required withholding. Payment shall be made within [2½ months] after the end of the year in which the Settlement Date occurs.[31]

(c)   *Dividend Equivalents.* If the Award Agreement provides for payment of Dividend Equivalents, then within 2½ months after the end of each year, the Participant will receive an amount in cash equal to the Dividend Equivalent credited during that year on each share of Phantom Stock subject to such Award.[32]

7.   DILUTION AND OTHER ADJUSTMENTS

In the event of any change in the outstanding shares of Common Stock by reason of any stock dividend or split, recapitalization, merger, consolidation, spin-off, reorganization, combination or exchange of shares, or other similar corporate change, the Administrator will make such

---

Act. State blue sky laws may also affect the ability to settle in stock. If Awards are settled in stock and the company is private, consider applicable transfer restrictions, call rights, and whether or not such shares would be subject to a shareholders' agreement. If shares are subject to any restrictions, the applicable restrictions should be referenced on the stock certificates.

31.   If Awards do not vest until the Settlement Date, and payment is made within 2½ months after the end of the year, then the Plan will satisfy the short-term deferral requirements of Code Section 409(A). If the Plan provides for earlier vesting of Awards, i.e., a vesting schedule is provided in Section 5(c), then the Plan cannot qualify for the short-term deferral. In this case, the Plan may provide for a payment date later than 2½ months after the end of the applicable year, if desired.

32.   This approach will satisfy the short-term deferral requirements of Code Section 409A. Alternatively, the plan could grant equivalent phantom shares of stock to be paid out upon the specified Settlement Date along with the underlying shares. Under Code Section 409A, however, such a grant is viewed as an additional deferral of compensation, for which a new Award Agreement would be required. Note that the requirements of Code Section 409A can be applied separately to dividend equivalents and the underlying phantom shares, so that dividend equivalents could be designed to be short-term deferrals even if the underlying phantom stock awards are viewed as deferred compensation under Code Section 409A.

adjustments, if any, as it in its sole discretion deems equitable in the number of shares of Common Stock with respect to which an Award held by any Participant is referenced, such adjustments to be conclusive and binding upon all parties concerned.

8. CANCELLATION OF AWARDS

The Administrator may cancel all or any part of an Award with the written consent of the Participant holding such Award. In the event of any cancellation, all rights of the former Participant in respect of such cancelled Award will terminate.

9. MISCELLANEOUS PROVISIONS

(a) *Assignment and Transfer*. Awards will not be transferable other than by will or the laws of descent and distribution and may be realized, during the lifetime of the Participant, only by the Participant or by his or her guardian or legal representative. No Award or interest or right therein shall be liable for the debts, contracts, or engagements of the Participant or his successors in interest or shall be subject to disposition by transfer, alienation, anticipation, pledge, encumbrance, assignment, or any other means whether such disposition be voluntary or involuntary or by operation of law by judgment, levy, attachment, garnishment, or any other legal or equitable proceedings (including bankruptcy), and any attempted disposition thereof shall be null and void and of no effect, except to the extent that such disposition is permitted by the preceding sentence.

(b) *No Right to Awards or Employment*. No Employee or other person will have any claim or right to be granted an Award. Neither the Plan nor any action taken hereunder will be construed as giving any Employee or Participant any right to be retained in the employ of the Company or any of its Subsidiaries.

(c) *General Creditor Status*. Obligations of the Company and its Subsidiaries under the Plan shall be unsecured and unfunded obligations, and the holders of Awards shall be general creditors of the Company.

(d)   *Withholding.* The Company and its Subsidiaries will have the right to deduct from payment of an Award any taxes required by law to be withheld from an Employee with respect to such payment.[33]

(e)   *Securities Laws.* Each Award will be subject to the condition that such Award may not be exercised if the Administrator determines that the exercise of such Award may violate the Securities Act or any other law or requirement of any governmental authority. The Company will not be deemed by any reason of the granting of any Award to have any obligation to register the Awards or shares underlying such Awards under the Securities Act or to maintain in effect any registration of such Awards or shares that may be made at any time under the Securities Act.

(f)   *No Strict Construction.* No rule of strict construction will be applied against the Company, the Administrator, or any other person in the interpretation of any of the terms of the Plan, any Award, or any rule or procedure established by the Administrator.

(g)   *Stockholder Rights.* A Participant will not have any dividend, voting, or other stockholder rights by reason of a grant of an Award or settlement of an Award.

(h)   *Severability.* Whenever possibility, each provision in the Plan and in every Award Agreement will be interpreted in such manner as to be effective and valid under applicable law, but if any provision of this Plan or any Award Agreement made thereunder will be held to be prohibited by or invalid under applicable law, then (i) such provision will be deemed amended to, and to have contained from the outset such language will be necessary to, accomplish the objectives of the provision as originally written to the fullest extent permitted by law, and (ii) all other provisions of the Plan and every Award Agreement will remain in full force and effect.

(i)   *Governing Law.* The Plan will be governed by and construed in accordance with the laws of the United States of America and, to the extent not inconsistent therewith, by the laws of the State of _____ without regard to conflicts of laws thereof.

---

33. This section could provide that payments may be accelerated to pay the taxes resulting from a failure to satisfy the requirements of Code Section 409A.

10. AMENDMENT AND TERMINATION

The Administrator may at any time amend, suspend, or terminate the Plan, provided that no such action will adversely affect any rights under any Awards theretofore granted or change the vesting applicable to an Award in a manner adverse to a Participant, except in accordance with Section 7.[34]

11. EFFECTIVE DATE OF THE PLAN

The Plan will become effective as of _____.

* * *

I hereby certify that the foregoing Plan was duly adopted by the Board of Directors of ABC Corporation on _____.

Executed on this _____ day of _____.

Secretary

---

34. Under Code Section 409A, the Plan can be terminated and payments accelerated at the discretion of the Company only if the Plan so provides and the Plan otherwise meets one of the following requirements: (1) all stock right plans must be terminated with respect to all participants, (2) distributions on account of termination can be made no earlier than 12 months after the termination, (3) all distributions must be made within 24 months of the termination, and (4) no new stock rights plans may be adopted within the five-year period after the termination. The Plan could also provide that it would be terminated within 12 months after a Change in Control, or upon corporate liquidation or with the approval of a bankruptcy court, as long as all substantially similar arrangements were terminated and all payments were made to Participants within 12 months after termination.

ABC CORPORATION
PHANTOM STOCK AWARD AGREEMENT

THIS PHANTOM STOCK AWARD AGREEMENT (the "Agreement"), made this _____ day of _____, 20___ (the "Grant Date"), between ABC Corporation, a _____ corporation (the "Company"), and _____ (the "Participant").

WITNESSETH:

WHEREAS, the Company maintains the ABC Corporation Phantom Stock Plan (the "Plan"), as it may hereafter be amended and continued, in order to attract and retain quality management personnel and provide its officers and other key employees with incentives to achieve long-term corporate objectives;

WHEREAS, the Participant is an officer or other key employee of the Company with responsibility for the management or administration of the Company's business;

WHEREAS, the Plan's Administrator has determined to grant Phantom Stock under the Plan to the Participant on the terms and conditions set forth below.

NOW, THEREFORE, in consideration of the various covenants and agreements herein contained, and intending to be legally bound hereby, the parties hereto agree as follows:

1.   *Award.*

    (a)   The Company hereby grants to Participant a total of _____ shares of Phantom Stock (the "Phantom Stock"), subject to the terms, restrictions, and other conditions of this Agreement and the Plan. Any term used herein and not defined shall have the meaning given such term in the Plan.

    (b)   The Phantom Stock ____ will or ____ will not have Dividend Equivalent rights.

2. *Vesting.*[1]

    (a) Provided in each case that no termination of employment has occurred prior to the applicable date, the Phantom Shares shall become vested as follows:[2]

Date	Percentage of phantom shares vested
Prior to _____ , ____ , _____	0%
On and after _____ , ____ , _____	___%
On and after _____ , ____ , _____	___%
On and after _____ , ____ , _____	___%
On and after _____ , ____ , _____	___%
On and after _____ , ____ , _____	___%

    (b) Notwithstanding subsection (a), the Company may, in its sole discretion, accelerate the vesting of Phantom Stock upon the occurrence of a [Change in Control or other event.][3]

    (c) No shares of Phantom Stock that are unvested at termination of employment shall thereafter become vested.[4]

3. *Expiration of Phantom Shares.* Notwithstanding any other provision in this Agreement, no payment shall be made with respect to any shares of Phantom Stock after the tenth anniversary of the date of this Agreement, and all shares of Phantom Stock then

---

1. To the extent that uniform vesting provisions are not provided in the Plan, they should be defined in each individual award agreement.

2. The following vesting feature is a basic time-based vesting schedule. The Company should consider whether vesting should be based on performance hurdles. The performance goals may be based on individual, unit, or Company performance. To the extent that performance goals are applied, the Award may constitute performance-based pay, which is subject to special rules under Internal Revenue Code Section 409A. See Chapter 4 of this book for a discussion of performance-based pay.

3. The Company may have uniform Vesting Date triggers set forth in the Plan, or, in the alternative, the triggers may be delineated and defined in this Agreement.

4. Consider whether or not full vesting should occur as a result of death, disability, retirement, or a change in control.

outstanding shall be canceled and will expire immediately as of such date.[5]

4.   *Settlement Dates.* Payment of vested Phantom Stock shall be made on the earlier of the Settlement Dates specified in Section 6(a) of the Plan and the following date:_____.[6]

5.   *No Right to Continued Employment.* Nothing in this Agreement or in the Plan shall confer upon the Participant any right to continue in the employment or other service of the Company or any Subsidiary or shall interfere with or restrict in any way the rights of the Company or any Subsidiary, which are hereby expressly reserved, to discharge the Participant at any time for any reasons whatsoever, with or without cause.

6.   *Award Subject to Plan.* Notwithstanding anything in this Agreement to the contrary, the terms of this Agreement shall be subject to the terms of the Plan, a copy of which may be obtained by the Participant from the office of the Company's Secretary. In the event of any inconsistency between this Agreement and the Plan, the Plan shall control.

7.   *Miscellaneous.*

   (a)   This Agreement may be executed in one or more counterparts, all of which taken together will constitute one and the same instrument.

   (b)   The terms of this Agreement may only be amended, modified, or waived by a written agreement executed by both of the parties hereto.

   (c)   The validity, performance, construction, and effect of this Agreement shall be governed by and construed in accordance with the laws of the State of _____, without regard to the conflict of laws thereof.

   (d)   This Agreement and the Plan constitute the entire agreement

---

5.   The Company should consider whether the Award should have a term limit.

6.   The Company should consider whether Participants will be permitted to elect a fixed payment date in addition to the Settlement Dates specified in the Plan.

between the parties hereto with respect to the Award granted herein.[7]

(e)   Except as otherwise herein provided, this Agreement shall be binding upon and shall inure to the benefit of the Company, its successors and assigns, and of Participant and Participant's personal representatives.

IN WITNESS WHEREOF, the parties have executed this Agreement as of the Grant Date.

ABC CORPORATION

By:
Name:
Title:

PARTICIPANT

Name:
Address:
Social Security Number:

---

7.   If the Participant has an employment agreement that governs the employment relationship, that employment agreement should also be referenced.

Stock Appreciation Rights Plan Documents

Robin Struve
Kay Kemp

The following documents are included on the CD-ROM that accompanies this book. These are sample documents that must be customized before being used. A company should consult with its own legal and accounting advisors before implementing any equity (or equity-equivalent) compensation plan. Before working with these documents, please read appendix A of this book for more information and important disclaimers.

ABC CORPORATION
STOCK APPRECIATION RIGHTS PLAN[1]

1. PURPOSE OF THE PLAN

The purpose of the ABC Corporation Stock Appreciation Rights Plan (the "Plan") is to:

(a) Promote the long-term financial interests and growth of ABC Corporation (the "Company") and its Subsidiaries (as defined below) by attracting and retaining management and personnel with the training, experience, and ability to enable them to make a substantial contribution to the success of the Company's business;

(b) To motivate key employees with an incentive to promote the long-term performance of the Company by tying their long-term incentives to the performance of the common stock of the Company; and

---

1. This Plan will be exempt from the requirements of Internal Revenue Code ("Code") Section 409A and guidance issued with respect thereto. Endnotes have been included, where appropriate, to describe applicable Plan provisions if Rights under the Plan are settled in cash and the Plan intends to comply with Code Section 409A.

(c)   To further the identity of interests of key management and personnel with those of the Company's stockholders in accordance with the terms of the Plan.

2.   DEFINITIONS

(a)   "Award Agreement" means the agreement entered into between the Company and the Participant evidencing the terms of a Right.

(b)   "Base Price" means an amount as determined by the Committee, but such amount will not be less than the Fair Market Value of a share of Common Stock on the Grant Date.

(c)   "Board" or "Board of Directors" means the Board of Directors of the Company as it may be constituted from time to time.

(d)   "Cause"[2] shall have the meaning set forth in any employment agreement between the Company or a Subsidiary and a Participant, and if the Participant and the Company or a Subsidiary are not parties to an employment agreement, then Cause shall mean a termination of the Employee's employment due to:

(i)   the commission by the Participant of an act of fraud against the Company or any Subsidiary thereof or embezzlement, the unauthorized disclosure of the Company's or a Subsidiary's confidential information which disclosure the Participant knew or reasonably should have known could have the potential to result in material damage to the Company or its Subsidiaries, or a breach of one or more of the following duties to the Company or a Subsidiary: (A) the duty of loyalty, (B) the duty not to take willful actions that would reasonably be viewed by the Company as placing the Participant's interest in a position adverse to the interest of the Company or a Subsidiary, (C) the duty not to engage in self-dealing with respect to the Company's or its Subsidiaries' assets, properties, or business opportunities, (D) the duty of honesty, or (E) any other fiduciary duty which the Participant owes to the Company or a Subsidiary;

---

2.   Conform the definition of Cause to other definitions of cause used by the Company. Consider whether to have forfeiture of Rights of a Participant due to termination for Cause.

(ii) a conviction[3] of the Participant (or a plea of nolo contendere in lieu thereof) for (A) a felony or (B) a crime involving fraud, dishonesty or moral turpitude;

(iii) intentional misconduct as an employee or other provider of services to the Company or a Subsidiary, including, but not limited to, knowing and intentional violation by the Participant of written policies of the Company and its Subsidiaries or specific directions of the Board or superior officers of the Company or a Subsidiary, which policies or directives are neither illegal (or do not involve illegal conduct) nor require the Participant to violate reasonable business ethical standards; or

(iv) the failure of the Participant, after written notice to render services in accordance with his employment other than for reasons of Disability, which failure is not cured within [10] days of receipt of such notice.

(e) [[4]"Change in Control" means the occurrence of any of the following events:

(i) the acquisition, directly or indirectly, by any "person" or "group" (as those terms are defined in Sections 3(a)(9), 13(d), and 14(d) of the Securities Exchange Act of 1934 (the "Exchange Act") and the rules thereunder) of "beneficial ownership" (as determined pursuant to Rule 13d-3 under the Exchange Act) of securities entitled to vote generally in the election of directors ("voting securities")[5] of the Company

---

3. Consider whether to use "commission of felony" rather than "conviction."

4. Consider whether or not acceleration of vesting is appropriate upon a Change in Control (CIC). The following definition is generally more relevant for a public company. However, it can be tailored to fit a private company sale also. If the Plan is intended to comply with Code Section 409A, this definition must conform to the requirements of that section.

5. The Company should consider whether this prong of the definition should be limited to the acquisition of *voting* securities or should apply to outstanding equity securities in general. If the latter, references to "voting securities" and "combined voting power" should be conformed throughout the definition.

that represent [20%][6] or more of the combined voting power of the Company's[7] then outstanding voting securities, other than

(A) an acquisition by a trustee or other fiduciary holding securities under any employee benefit plan (or related trust) sponsored or maintained by the Company or any person controlled by the Company or by any employee benefit plan (or related trust) sponsored or maintained by the Company or any person controlled by the Company, or

(B) an acquisition of voting securities by the Company or a corporation owned, directly or indirectly, by the stockholders of the Company in substantially the same proportions as their ownership of the stock of the Company,[8] or

---

6. The appropriate percentage will depend on a number of factors, including the Company's capital structure, whether there are shareholders that own a significant percentage of stock, whether the Company has a "poison pill" (and if so, what percentage will trigger the pill), and whether the Company uses its stock as currency in significant acquisitions or joint ventures. The range is typically between 15% and 50%.

7. It is important to make sure that the "Company" (as defined in the applicable document) is the appropriate entity to trigger the CIC. For example, an employment agreement or equity plan at the subsidiary level may define "Company" as the subsidiary entity, and a transaction involving the parent would not necessarily trigger a CIC. Consideration must therefore be given to whether the CIC should be triggered at the parent level, subsidiary level, or both.

8. An additional carve-out that the Company may want to consider here is "any acquisition of [voting securities or equity securities] directly from the Company." The rationale behind this carve-out is that a CIC should not be triggered if the Board or the Company, knowing that the acquisition will result in significant share ownership by the acquiring person, agrees to directly sell the shares to that person in a friendly transaction. Such a carve-out may be important to a company that uses its stock as currency in connection with joint ventures and other business acquisitions. Note that the inclusion of this carve-out should make it easier for the Company to agree to a lower percentage CIC threshold. Consideration should also be given to excepting acquisitions by persons who currently own a significant percentage of the Company's stock, especially if the Company's poison pill contains a similar carve-out for such persons.

(C) an acquisition of voting securities pursuant to a transaction described in clause (iii) below that would not be a Change in Control under clause (iii);[9]

Notwithstanding the foregoing, neither of the following events shall constitute an "acquisition" by any person or group for purposes of this clause (i): [(x) a change in the voting power of the Company's voting securities based on the relative trading values of the Company's then-outstanding securities as determined pursuant to the Company's Articles of Incorporation,[10] or (y)] an acquisition of the Company's securities by the Company that[, either alone or in combination only with the other event,] causes the Company's voting securities beneficially owned by a person or group to represent [20%] or more of the combined voting power of the Company's then outstanding voting securities; *provided, however,* that if a person or group shall become the beneficial owner of [20%] or more of the combined voting power of the Company's then-outstanding voting securities by reason of share acquisitions by the Company as described above and shall, after such share acquisitions by the Company, become the beneficial owner of any additional voting securities of the Company, then such acquisition shall constitute a Change in Control;

(ii) individuals who, as of the date hereof, constitute the Board (the "Incumbent Board") cease for any reason to constitute

---

9. When drafting a CIC definition, it is important to make sure that all subparts of the definition work together so that a transaction which is excepted from one prong does not unintentionally constitute a CIC under another less obvious prong. For example, a reverse triangular merger of equals or a "butterfly" merger that would not constitute a CIC under prong (iii) should not trigger a CIC under prong (i) by virtue of the acquisition of [20%] of the Company's voting securities (which would necessarily occur pursuant to such a merger).

10. Clause (x) is intended to carve-out instances where the voting power of the Company's securities could change based on the relative values of different series or classes of those securities (*e.g.*, in the case of a tracking stock). If applicable, consideration should also be given to including a carve-out relating to an acquisition of voting securities which results from the exchange or conversion of other securities.

at least a majority of the Board; *provided, however,* that any individual becoming a director subsequent to the date hereof whose election, or nomination for election by the Company's shareholders, was approved by a vote of at least a majority of the directors then comprising the Incumbent Board shall be considered as though such individual were a member of the Incumbent Board, but excluding, for this purpose, any such individual whose initial assumption of office occurs as a result of an actual or threatened election contest with respect to the election or removal of directors or other actual or threatened solicitation of proxies or consents by or on behalf of a person other than the Board;

(iii) the consummation[11] by the Company (whether directly involving the Company or indirectly involving the Company through one or more intermediaries) of (x) a merger, consolidation, reorganization, or business combination or (y) a sale or other disposition of all or substantially all of the Company's assets or (z) the acquisition of assets or stock of another entity,[12] in each case, other than a transaction

   (A) that results in the Company's voting securities outstanding immediately before the transaction continuing to represent (either by remaining outstanding or by being converted into voting securities of the Company or the person that, as a result of the transaction, controls, directly or indirectly, the Company or owns, directly or indirectly, all or substantially all of the Company's assets or otherwise succeeds to the business of the Company (the Company or such person, the "Succes-

---

11. Note that the *consummation* of the transaction (rather than shareholder approval) is a more appropriate trigger. In several recent high-profile cases (including one involving Sprint and one involving Northrop Grumman), shareholders have sued the company where a CIC was triggered by shareholder approval of a transaction that was never consummated.

12. Clause (z) is intended to address transactions (such as joint ventures) in which the Company uses its stock as currency.

sor Entity")) directly or indirectly, at least [50%][13] of the combined voting power of the Successor Entity's outstanding voting securities immediately after the transaction, and

(B) [after which more than 50% of the members of the board of directors of the Successor Entity were members of the Incumbent Board at the time of the Board's approval of the agreement providing for the transaction or other action of the Board approving the transaction,[14] and]

(C) after which no person or group beneficially owns voting securities representing [20%][15] or more of the combined voting power of the Successor Entity; *provided, however,* that no person or group shall be treated for purposes of this clause (C) as beneficially owning [20%] or more of combined voting power of the Successor Entity solely as a result of the voting power held in the Company [and the other entity][16] prior to the consummation of the transaction; or

(iv) a liquidation or dissolution of the Company.[17]

---

13. This carve-out is intended to except a "merger of equals" or a combination in which the Company's shareholders retain control. The percentage should generally be in the 40% to 60% range. A percentage at the lower end of this range might be appropriate where other components of the carve-out provide the Company with additional protection against the loss of control (such as a requirement that the Company's directors constitute a majority of the Board of the surviving entity).

14. The appropriateness of this type of provision will depend on the percentage used in the preceding clause (A). A less common provision might require that the Company's CEO be the CEO of the surviving entity following the CIC.

15. This percentage should generally be the same as the percentage in prong (i) of the definition. See notes 5 and 8 above.

16. Consider whether it would be appropriate to also exclude stock ownership by a person who also owns securities of the other entity.

17. In the case of a liquidation or dissolution, it might be more appropriate for the CIC to be triggered upon shareholder approval of the event.

[For purposes of clause (i) above, the calculation of voting power shall be made as if the date of the acquisition were a record date for a vote of the Company's shareholders, and for purposes of clause (iii) above, the calculation of voting power shall be made as if the date of the consummation of the transaction were a record date for a vote of the Company's shareholders.]

(f)   "Code" means the Internal Revenue Code of 1986, as amended.

(g)   "Committee" means the Board of Directors or a committee of the Board of Directors appointed to serve as the administrator of the Plan.

(h)   "Common Stock" means (i) the common stock of the Company, par value $_____ per share, as adjusted as provided in Section 7, or (ii) if there is a merger or consolidation and the Company is not the surviving corporation, the capital stock of the surviving corporation given in exchange for such common stock of the Company.

(i)   "Company" means ABC Corporation, a _____ corporation.

(j)   ["Director" means a member of the Board or a member of the Board of Directors of a Subsidiary who is not otherwise an Employee of the Company.][18]

(k)   "Disability" shall have the meaning set forth in the Company's long-term disability plan.

(l)   "Employee" shall mean any employee (as defined in accordance with the regulations and revenue rulings then applicable under Section 3401(c) of the Code) of the Company, or of any corporation or other entity which is then a Subsidiary, whether such employee is so employed at the time the Plan is adopted or becomes so employed subsequent to the adoption of the Plan.[19]

(m)   "Exchange Act" means the Securities Exchange Act of 1934, as amended, and any successor statutes or regulations of similar purpose or effect.

---

18. Consider whether directors should be allowed to participate.

19. A company may wish to include consultants within this definition.

(n) "Exercise Date" means the date on which the Participant elects to surrender his Right.[20]

(o) "Expiration Date" means the date on which a Right ultimately becomes unexercisable either by reason of the lapse of time or otherwise.[21]

(p) "Fair Market Value"[22] of a share of Common Stock as of a given date shall be [[23](i) the last sale price before the Grant Date, (ii)

---

20. If the Plan intends to comply with Code Section 409A, the Participant will not be permitted to exercise freely. Instead, as discussed in more detail below, the Plan will have to specify distribution events and dates, which cannot be changed after the associated Grant Date, except as permitted by Code Section 409A. Conforming changes must be made to the Plan to delete all references to exercises of Rights.

21. This section will not be applicable if the Plan is intended to comply with Code Section 409A.

22. This definition applies if Common Stock is traded under an established securities market as defined in Treas. Reg. § 1.897-1(m), which is generally any national securities exchange registered under Section 6 of the Securities Exchange Act of 1934, an officially sanctioned foreign exchange, or any over-the-counter market. If Common Stock is not traded on an established securities market, then Fair Market Value must be determined consistently using a reasonable method, based on the facts and circumstances as of the selected valuation date. A reasonable valuation method will most likely take into account the value of tangible and intangible assets, the present value of future cash flows, the market value of the Company's competitors, and other relevant factors. Three safe harbors for determining Fair Market Value are available under Code Section 409A: (1) an independent appraisal that meets the requirements for valuing stock help by an ESOP, if the valuation is issued not more than 12 months before the Right's Grant Date; (2) a formula price that is used to determine the price of Common Stock subject to transfer restrictions, provided that the formula price is used for all transfers of stock and for all purposes requiring valuation of the stock, including regulatory filings, loan covenants, and issuances to and repurchases of stock from individuals other than employees; and (3) for start-up companies with illiquid stock, a reasonable, good-faith valuation that is evidenced by a written report issued by someone with significant training in performing valuations. The Company will be deemed to use a valuation method consistently if the same method is used for all equity-based compensation arrangements, including for determining the Base Price and the Fair Market Value of the Right on the Exercise Date.

23. The Company should select, and the Plan document should set forth, one of the valuation methods described in this section.

the first sale price after the Grant Date, (iii) the closing price on the trading day before the Grant Date, (iv) the closing price on the Grant Date, or (v) an average price over a period of up to 30 days before or after the Grant Date.]

(q)   "Grant Date" means the date that is designated by the Committee as the date of grant of a Right.

(r)   "Participant" means an Employee [or Director] who has been granted a Right which has not been exercised, cancelled, or forfeited and which has not expired.

(s)   "Plan" means this ABC Corporation Stock Appreciation Rights Plan, as may be amended from time to time.

(t)   "Right" means a stock appreciation right entitling the Participant to the positive difference, if any, between the Fair Market Value of the Common Stock on the Exercise Date and the Base Price.

(u)   "Subsidiary" means (i) any corporation the majority of the voting power of all classes of stock entitled to vote or the majority of the total value of shares of all classes of stock of which is owned, directly or indirectly, by the Company, or (ii) any trade or business other than a corporation of which the majority of the profits interest, capital interest, or actuarial interest is owned, directly or indirectly, by the Company.

(v)   "Vesting Date" means the date o which a Right becomes fully exercisable by the Participant as provided in Section 5(b).

3.   ADMINISTRATION OF THE PLAN

(a)   The Plan will be administered by the Committee. The Committee may adopt its own rules of procedure, and the action of a majority of the Board or committee, as applicable, taken at a meeting or, to the extent permitted by law, taken without a meeting by a writing signed by such majority (or by all or such greater proportion of the members thereof if required by law), shall constitute action by the Committee. The Committee shall have the power, authority, and discretion to administer, construe, and interpret the Plan and Award Agreements, including without limitation, the discretion to determine which Employees and Directors shall be Participants and the terms and conditions, subject to the Plan, of the individual Award Agreements (including without limitation the Base Price and the vesting schedule, if any). The decisions and interpretations of the Committee with respect to any matter concerning the Plan shall be final, conclusive, and binding on all parties who have an interest in the Plan. Any such interpretations, rules, and administration shall be consistent with the basic purposes of the Plan.

(b) In its absolute discretion, the Committee may delegate to the Chief Executive Officer or other senior officers of the Company its duties under the Plan subject to any conditions and limitations as the Committee shall prescribe.

(c) The Committee may employ attorneys, consultants, accountants, appraisers, brokers, or other persons. The Committee, the Company and its Subsidiaries, and the officers and directors of the Company and its Subsidiaries shall be entitled to rely upon the advice, opinions, or valuations of any such persons. All actions taken and all interpretations and determinations made by the Committee in good faith shall be final and binding upon all Participants, the Company and its Subsidiaries, and all other interested persons. No member of the Committee shall be personally liable for any action, determination, or interpretation made in good faith with respect to the Plan, the Award Agreements, or the Rights, and all members of the Committee shall be fully protected by the Company with respect to any such action, determination, or interpretation.

4. PARTICIPATION

Participants will be determined by the Committee, in its sole discretion, from Employees and Directors who, in the Committee's judgment, have a significant opportunity to influence the growth of the Company or whose outstanding performance or potential merit further incentive and reward for continued employment and accomplishment.

5. RIGHTS

(a) *Grant of Rights.* The Committee may, in its sole discretion, at any time and from time to time grant Rights to any Employee or Director. Each award of Rights will be evidenced by an Award Agreement containing such terms and conditions, not inconsistent with the Plan, as the Committee will approve. Each award of Rights shall specify the number of shares to which such Rights apply, which number shall not be subject to change thereafter except as provided in Section 7 hereof.

(b) *Vesting.* Each Right vests and becomes fully exercisable by the Participant on the Vesting Date as specified by the Committee in the Award Agreement.[24] Unless otherwise specified by the Committee in the Award Agreement, the Vesting Date of each Right is [specify vesting provisions]; provided the Participant is an active employee of the Company or a Subsidiary on such date. [Notwithstanding the foregoing, a Participant shall vest and the Participant's Vesting Date shall be on the date of Participant's termination of employment with the Company and all subsidiaries due to (i) normal retirement on or after age 65, (ii) early retirement at the request of the Company or a Subsidiary, (iii) death, or (iv) Disability.][25]

(c) *Exercisability.*[26]

  (i) A Participant who is an active employee or director of the Company or a Subsidiary may exercise a Right on any date that is on or after the Vesting Date, but on or before the Ex-

---

24. A private company may want to consider limiting vesting to certain trigger events such as IPO, a sale, or other Change in Control which would produce liquidity for other shareholders.

25. Consider whether or not full vesting should occur as a result of death, Disability, or retirement.

26. If the Plan is intended to comply with Code Section 409A, then the Participant will not be permitted to freely exercise his or her Rights. Instead, the Plan (or the Award Agreement) will have to specify a fixed payment date or the applicable distribution dates under the Plan, which could include one or more of the following: separation from service (with a six-month wait for specified employees), death, disability, unforeseeable emergency, or a change in control (each as defined in Code Section 409A and applicable guidance). Once the distribution events have been specified, the Participant can elect to change the distribution date only if the following requirements are met: (1) the election is made at least 12 months before the scheduled payment, (2) the election does not become effective until 12 months after it is made, and (3) the delay is for an additional period of five years.

piration Date. If a Participant's employment or directorship with the Company and all Subsidiaries is terminated for any reason whatsoever, any Right granted pursuant to the Plan outstanding at the time, whether or not then vested, may, unless earlier terminated in accordance with its terms, or the occurrence of the Expiration Date, be exercised by the Participant or other person who acquired the right to exercise such Right, on or prior to the following date:

(A) [one year] after termination of employment, if termination of employment is due to death, Disability, or normal retirement on or after age 65; or

(B) [three months] after the date of termination of employment, if employment is terminated for any reason other than death, Disability, or normal retirement on or after age 65.[27]

(ii) Any Right not exercised within the applicable period as described above will be forfeited and become non-exercisable. Notwithstanding anything herein to the contrary, no Right may be exercised before the Vesting Date.

(iii) [If a Participant's employment [or directorship] is terminated for Cause, the Participant shall forfeit all Rights outstanding as of the date of such termination of employment or directorship, whether or not after the Vesting Date, and such Rights shall become unexercisable.][28]

(d) *Term.* The term of each Right will be 10 years from the Date of Grant, unless otherwise specified by the Committee in the Award Agreement.[29]

---

27. If the Company's Common Stock is not traded on an established securities market, consider the post-termination exercise period in light of the Fair Market Value determination. If the value is determined using a formula price, the post-exercise period or payment needs to take into account the timing for applying the formula and making the Fair Market Value determination.

28. Consider whether a forfeiture of Rights is appropriate upon termination for Cause.

29. Consider whether or not Rights should have a term limit, or whether Rights should only be triggered by certain events, such as a qualifying IPO, sale,

(e) *No Ordering.*[30] Rights may be exercised in any order, regardless of the Date of Grant or the existence of any other outstanding Right.

(f) *Whole or Partial Exercise.*[31] A Right may be exercised by a Participant, to the extent exercisable, in whole or in part.

(g) *Beneficiaries.* In the event of the death of a Participant, the person or persons to whom any Right will have been transferred by will or the laws of descent and distribution will have the right (during the appropriate period determined under this section) to exercise such Right in whole or in part.

(h) *Committee Discretion.* Notwithstanding the foregoing, the Committee may, if it believes circumstances warrant such action, authorize the exercise of a Right that would otherwise have terminated.[32]

---

or other Change in Control. Section 8 of this Agreement is an example of a Change in Control trigger event. If the Plan is intended to comply with Code Section 409A, the concept of a term limit will be inapplicable, as the Right will be automatically paid on the earliest (or latest) of the distribution events specified in the Plan.

30. This section will not be applicable if the Plan is intended to comply with Code Section 409A.

31. This section will not be applicable if the Plan is intended to comply with Code Section 409A.

32. If the Plan is intended to comply with Code Section 409A, the Committee will not be permitted to exercise discretion as to the time or form of payment under the Plan. If the Plan so provides, however, the Committee could delay a payment without violating Code Section 409A, in any of the following situations: (1) to preserve a deduction under Code Section 162(m); (2) if payment would violate a loan covenant or securities laws, (3) if a bona fide dispute exists over the Participant's right to payment, or (4) if immediate payment is administratively or economically impractical. In these cases, distribution must be made as soon as practicable after the obstacle has been removed. Note that payments may not be delayed for any of the aforementioned reasons with respect to amounts payable upon exercise of a Right that is exempt from the requirements of Code Section 409A.

6. MANNER OF EXERCISE[33]

(a) *Notice of Exercise.* To the extent an Right is vested and exercisable as provided in Section 5, a Participant (or if applicable, his or her beneficiary), may exercise all or any part of the Right by delivery of an exercise notice in the form and manner as set forth in the Award Agreement.

(b) *Settlement of Rights.* Upon exercise of a Right, the Participant (or if applicable, his or her beneficiary) will receive a lump sum payment[34], in cash,[35] less any required withholding, equal to the product of:

---

33. If the Plan is intended to comply with Code Section 409A, this section must reflect that payments are made automatically on the earliest or latest, as the Plan may provide, of the specified distribution events. This section also must specify the form and payment date applicable to each specified distribution event. Under Code Section 409A, regularly scheduled payments cannot be accelerated, except in limited circumstances. If desired, this section could provide for the following accelerations: (1) payment of a de minimum amount (under $10,000) could be made immediately upon separation from service; (2) payment could be made to comply with a qualified domestic relations order; or (3) if the Plan is maintained by an S corporation owned all or in part by an ESOP, payment could be made to avoid a nonallocation year under Code Section 409(p).

34. If the plan is intended to comply with Code Section 409A, the Plan could provide for payment in installments, or could permit the Participant to elect the applicable form of payment, provided this election is made no later than the Grant Date, subject to the same limits as apply to changes in the timing of distributions, as discussed in footnote 27. If installments are provided, then the Plan or the Award Agreement should specify whether interest will be credited on the unpaid balance, and if so, how such interest will be determined and how often it will be credited.

35. Rights also may settle in stock. However, if Rights are settled in stock, then the Rights will be considered "securities" for Federal and state securities law purposes, and either the Plan will need to be registered under the Securities Act of 1933 (the "Securities Act"), or the Plan must satisfy an exemption from registration such as Rule 701. State blue sky laws may also impact the ability to settle in stock. If a Company desires to settle Rights in stock, add the following language [or Common Stock with a Fair Market Value,...] and consider the implication of state and federal securities laws.

(i) the difference between the Fair Market Value of a share of Common Stock on the Exercise Date and the Base Price; and

(ii) the number of shares of Common Stock with respect to which the Right is being exercised.

7. DILUTION AND OTHER ADJUSTMENTS

In the event of any change in the outstanding shares of Common Stock by reason of any stock dividend or split, recapitalization, merger, consolidation, spin-off, reorganization, combination or exchange of shares, or other similar corporate change, the Committee will make such adjustments, if any, as it in its sole discretion deems equitable in the number of shares of Common Stock with respect to which an Right held by any Participant is referenced and the Base Price with respect to any Right, such adjustments to be conclusive and binding upon all parties concerned.

8. [CHANGE IN CONTROL

Upon a Change in Control, all outstanding Rights will become fully vested and exercisable. The Committee in its sole discretion may declare the date upon which a Change in Control occurs to be the Exercise Date for all outstanding Rights and will provide for the settlement of such Rights in accordance with Section 6.][36]

9. MISCELLANEOUS PROVISIONS

(a) *Assignment and Transfer*. Rights will not be transferable other than by will or the laws of descent and distribution and may be

---

36. Include only if vesting on Change in Control is desirable. Note that if the Plan intends to comply with Code Section 409A and a Change in Control is a specified distribution event, the Company cannot exercise discretion over whether to make payouts upon a Change in Control. However, if the Plan so provides, the Company can delay payments due on a Change in Control so long as payments are made on the same schedule and subject to the same conditions as apply to payments to shareholders or to the Company, as the case may be, and so long as all payments are made within five years of the Change in Control.

exercised or otherwise realized, during the lifetime of the Participant, only by the Participant or by his or her guardian or legal representative.

(b) *No Rights or Right to Employment.* No Employee or other person will have any claim or right to be granted a Right. Neither the Plan, nor any instrument executed pursuant to the Plan, nor any action taken hereunder will be construed as giving any Participant any right to be retained in the employ or remain as a Director of the Company or any Subsidiary.

(c) *General Creditor Status.* Obligations of the Company and its Subsidiaries under the Plan shall be unsecured and unfunded obligations, and the holders of Rights shall be general creditors of the Company.

(d) *Taxes.*[37] The Company or its Subsidiaries will have the right to deduct from settlement of a Right any taxes required by law to be withheld from a Participant with respect to such payment. The Company or its Subsidiaries may make such provisions as it deems appropriate to withhold any taxes the Company or its Subsidiaries determine it is required to withhold in connection with any such payment of a Right.

(e) *Securities Laws.* Each Award Agreement will be subject to the condition that such Right may not be exercised if the Committee determines that the exercise of such Right may violate the Securities Act of 1933 or any other law or requirement of any governmental authority. The Company will not be deemed by any reason of the granting of any Right to have any obligation to register the Rights or shares underlying such Rights under the Securities Act of 1933 or to maintain in effect any registration of such Rights or shares which may be made at any time under the Securities Act of 1933.

(f) *[Premature Termination.* The Company will not be obligated to make any payment of cash (or have any other obligation or li-

---

37. If the Plan is intended to comply with Code Section 409A, this section could provide that payments may be accelerated to pay the taxes resulting from a failure to satisfy the requirements of Code Section 409A.

ability) under any Right if the Committee determines that (i) the employment or directorship of the Participant with the Company or any Subsidiary will have been terminated for Cause, or (ii) the Participant will have engaged or may engage in employment or activities competitive with the Company, any of its Subsidiaries or contrary, in the opinion of the Committee, to the best interests of the Company.[38] After any such determination, the Participant will have no right under any such Right (regardless of whether such Participant will have delivered a notice of exercise prior to the making of such determination) to receive any payment at any time unless such determination will be rescinded by the Committee. Any Right may be terminated entirely by the Committee at the time of or any time subsequent to a determination by the Committee under this section which has the effect of eliminating the Company's obligation to pay such Right.]

(g) *Severability*. Whenever possible, each provision in the Plan and in every Award Agreement will be interpreted in such manner as to be effective and valid under applicable law, but if any provision of this Plan or any Award Agreement made thereunder will be held to be prohibited by or invalid under applicable law, then (i) such provision will be deemed amended to, and to have contained from the outset such language will be necessary to, accomplish the objectives of the provision as originally written to the fullest extent permitted by law and (ii) all other provisions of the Plan and every Award Agreement will remain in full force and effect.

(h) *No Strict Construction*. No rule of strict construction will be applied against the Company, the Committee or any other person in the interpretation of any of the terms of the Plan, any Right or any rule or procedure established by the Committee.

(i) *Stockholder Rights*. A Participant will not have any dividend, voting, or other stockholder rights by reason of a grant of a Right or settlement of a Right.

---

38. One should coordinate the non-compete clause with any other non-compete covenants the Company may have with its employees. Also, one needs to confirm that any non-compete covenants would be enforceable under applicable state law.

(j)   *Governing Law.* The Plan will be governed by and construed in accordance with the laws of the United States of America and, to the extent not inconsistent therewith, by the laws of the State of _____.

10. AMENDMENT AND TERMINATION

The Committee may at any time amend, suspend, or terminate the Plan, provided that no such action will adversely affect any rights under any Right theretofore granted or change the vesting applicable to a Right in a manner adverse to a Participant, except in accordance with Section 7.[39]

11. EFFECTIVE DATE OF THE PLAN

The Plan will become effective as of _____, 20___.

I hereby certify that the foregoing Plan was duly adopted by the Board of Directors of ABC Corporation on _____ _____, 20__.

Executed on this _____ day of _____, 20___.

Secretary

---

39. If the Plan is intended to comply with Code Section 409A, then the Plan can be terminated and payments accelerated at the discretion of the Company only if the Plan so provides and the Plan otherwise meets one of the following requirements: (1) all stock right plans must be terminated with respect to all participants, (2) distributions on account of termination can be made no earlier than 12 months after the termination, (3) all distributions must be made within 24 months of the termination, and (4) no new stock rights plans may be adopted within the five-year period after the termination. The Plan could also provide that it would be terminated within 12 months after a Change in Control, or upon corporate liquidation or with the approval of a bankruptcy court, as long as all substantially similar arrangements were terminated and all payments were made to Participants within 12 months after termination.

ABC CORPORATION STOCK APPRECIATION RIGHTS PLAN AWARD AGREEMENT[1]

This AWARD AGREEMENT, made as of the ___day of _____, 20___ (the "Grant Date"), by ABC Corporation, a _____ company (the "Company"), with _____ (the Participant"). This Agreement is made under the terms of the ABC Corporation Stock Appreciation Rights Plan, as amended from time to time (the "Plan"). The Plan, as it may hereafter be amended and continued, is incorporated herein by reference and made a part of this Agreement and shall control the rights and obligations of the Company and the Participant under this Agreement. Except as otherwise provided, terms used herein shall have the meaning provided in the Plan.

1. *Grant of Right.* The Company hereby grants to the Participant a Right with respect to _____ shares of Common Stock at a Base Price per Right of $_____, subject to the terms and conditions of the Plan and this Agreement.

2. *Vesting.*

    (a) The Participant shall vest in the Rights according to the following:

    (i) [Add description of vesting, either time-based, performance-based, or time- and performance-based]

    (b) No portion of the Right that is unvested upon the date when the Participant's employment[2] with the Company and all Subsidiaries is terminated shall thereafter become vested or exercisable.[3] [Notwithstanding the foregoing, if the Partici-

---

1. This Award Agreement and the underlying Plan will be exempt from the requirements of Internal Revenue Code ("Code") Section 409A and guidance issued with respect thereto. Notes have been included, where appropriate, to describe applicable provisions if Rights under the Plan are settled in cash and the Plan intends to comply with Code Section 409A.

2. If the Rights are granted to a Director, then the forfeiture should be based on a termination of directorship. Consider including a definition of termination of directorship.

3. The Company should consider the treatment of any unvested portion of Rights of a Participant upon termination of employment or directorship due to death or disability.

pant's employment with the Company and its subsidiaries is terminated for Cause, then the Participant shall forfeit all Rights, whether or not previously vested.][4]

(c) The installments provided for in Section 2(a) are cumulative. Each such installment which becomes vested and exercisable pursuant to Section 3 shall remain exercisable until it terminates pursuant to Section 3.

3. *Exercise and Term.*[5]

(a) The Right may be exercised during its term only to the extent vested.[6] Any portion of the Right in which the Participant is vested shall be exercisable until the earlier of:

(i) [one year][7] after the date of the Participant's termination of employment [or directorship], if termination is by reason of death or Disability [or normal retirement on or after age 65];

(ii) [three months] after the date the Participant's termination of employment, if terminated for any reason other

---

4. Include only if forfeiture for cause is desired. If forfeiture for cause is not included in the Plan document, this does not preclude use in the Award Agreement, but a definition of cause will need to be added to Award Agreement in that case. If the Employee has an employment agreement, the definition of cause should correspond to the definition in the employment agreement.

5. If the Plan intends to comply with Code Section 409A, the Participant will not be permitted to exercise freely. Instead, the Plan will have to specify distribution events and dates, which cannot be changed after the associated Grant Date, except as permitted by Code Section 409A. Conforming changes must be made to the Award Agreement to delete all references to exercises of Rights. In addition, this section should be expanded to permit the Participant to elect applicable distribution events, to the extent the Plan gives the Participant the right to make such elections.

6. Other restrictions on exercise such as only on Change in Control, IPO, or other events should be included here if applicable.

7. The Plan permits the Board to exercise its discretion and shorten any exercise period that is set forth in the Plan. If the Company desires shorter exercise periods, it should be included in this section. Also, the period for exercise can be same for regular termination vs. termination for death, disability, or retirement. None of these events need extend the exercise period.

than death, or Disability [or retirement on or after age 65]; or

(iii) the tenth anniversary of the Grant Date.

(b) Any exercisable portion of the Right may be exercised in whole or in part at any time prior to the time when the Right becomes unexercisable under Section 3(a).

(c) Any vested Right not exercised prior to its Expiration Date will be forfeited and will terminate.

(d) A vested Right may be exercised by completing a Right Exercise Notice in the form attached hereto as Exhibit A and returning it to _____ prior to its Expiration Date. The Right may not be exercised more than once with respect to any share of Common Stock related thereto.

4. *Payment.*[8] Payment shall be made in a cash lump sum (less any applicable withholding taxes) within 30 days of such exercise.[9]

5. *Miscellaneous.*

(a) *Successors.* This Agreement shall inure to the benefit of and be binding upon the parties hereto and their respective heirs, executors, administrators, successors, and permitted assigns.

---

8. SARs could be settled in stock as long as appropriate securities laws are satisfied. If a private company settles SARs in stock, consider the applicability of shareholders' agreements and appropriate call provisions upon termination of employment. If a SAR is to be settled in stock, then any requirements to become parties to shareholder agreements, restrictions on transfer, or call rights should be included in this section.

9. If the Plan intends to comply with Code Section 409A and payments are to be made in installments, then the following provision could be included here:

> The Participant shall receive payment of his or her Right in five equal annual installments commencing on XXX, with any unpaid balance accruing interest (compounded annually) at the interest rate publicly quoted by [Institution], or its successor from time to time as its prime rate.

> If the Plan permits Participants to elect the form of payment (either a lump sum or installment payments), then the Participant's election must be specified in the Award Agreement and may not be changed except as permitted under Code Section 409A.

(b) *Shareholder Rights.* Participant acknowledges that he/she does not have any rights as a shareholder of the Company by reason of a grant of the Right or settlement of the Right pursuant to the Plan.

(c) *Nontransferable.* The Right is not transferable other than by will or the laws of descent and distribution and may be realized, during the lifetime of the Participant, only by the Participant or by his or her guardian or legal representative.

(d) *Notices.* Notices required or permitted hereunder shall be given in writing and shall be deemed effectively given upon personal delivery or upon deposit in the United States mail by certified mail, with postage and fees prepaid, addressed to the Participant to his or her address shown in the Company's records, and to the Company at its principal executive office.

(d) *Rights Subject to Plan.* Notwithstanding anything in this Agreement to the contrary, the terms of this Agreement shall be subject to the terms of the Plan, a copy of which may be obtained by the Participant from the office of the Company's Secretary. In the event of any inconsistency between this Agreement and the Plan, the Plan shall control.

(e) *Governing Law; Severability.* The interpretation, performance and enforcement of this Agreement shall be governed by the laws of the State of _____ without regard to conflicts of law thereof.[10] The invalidity or unenforceability of any provision of this Agreement shall not affect the validity or enforceability of any other provision of this Agreement which shall remain in full force and effect.

---

10. The governing law of the Award Agreement should be same as the Plan.

In WITNESS WHEREOF, this Agreement has been executed and delivered by the parties hereto as of the Grant Date.

ABC CORPORATION
    By:
    Its:

PARTICIPANT
    (Participant)
    (Social Security Number)
    Residence Address:

EXHIBIT A
ABC CORPORATION
STOCK APPRECIATION RIGHTS PLAN
RIGHTS EXERCISE NOTICE

ABC Corporation
123 Yellow Brick Road
La La Land, OZ 99999

Attention: _____

Effective as of today, _____, the undersigned Participant hereby elects to exercise Participant's vested Right with respect to _____ shares of Common Stock (the "Rights") pursuant to the ABC Corporation Stock Appreciation Rights Plan and the Award Agreement dated _____.

I acknowledge that payment for the Rights will be made in accordance with the terms set forth in the Award Agreement and Plan, less any legally required withholdings.

Submitted by:
PARTICIPANT:

Address:

Restricted Stock Plan Documents

Robin Struve

The following documents are included on the CD-ROM that accompanies this book. These are sample documents that must be customized before being used. A company should consult with its own legal and accounting advisors before implementing any equity (or equity-equivalent) compensation plan. Before working with these documents, please read appendix A of this book for more information and important disclaimers.

ABC CORPORATION RESTRICTED STOCK PLAN

1. PURPOSE OF THE PLAN

ABC Corporation (the "Company"), a corporation organized under the laws of the state of _____, hereby adopts this Restricted Stock Plan (the "Plan"). The purposes of the Plan are:

(a) To further the growth, development, and financial success of the Company by providing additional incentives to certain of its employees who have been or will be given responsibility for the management or administration of the Company's business affairs, by assisting them to become owners of the common stock, par value $____ per share, of the Company (the "Common Stock").

(b) To enable the Company to retain the services of the type of professional, technical, and managerial employees considered essential to the long-range success of the Company by providing and offering them an opportunity to become owners of Common Stock.

2. DEFINITIONS

Whenever the following terms are used in the Program, they shall have the meaning specified below unless the context clearly indicates to the contrary. The masculine pronoun shall include the feminine and neuter and the singular shall include the plural, where the context so indicates.

(a)   "Board" shall mean the Board of Directors of the Company.

(b)   [[1]"Change in Control" means the occurrence of any of the following events:

  (i)   the acquisition, directly or indirectly, by any "person" or "group" (as those terms are defined in Sections 3(a)(9), 13(d), and 14(d) of the Securities Exchange Act of 1934 (the "Exchange Act") and the rules thereunder) of "beneficial ownership" (as determined pursuant to Rule 13d-3 under the Exchange Act) of securities entitled to vote generally in the election of directors ("voting securities")[2] of the Company that represent [20%][3] or more of the combined voting power of the Company's[4] then outstanding voting securities, other than

    (A)   an acquisition by a trustee or other fiduciary holding securities under any employee benefit plan (or related

---

1.   Include only if Change in Control (CIC) is one of the vesting date triggers as is provided in Section 7 of this Plan. The following definition is generally more relevant for a public company. However, can be tailored to fit a private company sale also.

2.   The Company should consider whether this prong of the definition should be limited to the acquisition of *voting* securities or should apply to outstanding equity securities in general. If the latter, references to "voting securities" and "combined voting power" should be conformed throughout the definition.

3.   The appropriate percentage will depend on a number of factors, including the Company's capital structure, whether there are shareholders that own a significant percentage of stock, whether the Company has a "poison pill" (and if so, what percentage will trigger the pill), and whether the Company uses its stock as currency in significant acquisitions or joint ventures. The range is typically between 15% and 50%.

4.   It is important to make sure that the "Company" (as defined in the applicable document) is the appropriate entity to trigger the CIC. For example, an employment agreement or equity plan at the subsidiary level may define "Company" as the subsidiary entity, and a transaction involving the parent would not necessarily trigger a CIC. Consideration must therefore be given to whether the CIC should be triggered at the parent level, subsidiary level, or both.

trust) sponsored or maintained by the Company or any person controlled by the Company or by any employee benefit plan (or related trust) sponsored or maintained by the Company or any person controlled by the Company, or

(B) an acquisition of voting securities by the Company or a corporation owned, directly or indirectly, by the stockholders of the Company in substantially the same proportions as their ownership of the stock of the Company,[5] or

(C) an acquisition of voting securities pursuant to a transaction described in clause (iii) below that would not be a Change in Control under clause (iii);[6]

Notwithstanding the foregoing, neither of the following events shall constitute an "acquisition" by any person or group for purposes of this clause (i): [(x) a change in the voting power of the Company's voting securities based on the relative trading values of the Company's then outstanding securities as determined pursuant to the Company's Articles of Incor-

---

5. An additional carve-out which the Company may want to consider here is "any acquisition of [voting securities or equity securities] directly from the Company." The rationale behind this carve-out is that a CIC should not be triggered if the Board or the Company, knowing that the acquisition will result in significant share ownership by the acquiring person, agrees to directly sell the shares to that person in a friendly transaction. Such a carve-out may be important to a company that uses its stock as currency in connection with joint ventures and other business acquisitions. Note that the inclusion of this carve-out should make it easier for the Company to agree to a lower percentage CIC threshold. Consideration should also be given to excepting acquisitions by persons who currently own a significant percentage of the Company's stock, especially if the Company's poison pill contains a similar carve-out for such persons.

6. When drafting a CIC definition, it is important to make sure that all subparts of the definition work together so that a transaction which is excepted from one prong does not unintentionally constitute a CIC under another less obvious prong. For example, a reverse triangular merger of equals or a "butterfly" merger that would not constitute a CIC under prong (iii) should not trigger a CIC under prong (i) by virtue of the acquisition of [20%] of the Company's voting securities (which would necessarily occur pursuant to such a merger).

poration,[7] or (y)] an acquisition of the Company's securities by the Company that[, either alone or in combination only with the other event,] causes the Company's voting securities beneficially owned by a person or group to represent [20%] or more of the combined voting power of the Company's then outstanding voting securities; provided, however, that if a person or group shall become the beneficial owner of [20%] or more of the combined voting power of the Company's then outstanding voting securities by reason of share acquisitions by the Company as described above and shall, after such share acquisitions by the Company, become the beneficial owner of any additional voting securities of the Company, then such acquisition shall constitute a Change in Control;

(ii) individuals who, as of the date hereof, constitute the Board (the "Incumbent Board") cease for any reason to constitute at least a majority of the Board; *provided, however,* that any individual becoming a director subsequent to the date hereof whose election, or nomination for election by the Company's shareholders, was approved by a vote of at least a majority of the directors then comprising the Incumbent Board shall be considered as though such individual were a member of the Incumbent Board, but excluding, for this purpose, any such individual whose initial assumption of office occurs as a result of an actual or threatened election contest with respect to the election or removal of directors or other actual or threatened solicitation of proxies or consents by or on behalf of a person other than the Board;

(iii) the consummation[8] by the Company (whether directly involving the Company or indirectly involving the Com-

---

7. Clause (x) is intended to carve-out instances where the voting power of the Company's securities could change based on the relative values of different series or classes of those securities (e.g., in the case of a tracking stock). If applicable, consideration should also be given to including a carve-out relating to an acquisition of voting securities that results from the exchange or conversion of other securities.

8. Note that the *consummation* of the transaction (rather than shareholder approval) is a more appropriate trigger. In several recent high-profile cases (including

pany through one or more intermediaries) of (x) a merger, consolidation, reorganization, or business combination or (y) a sale or other disposition of all or substantially all of the Company's assets or (z) the acquisition of assets or stock of another entity,[9] in each case, other than a transaction

(A) that results in the Company's voting securities outstanding immediately before the transaction continuing to represent (either by remaining outstanding or by being converted into voting securities of the Company or the person that, as a result of the transaction, controls, directly or indirectly, the Company or owns, directly or indirectly, all or substantially all of the Company's assets or otherwise succeeds to the business of the Company (the Company or such person, the "Successor Entity")) directly or indirectly, at least [50%][10] of the combined voting power of the Successor Entity's outstanding voting securities immediately after the transaction, and

[(B) after which more than 50% of the members of the board of directors of the Successor Entity were members of the Incumbent Board at the time of the Board's approval of the agreement providing for the transaction or other action of the Board approving the transaction,[11] and]

---

one involving Sprint and one involving Northrop Grumman), shareholders have sued the company where a CIC was triggered by shareholder approval of a transaction that was never consummated.

9. Clause (z) is intended to address transactions (such as joint ventures) in which the Company uses its stock as currency.

10. This carve-out is intended to except a "merger of equals" or a combination in which the Company's shareholders retain control. The percentage should generally be in the 40% to 60% range. A percentage at the lower end of this range might be appropriate where other components of the carve-out provide the Company with additional protection against the loss of control (such as a requirement that the Company's directors constitute a majority of the Board of the surviving entity).

11. The appropriateness of this type of provision will depend on the percentage used in the preceding clause (A). A less common provision might require that the Company's CEO be the CEO of the surviving entity following the CIC.

(C) after which no person or group beneficially owns voting securities representing [20%][12] or more of the combined voting power of the Successor Entity; provided, however, that no person or group shall be treated for purposes of this clause (C) as beneficially owning [20%] or more of combined voting power of the Successor Entity solely as a result of the voting power held in the Company [and the other entity][13] prior to the consummation of the transaction; or

(iv) a liquidation or dissolution of the Company.[14]

For purposes of clause (i) above, the calculation of voting power shall be made as if the date of the acquisition were a record date for a vote of the Company's shareholders, and for purposes of clause (iii) above, the calculation of voting power shall be made as if the date of the consummation of the transaction were a record date for a vote of the Company's shareholders.]

(c) "Code" shall mean the Internal Revenue Code of 1986, as amended.

(d) "Company" shall mean ABC Corporation, a _____ corporation.

(e) "Eligible Participants" shall mean all present and future officers and key Employees of the Company,[15] its subsidiaries and affiliates, as selected by the Board or an individual or entity to whom the Board has delegated its authority, who are expected to contribute to the Company's future growth and success.

(f) "Employee" shall mean any employee (as defined in accordance with the regulations and revenue rulings then applicable under

---

12. This percentage should generally be the same as the percentage in prong (i) of the definition. See notes 2 and 6 above.

13. Consider whether it would be appropriate to also exclude stock ownership by a person who also owns securities of the other entity.

14. In the case of a liquidation or dissolution, it might be more appropriate for the CIC to be triggered upon shareholder approval of the event.

15. The Company should consider whether to permit non-employee directors to participate in the Plan.

Section 3401(c) of the Code) of the Company, or of any corporation which is then a Parent or a Subsidiary, whether such employee is so employed at the time the Plan is adopted or becomes so employed subsequent to the adoption of the Plan.

(g) "Parent" shall mean any corporation, company, joint venture, partnership, or such other business entity, during any period in an unbroken chain of entities ending with the Company if each of the entities other than the Company then owns equity interests possessing 50% or more of the total combined voting power of all classes of equity interests in one of the other entities in such chain.

(h) "Participant" shall mean an Eligible Participant designated in writing by the Board as eligible to participate in the Plan.

(i) "Plan" shall mean this ABC Corporation Restricted Stock Plan.

(j) "Restricted Stock" shall mean shares of Common Stock granted or purchased under this Plan, which are subject to restrictions set forth in the Restricted Stock Agreement.

(k) "Restricted Stock Agreement" shall mean the agreement entered into between the Company and an Employee pursuant to which the Employee is granted the right to purchase Restricted Stock and which sets forth the terms and conditions applicable to the Restricted Stock.

(l) "Restricted Stock Award" shall mean a grant of Common Stock made by the Board, or an individual or entity operating under authority delegated by the Board, pursuant to the provisions of the Plan.

(m) "Subsidiary" shall mean any corporation, company, joint venture, partnership, or such other business entity, during any period in which it is a "subsidiary" to the Company as that term is defined by the Code.

3. PLAN ADMINISTRATION

(a) *Duties and Powers of the Board.* It shall be the duty of the Board to conduct the general administration of the Plan in accordance with its provisions.[16] The Board shall have the power and authority to interpret the Plan and to adopt such rules for the administration, interpretation, and application of the Plan as are consistent therewith and to interpret, amend, or revoke any such rules. The Board shall have the power and authority, in its sole discretion, to impose restrictions in addition to those otherwise required by the Plan and the Code. The Board may at any time, in its sole discretion, accelerate the time at which any or all restrictions or conditions will lapse or remove or change any and all restrictions or conditions previously imposed on Restricted Stock. All determinations and decisions made by the Board under any provision of the Plan or of any Restricted Stock granted thereunder shall be final, conclusive, and binding on all persons.

(b) *Delegation.* The Board may delegate to one or more of its respective members or to any other person or persons such ministerial duties as it may deem advisable.[17]

(c) *Expenses; Professional Assistance; Good Faith Actions.* All expenses and liabilities incurred by members of the Board in connection with the administration of the Plan shall be borne by the Company. The Board may employ attorneys, consultants, accountants, appraisers, brokers or other persons. The Board, the Company and its officers and directors shall be entitled to rely upon the advice, opinions or valuations of any such persons. All actions taken and all interpretations and determinations made by the Board in good faith shall be final and binding upon the Company, all Employees to whom Shares are sold, and all other interested persons. No member of the Board shall be personally liable for any action, determination, or interpretation made in good faith with respect to the Plan, and all members of the Board shall be fully protected

---

16. A committee may be named to administer the Plan, or the Board may delegate its administrative authority to a committee if desired. In many instances, the committee that administers the Plan is the Compensation Committee of a company. However, the Board may appoint a separate committee. In this case, the power to appoint the committee and the basic terms governing the committee and its members should be described in the Plan.

17. Depending on the size and nature of the Plan, the Company may require that all grants of Restricted Stock Award be approved or ratified by the Board.

by the Company in respect to any such action, determination, or interpretation.

4.   GRANT AND SALE OF SHARES

(a)   *Shares Subject to Plan.* Subject to Section 6, the Company is authorized to sell or otherwise grant to Participants in connection with the performance of services up to _____ shares of Common Stock (the "Shares") as Restricted Stock Awards, on such terms and conditions as may be fixed from time to time by the Board, in its sole and absolute discretion. The Company shall at all times reserve and keep available such number of Shares as shall be sufficient to satisfy the requirements of the Plan. To the extent that Shares of Restricted Stock are repurchased by the Company at their original purchase price, such Shares shall again become available for future sale under the Plan.

(b)   *Restricted Stock Awards.* In the event that the Board grants Restricted Stock to Participants pursuant to the Plan, the Board shall have the authority, in its sole and absolute discretion, to:

   (i)   select which Participant(s), if any, to whom such Shares of Restricted Stock are to be granted or sold; and

   (ii)   determine the number of Shares to be granted or sold to such Participant(s); and

   (iii)   determine the terms and conditions (including, without limitation, the purchase price, vesting and other restrictions applicable to the Restricted Stock) of such grant or sale, consistent with the Plan.[18]

(c)   *Restricted Stock Agreement.* The Board shall require a Participant to whom Restricted Stock is granted or sold pursuant to the Plan to enter into a written Restricted Stock Agreement with the Company, which shall be executed by such Participant and an authorized officer of the Company and which shall contain such terms and

---

18.   If the Company is to grant Restricted Stock Awards with uniform restrictions, the terms may be set forth in the Plan rather than in each individual Restricted Stock Agreement.

conditions as the Board shall determine, consistent with the Plan.[19]

(d) *Transfer Restrictions.* Shares acquired by a Participant upon the lapse of restrictions under the Restricted Stock Agreement shall be subject to the terms and conditions of a Stockholders Agreement.[20] In addition, the Board, in its sole discretion, may impose further restrictions on transferability of the Shares received upon the lapse of restrictions as it deems appropriate. Any such restriction shall be set forth in the respective Restricted Stock Agreement and may be referred to on the certificates evidencing such Shares.

5. DIVIDENDS

A Restricted Stock Award may provide the Participant with the right to receive dividend payments with respect to Restricted Stock prior to the lapse of the restrictions set forth in the Restricted Stock Agreement or this Plan.

6. ADJUSTMENTS UPON CHANGES IN CAPITALIZATION, MERGER OR ASSET SALE

(a) *Adjustments to Shares.* In the event that the Board determines that any dividend or other distribution (whether in the form of cash, Common Stock, other securities, or other property), recapitalization, reclassification, stock split, reverse stock split, reorganization, merger, consolidation, split-up, spin-off, combination, repurchase, liquidation, dissolution, or sale, transfer, exchange, or other disposition of all or substantially all of the assets of the Company, or exchange of Common Stock or other securities of the Company, issuance of warrants or other rights to purchase Common Stock or other securities of the Company, or other similar corporate

---

19. Private companies may also want to require that the Participant enter into a Stockholders Agreement.

20. A company should consider including this provision if the Shares acquired upon the lapse of restrictions are to be subject to rights and restrictions set forth in a Stockholders Agreement.

transaction or event, in the Board's sole discretion, affects the Common Stock such that an adjustment is determined by the Board to be appropriate in order to prevent dilution or enlargement of the benefits or potential benefits intended to be made available under the Plan, then the Board shall, in such manner as it may deem equitable, adjust any or all of:

(i)   the number and kind of shares of Shares (or other securities or property) with respect to which may be granted as Restricted Stock and purchased under the Plan; or

(ii)   the number and kind of Shares (or other securities or property) subject to outstanding Restricted Stock.

(b)   *Adjustment to Restricted Stock Awards.* In the event of any transaction or event described in Section 6(a), the Board, in its sole and absolute discretion, and on such terms and conditions as it deems appropriate, either by the terms of the Restricted Stock Agreement or by action taken prior to the occurrence of such transaction or event and either automatically or upon the Participant's request, is hereby authorized to take any one or more of the following actions whenever the Board determines that such action is appropriate in order to prevent dilution or enlargement of the benefits or potential benefits intended to be made available under the Plan or with respect to any Restricted Stock issued under the Plan or to facilitate such transaction or event:

(i)   To provide for either the purchase of any such Restricted Stock for an amount of cash equal to the amount that could have been realized if the Employee's rights to the Restricted Stock been fully vested or the replacement of such Restricted Stock with other rights or property selected by the Board in its sole discretion;

(ii)   To provide that such Restricted Stock be assumed by the successor or survivor corporation, or a parent or subsidiary thereof, or shall be substituted for by similar rights or awards covering the stock of the successor or survivor corporation, or a parent or subsidiary thereof, with appropriate adjustments as to the number and kind of shares and prices; and

(iii) To provide that immediately upon the consummation of such event the restrictions imposed under a Restricted Stock Agreement upon some or all Shares may be terminated and, in the case of Restricted Stock, some or all shares of such Restricted Stock may cease to be subject to repurchase, notwithstanding anything to the contrary in the Plan or the provisions of such Restricted Stock Agreement.

(iv) The existence of the Plan or any Restricted Stock Agreement shall not affect or restrict in any way the right or power of the Company or the stockholders of the Company to make or authorize any adjustment, recapitalization, reorganization, or other change in the Company's capital structure or its business, any merger or consolidation of the Company, any issue of stock or of options, warrants, or rights to purchase stock or of bonds, debentures, preferred or prior preference stocks whose rights are superior to or affect the Common Stock or the rights thereof or which are convertible into or exchangeable for Common Stock, or the dissolution or liquidation of the Company, or any sale or transfer of all or any part of its assets or business, or any other corporate act or proceeding, whether of a similar character or otherwise.

7. [EFFECT OF CHANGE IN CONTROL ON RESTRICTED STOCK AWARDS[21]

Subject to Section 6 (relating to the adjustment for Shares), and except as otherwise provided in the Plan or a Restricted Stock Agreement reflecting the applicable Restricted Stock Award, upon the occurrence of a Change in Control, all remaining restrictions on any Restricted Stock granted to a Participant pursuant to a Restricted Stock Award shall immediately lapse and become null and void. The Shares shall be offered to the party or parties causing the Change in Control for the consideration offered to all stockholders. Should such party acquire greater than ___% of the Company's common stock but not purchase any of Participant's

---

21. Include only if full vesting on Change in Control is desired.

shares, the Company shall do so for the same consideration or its cash equivalent, at the Company's discretion.][22]

8. NON-TRANSFERABILITY

For so long as it is subject to any restrictions pursuant to this Plan or a Restricted Stock Agreement, no Restricted Stock Award or interest or right therein or part thereof shall be liable for the debts, contracts, or engagements of the Participant or his or her successors in interest or shall be subject to disposition by transfer, alienation, anticipation, pledge, encumbrance, assignment, or any other means whether such disposition be voluntary or involuntary or by operation of law, by judgment, levy, attachment, garnishment, or any other legal or equitable proceedings (including bankruptcy), and any attempted disposition thereof shall be null and void and of no effect: provided, however, that nothing in this Section 6 shall prevent transfers by will or by the applicable laws of descent and distribution.

9. OTHER PROVISIONS

(a) *Amendment, Suspension, or Termination of the Plan.* The Plan may be wholly or partially amended or otherwise modified, suspended, or terminated at any time or from time to time by the Board; provided, however, that no amendment or termination shall impair the rights of any Participant to Restricted Stock or under a Restricted Stock Agreement, unless agreed to in writing and signed by the Company and the Participant.

(b) *Effect of Plan Upon Other Compensation Programs.* The adoption of the Plan shall not affect any other compensation or incentive plans in effect for the Company, any Parent, or any Subsidiary. Nothing in the Plan shall be construed to limit the right of the Company, any Parent, or any Subsidiary to establish any other forms of incentives or compensation for employees of the Company, any Parent, or any Subsidiary.

---

22. This provision should be tailored as appropriate based on the capitalization of the Company and the definition of Change in Control.

(c) *Continuation of Employment.* Nothing in the Plan or in any instrument executed pursuant to the Plan will confer upon any Participant any right to continue employment.[23]

(d) *Titles.* Titles are provided herein for convenience only and are not to serve as a basis for interpretation or construction of the Plan.

(e) *Conformity to Securities Laws.* The Plan is intended to conform to the extent necessary with all provisions of the Securities Act and the Exchange Act and any and all regulations and rules promulgated by the Securities and Exchange Commission thereunder to the extent the Company or any Participant is subject to the provisions thereof. Notwithstanding anything herein to the contrary, the Plan shall be administered, and Restricted Stock Awards shall be granted only in such a manner, as to conform to such laws, rules, and regulations. To the extent permitted by applicable law, the Plan and Restricted Stock Awards granted hereunder shall be deemed amended to the extent necessary to conform to such laws, rules, and regulations. As a condition precedent to the issuance of Shares pursuant hereto, the Company may require the Participant to take any reasonable action to comply with such laws, rules, and regulations.

(f) *Withholding.* The Company may make such provisions as it deems appropriate to withhold any taxes the Company determines it is required to withhold in connection with any Restricted Stock Award. The Company may require the Participant to satisfy any relevant tax requirements before authorizing any issuance of Shares to the Participant. Such settlement may be made in cash or Shares, at the discretion of the Board.[24]

(g) *Governing Law.* To the extent not preempted by federal law, the Plan shall be construed in accordance with and governed by the laws of the state of [_____].

---

23. If directors are eligible to participant in the Plan, include a provision that nothing in the Plan would confer upon any director any right to continue to serve on the Board.

24. Withholding on Shares should be only the minimum amount required to be withheld. Withholding from shares in excess of minimum required amount results in adverse accounting.

(h) *Severability.* In the event any portion of the Plan or any action taken pursuant thereto shall be held illegal or invalid for any reason, the illegality shall not affect the remaining parts of the Plan, and the Plan shall be construed and enforced as if the illegal or invalid provisions had not been included, and the illegal or invalid action shall be null and void.

10. EFFECTIVE DATE OF THE PLAN

The Plan will become effective as of _____, 20____.

I hereby certify that the foregoing Plan was duly adopted by the Board of Directors of ABC Corporation on _____ ___, 20__.

Executed on this ___ day of _____, 20___.

Secretary

ABC CORPORATION
RESTRICTED STOCK AGREEMENT

THIS RESTRICTED STOCK AGREEMENT (the "Agreement"), made this
_____ day of _____, 20___, between ABC Corporation,
a _____ corporation (the "Company"), and _____
_____ (the "Participant").

WITNESSETH:

WHEREAS, the Company maintains the ABC Corporation Restricted
Stock Plan (the "Plan") in order to attract and retain quality management personnel and provide its officers and other key employees with
incentives to achieve long-term corporate objectives;

WHEREAS, the Participant is an officer or other key employee of the
Company with responsibility for the management or administration
of the Company's business;

WHEREAS, the Company's Board of Directors has determined to
grant Restricted Stock under the Plan to the Participant on the terms
and conditions set forth below.

NOW, THEREFORE, in consideration of the various covenants and
agreements herein contained, and intending to be legally bound hereby,
the parties hereto agree as follows:

1.　*Award.*

　　(a)　The Company hereby grants to Participant a total of _____
　　　　_____ shares of common stock, $__ par value per share, of
　　　　the Company (the "Restricted Stock"), subject to the terms,
　　　　restrictions, and other conditions of this Agreement and the
　　　　Plan. Any term used herein and not defined shall have the
　　　　meaning given such term in the Plan.

　　(b)　[Within 30 days after the date hereof, Participant will make
　　　　an effective election with the Internal Revenue Service under
　　　　Section 83(b) of the Internal Revenue Code and the regula-

tions promulgated thereunder in the form of Exhibit A attached hereto.][1]

2. *Purchase Price.* [Participant shall deliver $_____ to the Company as the purchase price for such Restricted Stock.][2]

3. *Stock Certificates.* The Company shall cause the Restricted Stock to be issued and a stock certificate or certificates representing the Restricted Stock to be registered in the name of Participant or held in book entry form promptly upon execution of this Agreement, but if a stock certificate or certificates is issued, it shall be delivered to, and held in custody by, the Company until the applicable restrictions lapse at the times specified in Section 5 below, such Restricted Stock is forfeited as specified in Section 6 below, [or such Restricted Stock is repurchased by the Company as described in Section 6 below].[3]

4. *Restrictions.* Participant shall have all rights and privileges of a stockholder of the Company with respect to the Restricted Stock, including voting rights and the right to receive dividends paid with respect to such shares, except that the following restrictions shall apply:

---

1. Grants of Restricted Stock are taxed under Section 83 of the Internal Revenue Code of 1986, as amended (the "Code"), at the time of grant, or if the shares are subject to a "substantial risk of forfeiture" at the time such shares vest and are no longer subject to such substantial risk of forfeiture. Restricted Stock subject to vesting based on time or performance criteria is subject to a substantial risk of forfeiture. Section 83(b) of the Code allows the Participant to elect to be taxed at the time of grant instead of at vesting or when the restrictions lapse. The Company receives a tax deduction in the amount and at the same time the Employee recognizes ordinary income. Some companies require Participants to make Section 83(b) elections in order to accelerate the tax deduction for such grant.

2. Certain state security laws, known as "blue sky laws," or state corporate laws require that the Participant pay a certain amount for Restricted Stock. If applicable, include this provision with the appropriate purchase amount. In certain states, the Participant is required to pay par value for an award of shares of Restricted Stock.

3. Include repurchase language only if participant actually pays for the shares rather than straight grant.

(a) Until all restrictions lapse as provided in Section 5 below, shares of Restricted Stock granted to Participant pursuant to this Agreement are subject to reacquisition by the Company immediately upon a termination of Participant's employment with the Company, its Subsidiaries, or Parent (a "Termination of Employment") [other than from death, disability, normal retirement, early retirement with unreduced retirement benefits or with the consent of the Company early retirement without unreduced retirement benefits (each as determined by the Company in accordance with Company plans and policies), in which event all restrictions with respect to such shares of Restricted Stock shall immediately expire.][4]

(b) No Restricted Stock or any interest or right therein or part thereof shall be liable for the debts, contracts, or engagements of the Participant or his/her successors in interest or shall be subject to disposition by transfer, alienation, anticipation, pledge, hypothecation, encumbrance, assignment, or any other means, whether such disposition be voluntary or involuntary or by operation of law by judgment, levy, attachment, garnishment, or any other legal or equitable proceedings (including bankruptcy), any attempted disposition thereof shall be null and void and of no effect; provided, however, that this Section 4(b) shall not prevent transfers by will or by the applicable laws of descent and distribution. [Notwithstanding the foregoing, Participant may transfer the Restricted Stock without receipt of consideration thereof to Participant's spouse and any lineal descendant (whether natural or adopted) or antecedent, brother or sister, or the spouse of any of the foregoing (collectively, "Immediate Family"), any trust for the benefit of such Participant or such Participant's Immediate Family, any corporation or partnership in which such Participant or such Participant's Immediate Family (or trust(s) for any of their benefit) are the direct and beneficial owners of all of the equity interests (provided such Partici-

---

4. Full vesting upon death, disability, or retirement may be required under state blue sky laws. Modify as appropriate for blue sky laws, as well as intent of the Company.

pant's or Participant's Immediate Family or trust(s) for any of their benefit continue to be the direct and beneficial owners of all such equity interests), the personal representative of such Participant upon such Participant's death for purposes of administration of such Participant's estate or upon such Participant's incompetence for purposes of the protection and management of the assets of such Participant, and any retirement plan for the Participant.][5]

(c) [The Company will retain custody of all dividends and other distributions ("Retained Distributions") made or declared with respect to the Restricted Stock (and such Retained Distributions will be subject to the same restrictions, terms, and conditions as are applicable to the Restricted Stock) until such time, if ever, as the Restricted Stock with respect to which such Retained Distributions shall have been made, paid, or declared shall have become vested, and such Retained Distributions shall not bear interest or be segregated in separate accounts.][6]

5. *Lapse of Restrictions.* The restrictions set forth in Section 4 on shares of Restricted Stock shall lapse, and shares of Restricted Stock shall vest upon satisfaction of the following:

(a) [Time Lapse Only: Insert schedule for lapse of restrictions.][7]

(b) [Time and Performance Lapse: All restrictions on shares of Restricted Stock will lapse on _____, 20__;[8] provided,

---

5. A Company may permitted certain transfers such as those delineated here in order to permit the Participant to include the Restricted Stock in his or her tax planning. However, the Company should consider the administrative burden of such an accommodation prior to authorizing such transfers.

6. This provision should only be included if dividends are to be subject to same vesting restrictions as Restricted Stock.

7. The Board may have all restrictions lapse at one time, known as "cliff vesting," or the restrictions on shares of Restricted Stock may lapse incrementally in annual or quarterly installments.

8. To avoid adverse accounting treatment, the outside vesting date must be "reasonable." Most companies select an outside vesting date similar to that for its

however, that if prior to the Restricted Stock shall vest if the following performance goals are satisfied: (Insert description of Performance Goals)]

(c)   [Performance Lapse only: All restrictions on shares of Restricted Stock will lapse in the amounts set forth below based upon satisfaction of the following performance goals: (Insert description of Performance Goals and percentage vesting)][9]

6.   *Forfeiture/Purchase of Stock by the Company.*

(a)   Upon Termination of Employment, Participant shall forfeit any shares of Restricted Stock that remain subject to any restrictions set forth in Section 4. [The Company shall reacquire any shares of Restricted Stock that remain subject to any restrictions set forth in Section 4 upon Termination of Employment, by promptly paying to the Participant an amount equal to the product of $_____ times the number of shares of Restricted Stock reacquired.][10]

(b)   [In the event of a Change of Control (as defined in the Plan) that results in the vesting of shares of Restricted Stock, the Participant agrees to sell, and the Company shall purchase, any Shares owned by the Participant as of the Change of Control as provided in the Plan.][11]

---

option plan. If a company does not have an option plan, the company should consult with its independent accountants for a determination of a reasonable outside vesting date upon which all restrictions will lapse.

9.   Adverse accounting treatment for Restricted Stock may be triggered if a Company grants Restricted Stock for which restrictions lapse only based on achievement of performance targets. Companies desiring to implement performance only lapsing should consult with its legal counsel and independent accountants regarding the impact of such accounting treatment.

10.   Some state blue sky and corporate laws require the Company to repurchase unvested shares for a minimum of par value. This language should be included if repurchase is required by state law. Also, if Participant was required to purchase the Restricted Stock for a certain price, then consider providing for repurchase at a price equal to the lesser of the fair market value of the shares or the original purchase price.

11.   A Company should consider including this provision requiring the Participant to cash out shares in the event of a Change in Control. In addition, the

7. *Issuance of Stock Certificates for Shares.* The stock certificate or certificates representing the Restricted Stock shall be issued promptly following the execution of this Agreement and shall be delivered to the Corporate Secretary or such other custodian as may be designated by the Company, to be held until their release as provided in Section 3.[12] The certificates representing the Restricted Stock will bear a legend in substantially the form set forth below.

> THE SECURITIES REPRESENTED BY THIS CERTIFICATE ARE SUBJECT TO CERTAIN RESTRICTIONS AND MAY BE SUBJECT TO REACQUISITION BY THE COMPANY UNDER THE TERMS OF THAT CERTAIN RESTRICTED STOCK AGREEMENT BY AND BETWEEN ABC CORPORATION (THE "COMPANY") AND THE HOLDER OF THE SECURITIES. PRIOR TO LAPSE OF RESTRICTIONS AND VESTING OF OWNERSHIP IN THE SECURITIES, THEY MAY NOT BE DIRECTLY OR INDIRECTLY, OFFERED, TRANSFERRED, SOLD, ASSIGNED, PLEDGED, HYPOTHECATED OR OTHERWISE DISPOSED OF UNDER ANY CIRCUMSTANCES. COPIES OF THE ABOVE REFERENCED AGREEMENT ARE ON FILE AT THE OFFICES OF THE COMPANY AT [ADDRESS].[13]

8. *Tax Withholding.* Whenever the restrictions on Participant's rights to shares of Restricted Stock lapse pursuant to Section 5 of this Agreement, the Company shall notify Participant of the amount of tax that must be withheld by the Company under all applicable federal, state and local tax laws. Participant agrees to make arrangements with the Company to (a) remit a cash payment of the

---

Company should consider the "golden parachute" rules under Section 280G of the Code that might be implicated upon the acceleration of vesting of shares of Restricted Stock due to a Change in Control. The Company should consider whether a gross-up provision for the benefit of the Participant or a cap limiting the amount payable to the Participant pursuant to the Restricted Stock Agreement upon a Change in Control is appropriate.

12. If the shares are publicly traded, the Company's transfer agent may also be designated to hold the shares.

13. If the Participant is required to enter into a stockholders' agreement upon the lapse of restrictions, then the legend should also include a reference to restrictions in the stockholders agreement, if any.

required amount to the Company or (b) authorize the deduction of such amounts from Participant's compensation.

9.   *Securities Laws.*[14]

(a)   In connection with the grant of the Restricted Stock, Participant covenants, represents, and warrants to the Company that:

(i)   The Restricted Stock to be acquired by Participant pursuant to this Agreement will be acquired for Participant's own account and not with a view to, or intention of, distribution thereof in violation of the Securities Act of 1933 (the "Securities Act"), as amended, or any applicable state securities laws, and neither the Restricted Stock nor any other shares of capital stock of the Company issued or issuable directly or indirectly with respect to the Restricted Stock by way of dividend or split or in connection with a combination of securities, recapitalization, merger, consolidation, or other reorganization will be disposed of in contravention of the Securities Act, any applicable state securities laws and any procedures reasonably established by the Board to ensure compliance with the foregoing.

(ii)   Participant is an [executive officer, employee] of the Company, is familiar with the financial affairs of the Company, is sophisticated in financial matters, and is able to evaluate the risks and benefits of the investment in the Restricted Stock.

(iii) Participant is able to bear the economic risk of his investment in the Restricted Stock for an indefinite period of time because the Restricted Stock has not been registered under the Securities Act and, therefore,

---

14. The Participant may be required to make certain representations and covenants regarding his or her eligibility to acquire shares of Restricted Stock in order to meet certain exemptions from registration requirements under federal and state securities laws. A company should consult with legal counsel regarding federal and state securities laws that are applicable to grants of Restricted Stock to Participants.

cannot be sold unless subsequently registered under the Securities Act or an exemption from such registration is available.

(iv) Participant has had an opportunity to ask questions and receive answers concerning the terms and conditions of the offering of Restricted Stock and has had full access to such other information concerning the Company as he has requested.

(v) This Agreement constitutes the legal, valid, and binding obligation of Participant, enforceable in accordance with its terms, and the execution, delivery, and performance of this Agreement by Participant does not and will not conflict with, violate, or cause a breach of any agreement, contract, or instrument to which Participant is a party or any judgment, order, or decree to which Participant is subject.

10. *Conditions to Issuance of Stock Certificates.* The Company shall not be required to issue or deliver any certificate or certificates for shares of Restricted Stock pursuant to this Agreement prior to fulfillment of all of the following conditions:

(a) The admission of such shares to listing on all stock exchanges on which such class of stock is then listed;

(b) The completion of any registration or other qualification of such shares under any state or federal law or under rulings or regulations of the Securities and Exchange Commission or of any other governmental regulatory body, which the Board shall, in its sole discretion, deem necessary or advisable;

(c) The obtaining of any approval or other clearance from any state or federal governmental agency which the Board shall, in its sole discretion, determine to be necessary or advisable;

(d) The payment by the Participant of all amounts that, under federal, state or local tax law, the Company (or other employer corporation) is required to withhold upon issuance of Restricted Stock and/or the lapse or removal of any of the restrictions; and

(e) The lapse of such reasonable period of time as the Company may from time to time establish for reasons of administrative convenience.

11. *No Right to Continued Employment.* Nothing in this Agreement or in the Plan shall confer upon the Participant any right to continue in the employment or other service of the Company, any Parent, or any Subsidiary, or shall interfere with or restrict in any way the rights of the Company, any Parent, or any Subsidiary, which are hereby expressly reserved, to discharge the Participant at any time for any reasons whatsoever, with or without cause.

12. *Restricted Stock Subject to Plan.* Notwithstanding anything in this Agreement to the contrary, the terms of this Agreement shall be subject to the terms of the Plan, a copy of which may be obtained by the Participant from the office of the Company's Secretary.

13. *Miscellaneous.*

(a) This Agreement may be executed in one or more counterparts, all of which taken together will constitute one and the same instrument.

(b) The terms of this Agreement may only be amended, modified, or waived by a written agreement executed by both of the parties hereto.

(c) The validity, performance, construction, and effect of this Agreement shall be governed by and construed in accordance with the laws of the State of _____.

(d) This Agreement and the Plan constitute the entire agreement between the parties hereto with respect to the Restricted Stock Award granted herein.[15]

(e) Except as otherwise herein provided, this Agreement shall be binding upon and shall inure to the benefit of the Company, its successors and assigns, and of Participant and Participant's personal representatives.

---

15. If the Participant has an employment agreement that governs the terms of the Restricted Stock Award, the agreement should be referenced.

IN WITNESS WHEREOF, the parties have executed this Agreement on the date and year first above written.

ABC CORPORATION
 By:
 Name:
 Title:

PARTICIPANT
 Name:

EXHIBIT A
ELECTION UNDER SECTION 83(b) OF THE
INTERNAL REVENUE CODE OF 1986

The undersigned taxpayer hereby elects, pursuant to Section 83(b) of the Internal Revenue Code of 1986, as amended, to include in taxpayer's gross income for the current taxable year the amount of any compensation taxable to taxpayer in connection with taxpayer's receipt of the property described below:

1.   The name, address, taxpayer identification number and taxable year of the undersigned are as follows:

NAME: TAXPAYER: _____

SPOUSE: _____

ADDRESS: _____

_____

_____

IDENTIFICATION NO.: TAXPAYER: _____

SPOUSE: _____

TAXABLE YEAR: _____

2.   The property with respect to which the election is made is described as follows: _____ shares of Common Stock (the "Shares") of ABC Corporation (the "Company").

3.   The date on which the property was transferred is _____ _____.

4.   The property is subject to the following restrictions: The Shares may not be transferred and are subject to forfeiture under the terms of an agreement between the taxpayer and the Company.

These restrictions lapse upon the satisfaction of certain conditions contained in such agreement.

5.   The fair market value at the time of transfer, determined without regard to any restriction other than a restriction which by its terms will never lapse, of such property is: $_____ .

6.   The amount (if any) paid for such property is: $_____ .

The undersigned has submitted a copy of this statement to the person for whom the services were performed in connection with the undersigned's receipt of the above-described property. The transferee of such property is the person performing the services in connection with the transfer of said property.

The undersigned understands that the foregoing election may not be revoked except with the consent of the Commissioner.

Dated: _____

_____
Taxpayer

The undersigned spouse of taxpayer joins in this election.
Dated: _____

_____
Taxpayer

Performance Unit Plan Document

Helen H. Morrison
Kay Kemp

The following document is included on the CD-ROM that accompanies this book. This is a sample document that must be customized before being used. A company should consult with its own legal and accounting advisors before implementing any equity (or equity-equivalent) compensation plan. Before working with this document, please read appendix A of this book for more information and important disclaimers.

ABC CORPORATION
PERFORMANCE UNIT PLAN

1. PURPOSE OF THE PLAN

ABC Corporation (the "Company") has established the ABC Corporation Performance Unit Plan (the "Plan"). The purposes of the Plan are to:

(a) Reward key employees who contribute to the long-term growth and increased value of the Company;

(b) Attract, retain, and motivate key employees; and

(c) Provide long-term incentive compensation to key employees that is competitive with other similarly situated companies.

2. DEFINITIONS

"Award" means an award of Units to a Participant by the Committee in accordance with Article IV.

"Award Agreement" shall mean a written agreement evidencing any Award granted under the Plan.

"Board of Directors" means the Board of Directors of the Company.

"Cause"[1] shall mean (a) the continued failure by Participant to substantially perform Participant's duties with the Company (other than any such failure resulting from Participant's Disability), after a demand for substantial performance is delivered to Participant that specifically identifies the manner in which the Company believes that Participant has not substantially performed Participant's duties, and Participant has failed to resume substantial performance of Participant's duties on a continuous basis; (b) gross and willful misconduct during the course of employment (regardless of whether the misconduct occurs on the Company's premises), including, but not limited to, theft, assault, battery, malicious destruction of property, arson, sabotage, embezzlement, harassment, acts or omissions that violate the Company's rules or policies (such as breaches of confidentiality), or other conduct that demonstrates a willful or reckless disregard of the interests of the Company; or (c) Participant's conviction of a crime (including, without limitation, a misdemeanor offense) that impairs Participant's ability substantially to perform Participant's duties with the Company.

["Change in Control" means any of the following:][2]

"Change in Control Termination" means any termination of an Award by the Company pursuant to Section 6(d) following a Change in Control, provided that a termination or forfeiture of an Award or Units in accordance with Sections 6(e), 5(f), and 5(g) shall not constitute a Change in Control Termination.

"Code of Ethics" means the Company's Code of Ethics and the Company's Code of Ethics (a copy of which is attached hereto as Appendix A), in each case as in effect from time to time.

"Committee" means an oversight committee with respect to the Plan designated by the Board of Directors and comprised of individuals (which at all times shall include two members of senior management of the Company) recommended by the chief executive officer of the Company and the head of human resources of the Company.

---

1. The definition of "Cause" should conform to that definition in related compensation plans or employment agreements.

2. See the alternative definitions provided in this book's sample stock appreciation rights plan and phantom stock plan. If the Plan permits a deferral of the performance share award, then the definition of Change in Control must satisfy the requirements of Code Section 409A.

"Company"[3] has the meaning set forth in Section 1.

"Deferred Compensation Plan" means the ABC Corporation Deferred Compensation Plan or any successor deferred compensation plan hereafter adopted by the Company.

"Disability" means a Participant is, by reason of any medically determinable physical or mental impairment that can be expected to result in death or can be expected to last for a continuous period of at least 12 months, receiving disability benefits for a period of at least three months under the Company's long-term disability programs as in effect from time to time.

"EBITDA"[4] means, for any Fiscal Year, the Company's earnings determined after accrual of any expenses resulting from Incentive Payments but before accrual of interest expense, federal and state income taxes, and depreciation and amortization expenses, as determined by the Company's independent certified public accountants from the Company's financial statements, in accordance with the Company's regular method of accounting consistently applied, provided that (a) in determining EBITDA, all operations of the Company's private asset management group will be excluded, and (b) the Committee shall have the authority to adjust the EBITDA determination in accordance with Section 4(c).

"EBITDA Multiple" means 5.0, provided that the Committee may change the EBITDA Multiple in accordance with Section 4(b).[5]

"Effective Date" has the meaning set forth in Section 10(a).

"Estimated Unit Value" means, with respect to each Unit subject to an Award granted under the Plan, an amount equal to the future value of the Unit at the end of the five-year period following the Grant Date, assuming a 10% annual increase in the value of such Unit during such five-year period.[6]

---

3. The plan would typically include also a definition of "Subsidiary" or "Affiliate."

4. This performance unit plan is based on the company's EBITDA and the EBITDA multiple. As explained in the chapter on performance award plans, the performance measurement for a performance unit plan can be based on any financial or nonfinancial measurement selected by the company.

5. The company would select the appropriate EBITDA multiple. A 5.0 multiple is used only for illustrative purposes.

6. The performance period is set by the company. Generally, the performance period will be from three to five years. The growth rate is also set by the com-

["Exchange Act" means the Securities and Exchange Act of 1934, as amended.][7]

"Fiscal Year" means any fiscal year of the Company ending December 31.

"Grant Date" means, with respect to an Award, the date on which such Award is effective, as specified in the applicable Award Agreement.

"Grant Date Enterprise Value" means an amount determined by multiplying (a) EBITDA for the Fiscal Year ended immediately before the Grant Date of an Award, by (b) the EBITDA Multiple.

"Grant Date Unit Value" means, with respect to each Unit subject to an Award granted under the Plan, the amount determined by dividing (a) the Grant Date Enterprise Value, by (b) the Total Authorized Units.

"Incentive Payment" means a cash bonus payment made to a Participant in accordance with Section 7.

"Participant" means each employee of the Company to whom the Committee grants an Award pursuant to the Plan.

"Payout Date" means the date upon which the Company makes an Incentive Payment to a Participant.

"Performance Period" means, with respect to any Award, the five-year period from the first day of the Fiscal Year in which the Grant Date of such Award occurs through the last day of the Fiscal Year ending five years thereafter.[8]

["Person" shall have the meaning set forth in Sections 13(d)(3) and 14(d)(2) of the Exchange Act.][9]

"Plan" has the meaning set forth in Section 1.

"Retirement" means termination of employment with the Company by a Participant who is age 59½ or older and has 10 or more years of employment with the Company (based on the Person's latest date of

---

pany. The five-year performance period and 10% growth rate are used here for illustrative purposes only.

7. This term is generally used in the "Change in Control" definition.

8. The performance period is defined by the company and is typically between three to five years.

9. This term is generally used in the "Change in Control" definition.

hire by the Company).[10]

"Total Authorized Units" has the meaning set forth in Section 3(a).

"Unit Spread Value" means, with respect to each Unit subject to an Award granted under the Plan, an amount determined by subtracting (a) the Grant Date Unit Value from (b) the Valuation Date Unit Value, provided that the Unit Spread Value may not be less than zero.

"Units" means each of the phantom stock option units authorized under the Plan that may result in the Participant holding such units receiving an Incentive Payment equal to the Unit Spread Value.

"Valuation Date" means, with respect to any Award, either of the following dates, as applicable: (a) the last day of any Performance Period for such Award, or (b) the date upon which the employment of a Participant holding Vested Units subject to such Award is terminated as described in Section 6(b), (c) or (d).

"Valuation Date Enterprise Value" means an amount determined by multiplying (a) EBITDA for the applicable Valuation Year by (b) the EBITDA Multiple.

"Valuation Date Unit Value" means, with respect to each Unit subject to an Award granted under the Plan, the amount determined by dividing (a) the Valuation Date Enterprise Value by (b) the Total Authorized Units.

"Valuation Year" means (a) the Fiscal Year ended immediately before the applicable Valuation Date for an Award, if such Valuation Date occurs in the first six months of any Fiscal Year, and (b) the Fiscal Year ended immediately after the applicable Valuation Date for an Award, if such Valuation Date occurs in the last six months of any Fiscal Year. If the Valuation Date is the last day of the Fiscal Year, then the applicable Valuation Year shall be the Fiscal Year ending on that Valuation Date.

"Vested Units" means any Units that have vested pursuant to Section 6.

---

10. The "Retirement" date is used here for illustrative purposes only. If the Plan permits a deferral of the performance share award and the Company is a public company, then payments to a specified employee (as defined in Prop. Treas. Reg. § 1.409A-1(i)) will be subject to a 6-month wait.

3. AUTHORIZED UNITS; TRANSFERABILITY

(a) Authorized Units. The total number of Units that the Committee shall have authority to issue under the Plan shall be 250,000,000 (the "Total Authorized Units").[11]

(b) Adjustments. In the event of any reorganization, merger, consolidation, spin-off, or other corporate transaction or event affecting the Units that would be reasonably likely to result in the diminution or enlargement of any of the benefits or potential benefits intended to be made available under the Plan or any Award (if such diminution or enlargement would go beyond the effect of such event on a shareholder of an independent asset management company), the Committee shall, in such manner as it shall deem equitable or appropriate in order to prevent such diminution or enlargement of any such benefits or potential benefits, adjust any or all of (a) the number and type of Units that thereafter may be made the subject of Awards and (b) the number and type of Units subject to outstanding Awards.

(c) Nontransferability. No Award, Unit, or right thereunder shall be transferable by a Participant otherwise by will or the laws of decent and distribution. No Award, Unit or right thereunder may be pledged, alienated, attached, or otherwise encumbered, and any purported pledge, alienation, attachment, or encumbrance thereof shall be void and unenforceable against the Company.

4. ADMINISTRATION OF THE PLAN

(a) General. Subject to the terms and conditions of the Plan, the Committee shall have full power and authority to administer the Plan. The Committee shall (i) determine the employees of the Company to be granted Units under the Plan; (ii) determine the number of Units to be granted to each Participant; (iii) determine the time or times at which Units will be granted to Participants; (iv) interpret and administer the Plan and any award agreement; (v) establish,

---

11. The total number of units is dependent on the company's capital structure and the value of the grants.

amend, suspend, or waive such rules and regulations and appoint such agents as it shall deem appropriate for the proper administration of the Plan; and (vi) make any other determination and take any other action that the Committee deems necessary or desirable for the administration of the Plan. Without limiting the generality of the foregoing, the Committee shall make all determinations regarding the Grant Date Enterprise Value, the Grant Date Unit Value, the Valuation Date Enterprise Value, the Valuation Date Unit Value, the Unit Spread Value, the Estimated Unit Value, and the amount of any Incentive Payment.

(b) EBITDA Multiple. The Committee shall have the authority to change the EBITDA Multiple to reflect a shift in market-based multiples for companies in the institutional investment market similar to the Company, provided that the Committee may not change the EBITDA Multiple with respect to an Award after such Award has been granted.

(c) EBITDA. The Committee, in determining EBITDA, shall (i) consider whether or not to include or exclude in the determination of EBITDA any extraordinary, nonrecurring, or unusual items, (ii) give appropriate effect to any acquisitions or dispositions of businesses or assets by the Company, and (iii) give appropriate effect to any recurring, material change in revenue-sharing or other similar allocations between divisions or units of the Company, provided that any determination regarding the adjustment of EBITDA as a result of such items or events shall be made by the Committee within its sole discretion on a consistent basis that is equitable for Participants.

(d) Correction of Defects. The Committee may correct any defect, supply any omission, or reconcile any inconsistency in the Plan or any Award in the manner and to the extent it shall deem desirable to carry the Plan into effect.

(e) Committee Determinations Binding. Unless otherwise expressly provided in the Plan, all determinations, interpretations, and other decisions under or with respect to the Plan or any Award shall be within the sole discretion of the Committee, may be made at any time, and shall be final, conclusive, and binding upon any

Participant, any beneficiary or estate of any Participant, and any employee of the Company.

5. ELIGIBILITY; UNIT AWARDS

(a) Eligibility. The Committee shall determine eligibility for participation in the Plan based on its judgment of the impact of a key employee on the Company's performance and on prevailing market practice regarding eligibility in similar programs for like employees in comparable companies. To be eligible for an Award, an employee must have a satisfactory performance rating and not be in a formal disciplinary status.

(b) Grant of Awards. The Committee may award Units to key employees of the Company determined by the Committee to be eligible to become Participants at such times and in such amounts as the Committee determines. Awards may be granted to new employees of the Company at the time they commence employment with the Company, as determined by the Company within its sole discretion.

(c) Award Agreement. Upon each grant of Units to a Participant, the Committee will give the Participant written notice of such grant, and will require the Participant, as a condition to participation in the Plan, to execute and return an Award Agreement. Subject to the terms and conditions of the Plan, the Award Agreement may contain any provisions as the Committee, in its sole discretion, may require.

6. VESTING; FORFEITURE

(a) Standard Vesting. Subject to the terms and conditions of this Plan, any Award granted hereunder shall vest on the last day of the Performance Period applicable to such Award, provided the Participant is an active employee of the Company on that date.

(b) Vesting Upon Disability or Retirement. If a Participant ceases to be an employee of the Company before the last day of the Performance Period due to Disability or Retirement, such Participant shall become immediately vested as of the date of such Disability or Retirement in all of such previously unvested Units.

(c) Vesting Upon Death. If a Participant ceases to be an employee of the Company before the last day of the Performance Period due to death, the Participant's estate or beneficiaries shall become immediately vested as of the date of the Participant's death in all of such previously unvested Units.

(d) Vesting Upon Change in Control Termination. If a Participant has an Award terminated as a result of a Change in Control Termination before the last day of the Performance Period, such Participant shall become vested in all of such previously unvested Units immediately prior to such Change in Control Termination of the Award.

(e) Forfeiture. If a Participant ceases to be an employee of the Company for any reason other than Disability, Retirement, or death prior to the vesting of any Units pursuant to this Section 6, all of Participant's rights to any unvested Units shall be immediately and irrevocably forfeited.

(f) Termination for Cause. Notwithstanding any other provision of this Plan, if a Participant's employment with the Company is terminated for Cause, the Participant shall immediately forfeit all outstanding Awards and Units (whether vested or unvested) and any rights to receive Incentive Payments thereunder.

(g) Breach of Code of Ethics. Notwithstanding any other provision of the Plan, if a Participant fails to comply in any material respect with the Code of Ethics (for any reason other than inadvertence), the Committee may immediately terminate any or all outstanding Awards and Units (whether vested or unvested) and any rights to receive Incentive Payments thereunder. In the event of such failure, the Committee may also reduce or defer any or all outstanding Awards and Units and any rights to receive Incentive Payments thereunder. All determinations of whether the Code of Ethics has been breached in any material respect and whether such breach was inadvertent shall be made by the Committee after receiving a recommendation with respect to such determination from the Company's Board of Directors.

7.   INCENTIVE PAYMENT

(a)   Payout at End of Performance Period. If a Participant is employed by the Company on the last day of the Performance Period applicable to an Award held by the Participant, the Company shall make an Incentive Payment to the Participant with respect to all Vested Units subject to the Award. Subject to Section 8, such Incentive Payment shall be made within 2-1/2 months after the end of the Performance Period.

(b)   Payments on Termination. Unless a Participant's Vested Units subject to an Award are forfeited pursuant to Section 6, if such Participant's employment with the Company is terminated due to death, Disability or Retirement, or a Change in Control Termination occurs, the Company shall make an Incentive Payment with respect to such Vested Units (including Units that become vested as a result of the termination of employment or a Change in Control Termination pursuant to Section 6). Such Incentive Payment shall be made (i) within 2-1/2 months after the end of the month in which the date of termination of employment or the Change in Control Termination occurs, if such date occurs during the first six months of any Fiscal Year, or (ii) within 2-1/2 months after the end of the applicable Valuation Year, if the date of termination of employment or the Change in Control Termination occurs during the last six months of such Fiscal Year.

(c)   Amount of Incentive Payment Generally. If any Award vests for any reason other than as a result of a Change in Control Termination, the amount of any Incentive Payment made with respect to such Award pursuant to this Section 7 shall be determined by multiplying (a) the Unit Spread Value applicable to the Units with respect to which an Incentive Payment is being made by (b) the number of Units with respect to which such Incentive Payment is being made.

(d)   Amount of Incentive Payment Following a Change in Control Termination.[12] If any Award vests as a result of a Change in Control Termination occurring within the 24-month period following the

---

12.   The employer must determine the appropriate formula for calculating the value to be paid upon a change in control.

Grant Date, the amount of any Incentive Payment with respect to such Award pursuant to this Section 7 shall be determined by multiplying [(a) the greater of (i) the Unit Spread Value or (ii) 60% of the Estimated Unit Value, by (b) the number of Units with respect to which such Incentive Payment is being made]. If any Award vests as a result of a Change in Control Termination occurring after the end of the 24-month period following the Grant Date, the amount of any Incentive Payment with respect to such Award pursuant to this Section 7 shall be determined by multiplying (x) the Unit Spread Value by (y) the number of Units with respect to which such Incentive Payment is being made.

(e) Form of Payment. Any Incentive Payments shall be made in single lump sum cash payment. Payment shall be made by direct deposit to the Participant's checking account if the Participant has authorized the direct deposit of salary and wages paid by the Company. If the Participant has not authorized such direct deposit, Incentive Payments shall be made by check.

(f) Tax Withholding. The Company shall have the right to deduct from all amounts paid pursuant to the Plan any taxes required by law to be withheld with respect to Incentive Payments. Any amounts so withheld shall be treated as paid to the Participant (or the Participant's beneficiary or estate, if applicable) for all purposes of the Plan.

(g) Value of Units. After the first year of any Performance Period applicable to an Award, the Company shall notify the Participant holding such Award in writing of the Unit Spread Value of a Unit subject to the Award.

8.   DEFERRAL ELECTION[13]

Within the time period designated by the Committee, but in no event later than six months before the end of the applicable Performance

---

13. Such a deferral election is an optional provision. As noted, if the plan permits the deferral of the performance award, then the plan will be subject to the requirements of Code Section 409A. If no deferral election is offered, then the plan will meet the "short-term deferral" exception because awards are paid

Period (or such earlier date as may be specified by the Committee), the Participant may elect to defer all or a portion (in increments of 25%) of the amount that the Participant is entitled to received under the applicable Award in accordance with the terms of the Deferred Compensation Plan, provided that no deferral election may be made with respect to amounts less than $5,000. A deferral election shall be irrevocable and shall be in writing on a form provided by the Committee. Amounts deferred under this Section shall become subject to all terms and conditions of the Deferred Compensation Plan, and shall be paid to the Participant pursuant to the provisions of said Plan.

9. CODE OF ETHICS[14]

In consideration of each Award made to a Participant, each Participant will be required to be familiar with the Code of Ethics and comply with the letter and spirit of the Code of Ethics at all times. Without limiting the generality of the foregoing, no Participant shall pay or offer to pay any part of such Participant's compensation or any other money to any customer or agent or representative of a customer as an inducement or reward for doing business with the Company.

10. TERM; AMENDMENT

(a)   Term. This Plan shall be effective as of January 1, 20__ (the "Effective Date"). The Plan shall continue in effect from the Effective Date until December 31, 20__, unless terminated as of an earlier date by the Committee.[15] Any Award granted during the term of the Plan may extend beyond the end of such term. The authority of the Committee provided with respect to the Plan and any Awards, as well as the authority of the Committee to amend the Plan, shall extend beyond the termination of the Plan with respect to outstanding Awards.

---

within 2½ months after they vest; in this case, the plan will not be subject to Code Section 409A.

14. Provisions of this sort relating to the employer's "Code of Ethics" are likely to become more prevalent following the recent corporate governance scandals.

15. The power to terminate the plan may rest with the board of directors, the CEO, or the committee that administers and oversees the plan.

(b) Amendments. The Committee may amend, alter, suspend, discontinue, or terminate the Plan at any time and from time to time.[16] No outstanding Award may be amended, altered, suspended, discontinued, or terminated, prospectively or retroactively, without the written consent of the Participant or beneficiary thereof, except as otherwise provided herein.

11. GENERAL PROVISIONS

(a) No Rights to Awards. No employee shall have any claim to be granted any Award under the Plan, and there is no obligation for uniformity of treatment of Participants or their beneficiaries under the Plan.

(b) Award Agreements. No Participant will have rights under an Award granted to such Participant unless and until an Award Agreement shall have been duly executed on behalf of the Company.

(c) No Limit on Other Compensation Arrangements. Nothing contained in the Plan shall prevent the Company from adopting or continuing in effect other or additional compensation arrangements, and such arrangements may be either generally applicable or applicable only in specific cases.

(d) No Right to Employment, Etc. The grant of an Award shall not be construed as giving a Participant the right to be retained in the employ of the Company. In addition, the Company may at any time dismiss a Participant from employment free from any liability or any claim under the Plan, unless otherwise expressly provided in the Plan or in any Award Agreement.

(e) Governing Law. The validity, construction, and effect of the Plan and any rules and regulations relating to the Plan shall be determined in accordance with the laws of the State of _____.

(f) Severability. If any provision of the Plan or any Award is or becomes or is deemed to be invalid, illegal, or unenforceable in any jurisdiction or would disqualify the Plan or any Award under any

---

16. The authority to amend the plan may be held by the board of directors, the CEO, or the committee.

law deemed applicable by the Committee, such provision shall be construed or deemed amended to conform to applicable laws, or if it cannot be so construed or deemed amended without, in the determination of the Committee, materially altering the purpose or intent of the Plan or the Award, such provision shall be stricken as to such jurisdiction or Award, and the remainder of the Plan or any such Award shall remain in full force and effect.

(g)   Unfunded Plan; No Trust or Fund Created. The Plan shall at all times be entirely unfunded, and no provision shall at any time be made with respect to segregating assets of the Company for the payment of any amounts that may become due hereunder. Neither the Plan nor any Award shall create or be construed to create a trust or separate fund of any kind or a fiduciary relationship between the Company and a Participant or any other Person. To the extent that any Person acquires a right to receive payments from the Company pursuant to an Award, such right shall rank *pari passu* the rights of any unsecured general creditor of the Company.

(h)   Beneficiary Designation. Each Participant may, from time to time, name a beneficiary or beneficiaries to whom any amount the Participant is entitled to receive under the Plan is to be paid in the event of the Participant's death prior to the payment of such amount. Each designation made by a Participant shall revoke all prior designations made by such Participant, shall be in writing on a form provided by the Committee, and will be effective only when delivered by the Participant to the Company during the Participant's lifetime. If a Participant fails to designate a beneficiary pursuant to this subsection, any amounts due to the Participant under the Plan in the event of the Participant's death shall be paid to the Participant's estate.

(i)   Headings. Headings are given to the Sections and subsections of the Plan solely as a convenience to facilitate reference. Such headings shall not be deemed in any way material or relevant to the construction or interpretation of the Plan or any provision thereof.

I hereby certify that the foregoing Plan was duly adopted by the Board of Directors of ABC Corporation on _____ _____, 20__.

Executed on this _____ day of _____, 20___.

_____

Secretary

Direct Stock Purchase Plan Documents

David R. Johanson

The following documents are included on the CD-ROM that accompanies this book. These are sample documents that must be customized before being used. A company should consult with its own legal and accounting advisors before implementing any equity (or equity-equivalent) compensation plan. Before working with these documents, please read appendix A of this book for more information and important disclaimers.

STOCK PURCHASE AGREEMENT

THIS AGREEMENT is made and entered into as of April __, 20__, between ABC Company, a _____ corporation (the "Corporation"), and Jane Doe (the "Purchaser").

RECITALS:

A.   The Purchaser has elected to purchase _____ shares of the Corporation's Common Stock for an aggregate purchase price of $_____.

B.   The Purchaser has agreed to grant the Corporation the option to repurchase such shares under certain circumstances.

NOW, THEREFORE, in consideration of the mutual covenants exchanged, the parties agree as follows:

I.   *Exercise of Option.*

   (a)   *Exercise.* The Purchaser hereby agrees to purchase _____ shares of the Corporation's Common Stock (the "Shares") at a purchase price of _____ and No/100 Dollars ($_____) per share (the "Purchase Price").

(b) *Payment.* Concurrently with the delivery of this Agreement to the Corporation, the Purchaser shall pay the consideration for the Shares purchased hereunder and shall deliver any additional documents that may be required by the Corporation as a condition to such exercise.

2. *Repurchase Option.* [Depending upon the applicable state securities laws, this section may need to be edited or eliminated entirely in order to properly create a broad-based equity incentive plan.]

(a) *Shares Subject to Repurchase.* The Purchaser hereby grants to the Corporation the option (the "Repurchase Option") to repurchase all or part of the Shares, upon the occurrences set forth in subsection (b).

(b) *Occurrences Permitting Exercise.* The Corporation may exercise the Repurchase Option upon [the Purchaser's purchase of the Corporation's Common Stock—this should be edited to fit the particular circumstances of a targeted or broad-based equity incentive plan and may have to be deleted entirely in some cases] ("Offering Event").

(c) *Exercise of Repurchase Option.* On or after the occurrence of an Offering Event, the Corporation may exercise the Repurchase Option by delivering a notice pursuant to Section 15 of this Agreement to the Purchaser (or his permitted transferee or legal representative, as the case may be). The Corporation's notice to the Purchaser shall indicate the Corporation's election to exercise its Repurchase Option and the number of Shares to be purchased by the Corporation or the Corporation's designee, who shall be identified in such notice, and the notice shall set forth a date for closing not later than thirty (30) days from the date of the giving of such notice.

(d) *Closing for Repurchase of Shares.* The closing for the repurchase of the Shares pursuant to the exercise of the Repurchase Option shall take place at the Corporation's principal offices. At the closing, the holder of the certificate(s) representing the Shares being transferred shall deliver such certificate or certificates evidencing the Shares to the Corporation, duly endorsed for transfer, and the Corporation (or its designee) shall tender payment of the purchase price for the Shares being purchased. The purchase price for the Shares shall be payable (i) in full in cash, or by certified check or cashier's check or (ii) by the issuance of a promissory note payable over ten years at a commercially reasonable rate of interest; provided, however, that the Corporation may elect to offset against and deduct from any payment of the purchase price any indebtedness then owed by the Purchaser to the Corporation. The Corporation's Board of Directors shall determine in its sole discretion whether the purchase price shall be payable under method (i) or (ii). [The purchase price for the Shares shall be the Purchase Price in the event of the Purchaser's voluntary termination of employment with the Corporation without Good Reason (as defined in the Purchaser's Employment Agreement with the Corporation) or termination by the Corporation with Cause (as defined in the Purchaser's Employment Agreement with the Corporation).] For all other purposes, the purchase price for the Shares shall be the [insert formula price or "book value" of the Shares (as determined in accordance with generally accepted accounting principles)], as established by the Corporation's Board of Directors with the advice of legal counsel and the Corporation's independent certified public accountants or the Corporation's independent appraiser and/or financial adviser. [In California, the following "purchase price" provision should be added in order for capital stock to be issued to a broad-based group of employees pursuant to this type of standard agreement: For all other purposes, the purchase price for the Shares shall be the "fair value" of the Shares established by the Corporation's Board of Directors pursuant to Title 10, Section 260.140.50 of the California Code of Regulations and shall be determined in accordance with Section 2.(j) of the Plan.]

[Alternative Section 2 for broad-based equity incentive plans:]

[2.   *Right of First Refusal.* The Shares shall be subject to a "right of first refusal" in favor of the Corporation. The right of first refusal shall provide that, prior to any subsequent transfer, the Shares must first be offered for purchase in writing to the Corporation at the then "purchase price." A bona fide written offer from an independent prospective buyer shall be deemed to be the "purchase price" for this purpose. The Corporation shall have a total of 14 days to exercise the right of first refusal on the same terms offered by a prospective buyer. The Corporation's Board of Directors may establish reasonable additional procedures relating to this right of first refusal.]

3.   *Restrictions on Transfer.*

    (a)   Except as provided in Section 2 or in this Section 3, the Purchaser shall not sell, assign, transfer, pledge, or otherwise dispose of any of the Shares, or any right or interest therein, either voluntarily or involuntarily.

    (b)   *Gift of Shares.* Notwithstanding any other term of this Section 3, the Purchaser may make a gift of all or part of the Shares to any of his parents, brothers or sisters, spouse or issue, or to a trust for his or their exclusive benefit. The donee or donees shall hold such Shares subject to all provisions of this Agreement.

    (c)   *Nullification of Improper Transfer.* Any transfer by the Purchaser in violation of this Section shall be null and void and of no effect.

4.   *Adjustments.* If, from time to time during the term of this Agreement: (i) there is any stock dividend, distribution, or dividend of cash or property, stock split, or other change in the character or amount of any of the outstanding securities of the Corporation; or (ii) there is any consolidation, merger or sale of all, or substantially all, of the assets of the Corporation; or (iii) the Shares are converted into any other class of securities by capital reorganization or recapitalization; then, in such event, any and all new, substituted or additional securities, cash or other property to which the Purchaser is entitled by reason of his ownership of the Shares shall be immediately subject to the Repurchase Option and the other terms of this Agreement. While the total Purchase Price shall remain the same after any such event, the Purchase Price per share shall be appropriately adjusted.

5. *Legends.*

   (a) *Endorsement on Certificates.* The certificates representing the Shares subject to this Agreement shall be endorsed with a legend substantially in the following form:

   THE SHARES REPRESENTED BY THIS CERTIFICATE MAY BE TRANSFERRED ONLY IN ACCORDANCE WITH THE TERMS OF A STOCK PURCHASE AGREEMENT BETWEEN THE CORPORATION AND THE REGISTERED HOLDER OR HIS PREDECESSOR IN INTEREST, A COPY OF WHICH MAY BE OBTAINED UPON WRITTEN REQUEST TO THE SECRETARY OF THE CORPORATION. THE AGREEMENT MAY BE INSPECTED AT THE PRINCIPAL OFFICE OF THE CORPORATION DURING NORMAL BUSINESS HOURS.

   (b) *Termination of All Restrictions.* In the event the restrictions imposed by this Agreement shall be terminated as herein provided, a new certificate or certificates representing the Shares shall be issued, on request, without the legend referred to in Section 6(a).

   (c) *Securities Law Legends.* Any transfer or sale of the Shares is further subject to all restrictions on transfer imposed by state or Federal securities laws. Accordingly, it is understood and agreed that the certificates representing the Shares shall bear any legends required by such state or Federal securities laws.

6. *Dissolution of Marriage.*

   (a) *Purchase of Shares from Former Spouse.* In the event of the dissolution of the Purchaser's marriage, including a decree of divorce or judgment of dissolution or separate maintenance, or under a property settlement or separation agreement, the Purchaser shall have the right and option to purchase from his or her spouse all of the Shares (i) awarded to the spouse pursuant to a decree of dissolution of marriage or any other order by any court of competent jurisdiction and/or any property settlement agreement (whether or not incorporated by reference in any such decree), or (ii) gifted to the spouse by the Purchaser prior to the dissolution, at the fair market value of such Shares on the date such shares are transferred to the spouse as determined by the Corporation's Board of Directors, upon the terms set forth below. The Purchaser shall exercise his or her right, if at all, within thirty (30) days following the entry of any such decree or property settlement agreement by delivery to the Purchaser's former spouse of written notice of exercise, specifying the number of Shares the Purchaser elects to purchase. The purchase price for the Shares shall be paid by delivery of a promissory note for the purchase price bearing interest at the rate of ten percent (10%) per annum payable in four (4) equal annual installments of principal and interest, commencing on the anniversary date of the exercise of the option; *provided, however,* that if, subsequent to the date any or all of the Shares is awarded to the Purchaser's former spouse as provided above, the Corporation exercises its Repurchase Option with respect to any or all of the Shares so awarded, the amount remaining due under such promissory note shall be reduced by the difference between the fair market value of such Shares determined as set forth above and the amount received by the Purchaser for such Shares upon exercise by the Corporation of the Repurchase Option.

(b) *Transfer of Rights to Corporation.* In the event the Purchaser does not exercise his or her right to purchase all of the Shares awarded to the Purchaser's former spouse, the Purchaser shall provide written notice to the Corporation of the number of Shares available for purchase and the purchase price of such Shares determined in accordance with Section 7(a) within thirty (30) days of the entry of the decree or property settlement agreement. The Corporation shall then have the right to purchase any of the Shares not acquired by the Purchaser directly from the Purchaser's former spouse in the manner provided in Section 2 above at the same price and on the same terms that were available to the Purchaser.

(c) *Shares Subject to Repurchase by Corporation.* Notwithstanding any other provisions of this Agreement, all of the Shares held by the Purchaser's spouse or former spouse will be subject to the Repurchase Option as such term is defined in Section 2, and all other provisions of this Agreement.

7. *Consent of Spouse.* If the Purchaser is married on the date of this Agreement, the Purchaser's spouse shall execute a Consent of Spouse in the form attached hereto, effective on the date hereof. Such consent shall not be deemed to confer or convey to the spouse any rights in the Shares that do not otherwise exist by operation of law or the agreement of the parties. If the Purchaser should marry or remarry subsequent to the date of this Agreement, the Purchaser shall within thirty (30) days thereafter obtain his or her new spouse's acknowledgment of and consent to the existence and binding effect of all restrictions contained in this Agreement by signing a Consent of Spouse in the form attached hereto.

8. *Compliance With Income Tax Laws.*

    (a) *Withholding Tax.* The Purchaser authorizes the Corporation to withhold in accordance with applicable law from any compensation payable to him or her any taxes required to be withheld by federal, state, or local laws as a result of the purchase of the Shares. Furthermore, in the event of any determination that the Corporation has failed to withhold a sum sufficient to pay all withholding taxes due in connection with the purchase of the Shares, the Purchaser agrees to pay the Corporation the amount of such deficiency in cash within five (5) days after receiving a written demand from the Corporation to do so, whether or not the Purchaser is an employee of the Corporation at that time.

    [Sections 9. and 10. of this standard agreement are typically intended to be used in connection with purchases of capital stock by executive employees and may not be applicable with respect to a broad-based equity incentive plan.]

9. *Purchaser's Representations.* In connection with the purchase of the Shares, the Purchaser hereby represents and warrants to the Corporation as follows:

(a) *Investment Intent; Capacity to Protect Interests.* The Purchaser is purchasing the Shares solely for his or her own account for investment and not with a view to or for sale in connection with any distribution of the Shares or any portion thereof and not with any present intention of selling, offering to sell or otherwise disposing of or distributing the Shares or any portion thereof in any transaction other than a transaction exempt from registration under the Securities Act of 1933, as amended (the "Act"). The Purchaser also represents that the entire legal and beneficial interest of the Shares is being purchased, and will be held, for the Purchaser's account only, and neither in whole or in part for any other person. The Purchaser either (i) has a pre-existing business or personal relationship with the Corporation or any of its officers, directors or controlling persons, or (ii) by reason of the Purchaser's business or financial experience or the business or financial experience of the Purchaser's professional advisors who are unaffiliated with and who are not compensated by the Corporation or any affiliate or selling agent of the Corporation, directly or indirectly, could be reasonably assumed to have the capacity to evaluate the merits and risks of an investment in the Corporation and to protect the Purchaser's own interests in connection with this transaction.

(b) *Information Concerning Corporation.* The Purchaser has heretofore discussed the Corporation and its plans, operations, and financial condition with the Corporation's officers and has heretofore received all such information as the Purchaser has deemed necessary and appropriate to enable the Purchaser to evaluate the financial risk inherent in making an investment in the Shares, and the Purchaser has received satisfactory and complete information concerning the business and financial condition of the Corporation in response to all inquiries in respect thereof.

(c) *Economic Risk.* The Purchaser realizes that the purchase of the Shares will be a highly speculative investment and involves a high degree of risk, and the Purchaser is able, without impairing his or her financial condition, to hold the Shares for an indefinite period of time and to suffer a complete loss on the Purchaser's investment.

(d) *Restricted Securities.* The Purchaser understands and acknowledges that:

    (i) the sale of the Shares has not been registered under the Act, and the Shares must be held indefinitely unless subsequently registered under the Act or an exemption from such registration is available and the Corporation is under no obligation to register the Shares;

    (ii) the stock certificate representing the Shares will be stamped with the legends specified in Section 5 hereof; and

    (iii) the Corporation will make a notation in its records of the aforementioned restrictions on transfer and legends.

(e) *Disposition under Rule 144.* The Purchaser understands that the Shares are restricted securities within the meaning of Rule 144 promulgated under the Act; that unless the Shares have been issued pursuant to Rule 701 promulgated under the Act the exemption from registration under Rule 144 will not be available in any event for at least one year from the date of purchase and payment of the Shares (AND THAT PAYMENT BY A NOTE IS NOT DEEMED PAYMENT UNLESS IT IS SECURED BY ASSETS OTHER THAN THE SHARES), and even then will not be available unless: (i) a public trading market then exists for the Common Stock of the Corporation; (ii) adequate information concerning the Corporation is then available to the public; and (iii) other terms and conditions of Rule 144 are complied with; and that any sale of the Shares may be made only in limited amounts in accordance with such terms and conditions.

(f) *Further Limitations on Disposition.* Without in any way limiting his representations set forth above, the Purchaser further agrees that he shall in no event make any disposition of all or any portion of the Shares unless and until:

      (i) (A) There is then in effect a Registration Statement under the Act covering such proposed disposition and such disposition is made in accordance with said Registration Statement; *or*, (B)(1) the Purchaser shall have notified the Corporation of the proposed disposition and shall have furnished the Corporation with a detailed statement of the circumstances surrounding the proposed disposition, (2) the Purchaser shall have furnished the Corporation with an opinion of the Purchaser's counsel to the effect that such disposition will not require registration of such shares under the Act, *and* (3) such opinion of the Purchaser's counsel shall have been concurred in by counsel for the Corporation and the Corporation shall have advised the Purchaser of such concurrence; *and,*

      (ii) The Shares proposed to be transferred are not subject to the Repurchase Option set forth in Section 2 hereof or any other restrictions under this Agreement.

10. *"Market Stand-Off" Agreement.* The Purchaser hereby agrees that he or she shall not, to the extent reasonably requested by the Corporation and an underwriter of Common Stock (or other securities) of the Corporation, sell or otherwise transfer or dispose (other than to donees who agree to be similarly bound) of any Shares during the one hundred eighty (180)-day period following the effective date of a registration statement of the Corporation filed under the Securities Act; provided, however, that: (a) all officers and directors of the Corporation and all other persons with registration rights enter into similar agreements; and (b) such agreement shall be applicable only to the first such registration statement of the Corporation which covers shares (or securities) to be sold on its behalf to the public in an underwritten public offering. Such agreement shall be in writing in a form satisfactory to the Corporation and such underwriter. In order to enforce the foregoing covenant, the Corporation may impose stop-transfer instructions with respect to the Shares of each Shareholder (and the shares or securities of every other person subject to the foregoing restriction) until the end of such one hundred eighty (180)-day period.

11. *Enforcement.* The Purchaser agrees that a violation on his or her part of any of the terms of this Agreement [(other than those contained in Section 10 above)] may cause irreparable damage to the Corporation, the exact amount of which is impossible to ascertain, and for that reason agrees that the Corporation shall be entitled to a decree of specific performance of the terms hereof or an injunction restraining further violation, such right to be in addition to any other remedies of such parties.

12. *Controlling Provisions.* To the extent that there may be any conflict between the provisions of this Agreement and the provisions contained in the Corporation's bylaws on the transfer or restriction on transfer of Shares, the terms of this Agreement shall be controlling.

13. *Notices.* All notices and other communications required or permitted hereunder shall be in writing and shall be deemed effectively given upon personal delivery or within 72 hours after mailing, if mailed by first-class mail, registered or certified, postage prepaid, and properly addressed. Notice to be given to the Corporation shall be delivered or addressed to the Corporation at its principal place of business; notice to be given to a holder of Shares shall be delivered or addressed to such holder at his or her or its address set forth on the signature page of this Agreement or at another address if given to the Secretary of the Corporation for the purpose of notice or, if no address is given, in care of the Corporation at its principal place of business.

14. *Binding Effect.* This Agreement shall inure to the benefit of the Corporation and its successors and assigns and, subject to the restrictions on transfer set forth herein, be binding upon the Purchaser, his permitted transferees, heirs, legatees, executors, administrators, and legal successors, who shall hold the Shares subject to the terms hereof. The Corporation may assign its rights under the terms of this Agreement without the consent of the Purchaser.

15. *Entire Agreement.* This Agreement supersedes all previous written or oral agreements between the parties regarding the subject matter hereof, and constitutes the entire agreement of the parties regarding such subject matter. This Agreement may not be modified

or terminated except by writing executed by all of the parties hereto.

16. *Not Employment Contract.* Nothing in this Agreement shall affect in any manner whatsoever the right or power of the Purchaser or the Corporation to terminate the Purchaser's employment, for any reason or for no reason, with or without cause, subject to the provisions of applicable law. This Agreement is not an employment contract.

17. *Counterparts.* This Agreement may be executed in counterparts, each of which shall be deemed to be an original, but all of which together shall constitute one and the same instrument.

18. *Governing Law.* This Agreement, together with the exhibits hereto, shall be governed by and construed under the laws of the State of _____, as such laws are applied to contracts entered into by residents of such state and performed in such state. All parties to this Agreement agree that exclusive jurisdiction to enforce any of the terms of this Agreement shall reside in the courts in the state of _____ (including the federal courts situated therein). The Purchaser specifically agrees that unless the Corporation determines otherwise, any actions to enforce any of the terms of this Agreement will first be brought in the courts of _____ County, _____.

19. *Attorneys' Fees.* In the event of arbitration or litigation brought by either party to enforce the provisions of this Agreement or for damages based upon the breach thereof, the prevailing party shall be entitled to recover his costs and reasonable attorneys' fees, as determined by the court.

20. *Severability.* If any provision of this Agreement is held by a court of competent jurisdiction to be invalid, void or unenforceable, the remaining provisions shall nevertheless continue in full force and effect without being impaired or invalidated in any way and shall be construed in accordance with the purposes and tenor and effect of this Agreement.

IN WITNESS WHEREOF, the parties have executed this Agreement on the date first above written.

CORPORATION:
    ABC COMPANY, a _____ corporation
    By:
    Title:

PURCHASER:
    [Name]
    Address:

CONSENT OF SPOUSE

I, _____, spouse of Jane Doe, acknowledge that I have read the Stock Purchase Agreement dated as of _____ __, 20__, to which this Consent is attached (the "Agreement") and that I know its contents. I am aware that by its provisions (a) my spouse and ABC Company (the "Corporation") have the option to purchase all the Shares of the Corporation of which I may become possessed as a result of a gift from my spouse or a court decree and/or any property settlement in any domestic litigation, (b) the Corporation has the option to purchase certain Shares of the Corporation which my spouse owns pursuant to the Agreement, including any interest I might have therein, upon termination of his or her employment under circumstances set forth in the Agreement, and (c) certain other restrictions are imposed upon the sale or other disposition of the Shares.

I hereby agree that my interest, if any, in the Shares subject to the Agreement shall be irrevocably bound by the Agreement and further understand and agree that any community property interest I may have in the Shares shall be similarly bound by the Agreement.

I agree to the sale and purchase described in Section 6 of the Agreement, and I hereby consent to the sale of the Shares by my spouse or his legal representative in accordance with the provisions of the Agreement. Further, as part of the consideration for the Agreement, I agree that at my death, if I have not disposed of any interest of mine in the Shares by an outright bequest of such Shares to my spouse, then my spouse and the Corporation shall have the same rights against my legal representative to purchase any interest of mine in the Shares as they would have had pursuant to Section 6 of the Agreement if I had acquired the Shares pursuant to a court decree in domestic litigation.

I am aware that the legal, financial and related matters contained in the Agreement are complex and that I am free to seek independent professional guidance or counsel with respect to this Consent. I have either sought such guidance or counsel or determined after reviewing the Agreement carefully that I will waive such right.

Dated as of the _____ day of _____, 20__.

Index

About the Authors

Joe S. Adams is a partner at McDermott, Will & Emery LLP based in the firm's Chicago office. As a member of the Employee Benefits department, Joe has substantial experience advising clients regarding executive and incentive compensation programs such as employment agreements, stock-based compensation, nonqualified deferred compensation, and SERPs. Joe is a frequent speaker and author on topics related to executive compensation and employee benefits.

Barbara Baksa is the executive director of the National Association of Stock Plan Professionals (NASPP). She is a frequent speaker on equity compensation-related topics and has spoken at NCEO, NASPP, and other industry events. In addition to her speaking engagements, she has authored several white papers on equity compensation-related topics and has contributed chapters to four books on equity compensation. She is a Certified Equity Professional (CEP) and serves on the Certified Equity Professional Institute's advisory board.

Clare Hatfield is a consultant at Sibson Consulting. Ms. Hatfield's consulting experience has been in both the performance and reward and in the change side of client organizations, focusing mainly on executive compensation and top-team development initiatives. Her specific experience includes developing and implementing reward programs for senior executives and key employees and designing executive change workshops. Based in the U.K., Ms. Hatfield has served clients in various industries, including professional and financial services, real estate management, and leisure and hospitality services.

Daniel N. Janich is the managing principal of Janich Law Group, a law firm serving employers and executives in employee benefits, executive compensation, and wealth management. He has extensive experience designing and implementing equity compensation plans; negotiating executive employment agreements, separation agreements, and compensation packages; and litigating employee benefits and executive compensation claims. Mr. Janich has spoken at the annual conferences of the NASPP, the NCEO, and the American Bar Association. He has contributed articles to the *Journal of Employee Ownership Law and Finance, Workspan, Family Advocate,* and *Profit Sharing,* and chapters to *Beyond Stock Options, Selected Issues in Equity Compensation,* and *ERISA Litigation.* A former chair of the Chicago Bar Association's Employee Benefits Committee, Mr. Janich is currently associate senior editor of *Employee Benefits Law* and co-chair of the Reporting and Disclosure Subcommittee of the ABA Labor and Employment Law Section's Employee Benefits Committee. Mr. Janich received a B.A. degree cum laude in history from Marian College, Indianapolis; a J.D. degree from John Marshall Law School, Chicago; and an LL.M. in taxation from DePaul University, Chicago.

David R. Johanson is the managing attorney and counselor at law with Johanson Berenson LLP, which has offices in Napa and Pasadena, California; Washington, D.C.; Arlington and Great Falls, Virginia; and Cary, North Carolina. Johanson Berenson LLP represents publicly traded and closely held corporations, serving as general and special counsel to various types of entities. The firm's practice focuses on a broad range of business and corporate matters, including employee ownership, ESOPs, ESOP transactions, executive compensation (including various types of stock option plans and deferred compensation), business succession and related tax and estate planning, general corporate matters, defense litigation, and various types of merger and acquisition transactions. A substantial portion of the firm's practice involves the structuring and financing of ESOP transactions and the involvement of ESOPs in corporate mergers, acquisitions, restructurings, and ownership transitions. The firm represents individual and institutional trustees and other fiduciaries, sellers, companies, and employee groups (including management and collectively bargained employees) in ESOP transactions. The firm is actively involved in promoting and advancing employee ownership throughout the United States. Mr. Johanson is general counsel to the NCEO's board of directors and a member of the editorial board of the NCEO's *Journal of Employee Ownership Law and Finance.*

Blair Jones is a managing principal at Semler Brossy Consulting Group, a compensation consulting firm. She has been an executive compensation consultant since 1991 and has worked extensively across industries, including healthcare, automotive, retail, professional services, heavy equipment manufacturing, and consumer products. She has particularly deep expertise working with companies in transition. Blair started her consulting career at Bain & Company, and before joining Semler Brossy, she was the practice leader in Leadership Performance and Rewards at Sibson Consulting.

Kay Kemp is an associate director in the Compensation and Benefits Advisory Services practice of McDermott Will & Emery LLP. Her practice focuses on U.S. employee benefit plans, nonqualified deferred compensation plans, equity-based compensation plans, and ESOPs. Kay is a graduate of Northwestern University and has a master's of business administration degree from the University of Chicago.

Helen H. Morrison is a principal at Deloitte Tax LLP, the leader of the firm's Employee Benefits Tax Practice Group in Chicago, and the national leader of the firm's ESOP Advisory Services Practice. She has authored or co-authored many articles and books on ESOPs and executive and broad-based compensation programs. She is an adjunct professor of employee benefits and executive compensation for John Marshall Law School's master of tax program and is a frequent speaker at professional and trade group conferences, including those of the NCEO. Before joining Deloitte, Ms. Morrison was a partner in the Employee Benefits Group at McDermott Will & Emery.

Corey Rosen is the executive director and cofounder of the National Center for Employee Ownership (NCEO), a private, nonprofit membership, information, and research organization in Oakland, CA. The NCEO is widely considered to be the authoritative source on broad-based employee ownership plans. He cofounded the NCEO in 1981 after working for five years as a professional staff member in the U.S. Senate, where he helped draft legislation on employee ownership plans. Before that, he taught political science at Ripon College. He is the author or coauthor of many books and over 100 articles on employee ownership, and coauthor (with John Case and Martin Staubus) of *Equity: Why Employee Ownership Is Good for Business* (Harvard Business School Press, 2005). He was the subject of an extensive interview in *Inc.* magazine in August 2000; has appeared frequently on CNN, PBS, NPR, and other network programs; and is regularly quoted in the *Wall Street Journal,* the *New York Times,* and other leading publications. He has a Ph.D. in political science from Cornell University and serves on the advisory board of the Certified Equity Professional Institute.

Martin Staubus is the director of consulting for the Beyster Institute at the Rady School of Management, University of California, San Diego. He has more than 20 years of experience in employee ownership, human resources, law, and organizational development. Trained as an attorney, Mr. Staubus has served as a practicing lawyer, a consultant, and a corporate VP of human resources. His career includes service as a policy analyst for Labor Secretary Robert Reich, legal advisor to the California State Labor Relations Board, and deputy director of the ESOP Association. He is a member of the NCEO's board of directors. Martin holds a B.A. in economics from the University of California, Berkeley; an M.B.A. in organizational development from George Washington University, Washington D.C.; and a law degree from Golden Gate University, San Francisco.

Robin L. Struve is a partner in the tax department of Latham & Watkins LLP. She advises U.S. and multinational companies regarding the application of U.S. tax, ERISA, securities, and other laws to employee benefit plans and executive compensation matters. A substantial portion of Ms. Struve's practice includes the structuring, drafting, amendment, termination, and legal compliance of benefit plans, with a focus on nonqualified deferred compensation plans, equity-based compensation plans (including plans for non-corporate entities such as LLCs and partnerships), and bonus plans for both public and private companies. Ms. Struve holds a J.D. from Harvard University and a B.A. from the University of Colorado, with distinction. She is the author of several articles on ESOPs as well as a frequent speaker on a variety of executive compensation and employee benefit plan topics.

About the NCEO

The National Center for Employee Ownership (NCEO) is widely considered to be the leading authority in employee ownership in the U.S. and the world. Established in 1981 as a nonprofit information and membership organization, it now has over 2,500 members, including companies, professionals, unions, government officials, academics, and interested individuals. It is funded entirely through the work it does.

The NCEO's mission is to provide the most objective, reliable information possible about employee ownership at the most affordable price possible. As part of the NCEO's commitment to providing objective information, it does not lobby or provide ongoing consulting services. The NCEO publishes a variety of materials on employee ownership and participation, holds dozens of seminars, Webinars, and conferences on employee ownership annually, and offers a variety of online courses. The NCEO's work includes extensive contacts with the media, both through articles written for trade and professional publications and through interviews with reporters. It has written or edited several books for outside publishers. The NCEO maintains an extensive Web site at *www.nceo.org*.

See the following page for information on membership benefits and fees. To join, see the order form at the end of this section, visit our Web site at *www.nceo.org*, or telephone us at 510-208-1300.

Membership Benefits

NCEO members receive the following benefits:

- The bimonthly newsletter *Employee Ownership Report*, which covers ESOPs, equity compensation, and employee participation.
- Access to the members-only area of the NCEO's Web site, which includes a searchable database of well over 200 NCEO members

who are service providers in this field, plus many other resources, such as a searchable newsletter archive and a discussion forum; a stock plan glossary; legislative/regulatory updates; and case studies organized by plan type and company type.

- Substantial discounts on publications, online courses, and events produced by the NCEO.

- Free access to live Webinars on ESOPs and related topics.

- The right to contact the NCEO for answers to general or specific questions regarding employee ownership.

An introductory NCEO membership costs $80 for one year ($90 outside the U.S.) and covers an entire company at all locations, a single professional offering services in this field, or a single individual with a business interest in employee ownership. Full-time students and faculty members who are not employed in the business sector may join at the academic rate of $35 for one year ($45 outside the U.S.).

Selected NCEO Publications

The NCEO offers a variety of publications on all aspects of employee ownership and participation. Below are some of our main publications.

We publish new books and revise old ones on a yearly basis. To obtain the most current information on what we have available, visit us on the Web at *www.nceo.org* or call us at 510-208-1300.

Equity Compensation

- This book, *Beyond Stock Options*, is a complete guide, including annotated model plans, to phantom stock, restricted stock, stock appreciation rights, performance awards, and more. Includes a CD with plan documents.

    $35 for NCEO members, $50 for nonmembers

- *The Stock Options Book* is a straightforward, comprehensive overview covering the legal, accounting, regulatory, and design issues involved in implementing a stock option or stock purchase plan.

    $25 for NCEO members, $35 for nonmembers

- *Selected Issues in Equity Compensation* is more detailed and specialized than *The Stock Options Book*, with chapters on issues such as repricing, securities issues, and evergreen options.

    $25 for NCEO members, $35 for nonmembers

- *Accounting for Equity Compensation* is a guide to the accounting rules that govern equity compensation programs in the U.S.

    $35 for NCEO members, $50 for nonmembers

- *The Stock Administration Book* is a comprehensive guide to administering stock options and other equity compensation plans. It includes a CD with templates for immediate use.

    $50 for NCEO members, $75 for nonmembers

- *The Law of Equity Compensation* reviews and analyzes case law, statutory, and regulatory law developments in recent years.

    $25 for NCEO members, $35 for nonmembers

- *Equity-Based Compensation for Multinational Corporations* describes how companies can use stock options and other equity-based programs across the world to reward a global work force. It includes a country-by-country summary of tax and legal issues as well as a detailed case study.

    $25 for NCEO members, $35 for nonmembers

- *Incentive Compensation and Employee Ownership* takes a broad look at how companies can use incentives, ranging from stock plans to cash bonuses to gainsharing, to motivate and reward employees.

    $25 for NCEO members, $35 for nonmembers

- *Tax and Securities Sources for Equity Compensation* is a compilation of statutory and regulatory material relevant to the study of equity compensation.

    $35 for NCEO members, $50 for nonmembers

- *Equity Compensation in a Post-Expensing World* presents strategies for companies in the new accounting environment.

    $25 for NCEO members, $35 for nonmembers

Employee Stock Ownership Plans (ESOPs)

- *The ESOP Reader* is an overview of the issues involved in establishing and operating an ESOP. It covers the basics of ESOP rules, feasibility, valuation, and other matters, and includes brief case studies.

  $25 for NCEO members, $35 for nonmembers

- *Selling to an ESOP* is a guide for owners, managers, and advisors of closely held businesses, with a particular focus on the tax-deferred Section 1042 "rollover" for C corporation owners.

  $25 for NCEO members, $35 for nonmembers

- *Leveraged ESOPs and Employee Buyouts* discusses how ESOPs borrow money to buy out entire companies, purchase shares from a retiring owner, or finance new capital.

  $25 for NCEO members, $35 for nonmembers

- *ESOP Valuation* brings together and updates where needed the best articles on ESOP valuation that we have published in our *Journal of Employee Ownership Law and Finance*, described below.

  $25 for NCEO members, $35 for nonmembers

- *ESOPs and Corporate Governance* covers everything from shareholder rights to the impact of Sarbanes-Oxley to choosing a fiduciary.

  $25 for NCEO members, $35 for nonmembers

- *The ESOP Communications Sourcebook* provides ideas for and examples of communicating an ESOP to employees and customers. It includes a CD with communications materials, including many documents that readers can customize for their own companies.

  $35 for NCEO members, $50 for nonmembers

- *Model ESOP* provides a sample ESOP plan, with alternative provisions given to tailor the plan to individual needs. It also includes a section-by-section explanation of the plan and other supporting materials.

  $50 for NCEO members, $75 for nonmembers

- *Executive Compensation in ESOP Companies* discusses executive compensation issues, special ESOP considerations, and the first-ever survey of executive compensation in ESOP companies.

  $25 for NCEO members, $35 for nonmembers

- *S Corporation ESOPs* introduces the reader to how ESOPs work and then discusses the legal, valuation, administrative, and other issues associated with S corporation ESOPs.

  $25 for NCEO members, $35 for nonmembers

- *How ESOP Companies Handle the Repurchase Obligation* has essays and recent research on the subject.

  $25 for NCEO members, $35 for nonmembers

Other

- *Section 401(k) Plans and Employee Ownership* focuses on how company stock is used in 401(k) plans, both in stand-alone 401(k) plans and combination 401(k)–ESOP plans ("KSOPs").

  $25 for NCEO members, $35 for nonmembers

- *Employee Ownership and Corporate Performance* reviews the research that has been done on the link between company stock plans and various aspects of corporate performance.

  $25 for NCEO members, $35 for nonmembers

- *The Journal of Employee Ownership Law and Finance* is the only professional journal solely devoted to employee ownership. Articles are written by leading experts and cover ESOPs, stock options, and related subjects in depth.

  One-year subscription (four issues):
  $75 for NCEO members, $100 for nonmembers

To join the NCEO as a member or to order publications, use the order form on the following page, order online at www.nceo.org, or call us at 510-208-1300. If you join at the same time you order publications, you will receive the members-only publication discounts.

Order Form

This book is published by the National Center for Employee Ownership (NCEO). You can order additional copies online at our Web site, *www. nceo.org;* by telephoning the NCEO at 510-208-1300; by faxing this page to the NCEO at 510-272-9510; or by sending this page to the NCEO at 1736 Franklin Street, 8th Floor, Oakland, CA 94612. If you join as an NCEO member with this order, or are already an NCEO member, you will pay the discounted member price for any publications you order.

Name

Organization

Address

City, State, Zip (Country)

Telephone   Fax   Email

Method of Payment: ❏ Check (payable to "NCEO")   ❏ Visa   ❏ M/C   ❏ AMEX

Credit Card Number

Signature   Exp. Date

Checks are accepted only for orders from the U.S. and must be in U.S. currency.

Title	Qty.	Price	Total

Tax: California residents add 8.75% sales tax (on publications only, not membership)
Shipping: In the U.S., first publication $5, each add'l $1; elsewhere, we charge exact shipping costs to your credit card, plus a $10 handling surcharge; no shipping charges for membership
Introductory NCEO Membership: $80 for one year ($90 outside the U.S.)

Subtotal	$
Sales Tax	$
Shipping	$
Membership	$
TOTAL DUE	$